E-Procurement in Emerging Economies:
Theory and Cases

Ashis K. Pani
XLRI, India

Amit Agrahari
SETLabs – Infosys Technologies Ltd, India

IDEA GROUP PUBLISHING
Hershey • London • Melbourne • Singapore

Acquisition Editor:	Kristin Klinger
Senior Managing Editor:	Jennifer Neidig
Managing Editor:	Sara Reed
Assistant Managing Editor:	Sharon Berger
Development Editor:	Kristin Roth
Copy Editor:	Susanna Svidunovich
Typesetter:	Amanda Appicello
Cover Design:	Lisa Tosheff
Printed at:	Yurchak Printing Inc.

Published in the United States of America by
Idea Group Publishing (an imprint of Idea Group Inc.)
701 E. Chocolate Avenue, Suite 200
Hershey PA 17033-1240
Tel: 717-533-8845
Fax: 717-533-8661
E-mail: cust@idea-group.com
Web site: http://www.idea-group.com

and in the United Kingdom by
Idea Group Publishing (an imprint of Idea Group Inc.)
3 Henrietta Street
Covent Garden
London WC2E 8LU
Tel: 44 20 7240 0856
Fax: 44 20 7379 0609
Web site: http://www.eurospanonline.com

Library of Congress Cataloging-in-Publication Data

E-procurement in emerging economies : theory and cases / Ashis K. Pani and Amit Agrahari, editors.
    p. cm.
  Summary: "This book presents issues such as legal, technical, cultural and social analysis on e-Procurement, and offers technical and managerial solutions to professionals in different emerging economies and industries"-- Provided by publisher.
  ISBN 1-59904-153-7 (hardcover) -- ISBN 1-59904-154-5 (softcover) -- ISBN 1-59904-155-3 (ebook)
  1. Industrial procurement--Developing countries. 2. Industrial procurement--Electronic information resources. 3. Business logistics--Developing countries. 4. Business logistics--Electronic information resources. I. Pani, Ashis Kumar. II. Agrahari, Amit, 1978- III. Title: Eprocurement in emerging economies.
  HD39.5.E16 2007
  658.7'202854678--dc22
                              2006033751
British Cataloguing in Publication Data
A Cataloguing in Publication record for this book is available from the British Library.

E-Procurement in Emerging Economies:
Theory and Cases

Table of Contents

Section III: Analyzing Adoption

Section IV: Technical Perspective

Preface

The Internet is an enabler. It has enabled us to break free of time and space barriers. This has resulted in the emergence of a new economy. Despite the initial confusions and the dot com burst, the value of the Internet as an enabler cannot be questioned. However, its impact on emerging economies is not well understood. We believe that the value that the Internet can bring into these economies is far greater as compared to what it has brought to developed economies. Business-to-business (B2B) transactions, enabled by the Internet, are what we will study in this book. When enabled by the Internet, we can see various facades of B2B transactions. Different areas, usually overlapping, have emerged in this space, such as: reverse auction, online bidding, e-purchase, e-sourcing, supplier relation management, and so forth. However, we have taken the liberty to ignore the differences and used an umbrella term of "e-procurement." E-procurement is defined as the usage of Web-based functions and services that allow employees of a buying organization to purchase goods and services, and allow suppliers to manage and communicate the fulfillment of those purchase orders which have been submitted (Rayport & Jaworski, 2002). Typically, an e-procurement tool provides functionalities such as: catalog management; requisition, control, and approval; receiving and exception processing; financials and payment processing; logistics and supply-chain management (Subramani, 1999).

What is an emerging economy? The term "emerging markets" was coined in the early 1980s by Antoine W. van Agtmael to describe nations with low-to-middle per capita incomes and that are instituting economic development and reform programs which will allow them to "emerge" into the arena of global economic competitiveness (Agtmael, 1984). Emerging economies are characterized as transitional, meaning they are in the process of moving from a closed to an open economy while building accountability within the system. Thus despite the difference in income level, bigger economies such as India and China are clubbed with smaller economies such as Slovenia, because they are all transitional. This characteristic makes emerging economies a high risk and higher return economies. Changes in economic systems have also resulted in changes in people, processes, culture, social fabric, and so forth. These changes have brought in new work ethics and standards. Thus, studying e-procurement in an emerging economies' context could be very interesting.

Why should we study e-procurement from an emerging economies' perspective? Manufacturing and services are being outsourced to places which are specialized in performing these activities or can perform it at the lowest possible cost. The Internet has enabled organizations to accept an order from a customer, decompose it into pieces, and forward those pieces to suppliers spread across the globe. Increasingly, these manufacturers are located in emerging economies. Thus any e-procurement initiative needs to be understood from the emerging economies perspective. Further, time and space barriers are more prevalent in emerging economies as compared to developed economies. Hence, if applied well, e-procurement can bring in unprecedented benefits to these economies. As illustrated in the chapter contributed by Dr. Somasundaram, in emerging economies, government procurement runs into billions of dollars, with rampant corruption in the process. For example, in 2004-2005, the government of India procured goods and services worth approximately US$100 billion. If it can save only 10% in this process, the resultant savings will be approximately 32% of its fiscal deficit.

This book will focus, primarily, on e-procurement usage in emerging economies. Literature on e-procurement is synthesized from the experience of developed economies, and hence the theory is also grounded in the same context. However, socio-economic context in emerging economies is different from that of developed economies. Hempel and Kwong (2001) argued that there is a fundamental difficulty in applying the Western best practices in e-commerce to Asian economies because of differences in business and cultural assumptions. For example, several infrastructural facilities that are taken for granted in developed economies are not available in emerging economies. Our case study on Indian steel industry (Pani & Agrahari, 2004) also suggests that in emerging economy inter-mediators offer services such as working capital management, logistics, and so forth. Hence when an e-procurement initiative tries to disintermediate the market, it has to create all services that intermediators used to offer. This might be an expensive proposition since existing infrastructure is poor.

Although we will study e-procurement, we will not limit ourselves to e-procurement alone, for procurement does not happen in a vacuum. It is important to understand the context in which e-procurement occurs. Issues such as overall industry structure, political environment, and societal and organizational culture are some of the issues that a procurement manager should be aware of. For example, in countries like India and China, trade is mainly conducted in a close-knit social network. Thus a supplier who is not included in these networks has very little chance to participate in trade. An e-market will force itself in challenging such a network and may not be received very well. Similarly, digital divide is another important phenomenon that needs to be understood before any e-procurement initiative can be undertaken.

Information systems shape and gets shaped by the environment in which they operate. This book is an attempt to understand how e-procurement is being shaped in emerging economies. Grounded in the socio-technical reality of emerging economies, this book tries to touch upon various issues such as culture, digital divide, country characteristics, and technologies used in various countries. Contributors from Italy, China, India, Turkey, Slovenia, Australia, and the United Kingdom have brought in case studies and theoretical insight on e-procurement and its implications for emerging economies. This book thus covers the entire gamut of issues that are relevant to understand *how Web-based function and services affect buyer-supplier interactions in emerging economies.*

Chapter Organization

This book tries to assimilate the knowledge on e-procurement initiatives in emerging economies. Authors from various part of the world have contributed excellent chapters on various issues. These chapters are divided into four sections. The first section elaborates on theoretical underpinnings, and presents an overview of the concept of e-procurement. E-procurement can be analyzed using various lenses such as transaction cost economics, inter-organizational interdependencies, value chain, and so forth. Both chapters in this section have tried to touch upon these theoretical lenses. In the first chapter, Pani has offered a detailed overview of existing literature on EDI, IOIS, and e-procurement. This chapter looks into prior research on inter-organizational information systems, electronic data interchange, and procurement to develop a research framework and identify research issues in e-procurement. It is argued that supply market characteristics and product characteristics can explain the emergence of various types of the e-procurement model. Further, these e-procurement models have different impacts on inter-organizational relationships and amount of value generated. However, these impacts are moderated by adoption and implementation risks.

In the second chapter, Vaidya has argued that the focus of the majority of research on e-procurement has been on the possible impact of e-procurement adoption on the buyer's interaction with the suppliers, whereas very little has been discussed about e-procurement assimilation. This chapter looks beyond the decision of adoption of the technology, investigating the environmental conditions that may influence the successful assimilation of e-procurement in the public sector organizations. Using institutional theory and building on prior research on the theories of technology assimilation, this chapter investigates the institutional factors that enable higher levels of e-procurement assimilation in the public sector, and also argues that the e-procurement benefits greatly depend on the operational and strategic organizational assimilation of e-procurement with different levels of success. This chapter also discusses the need to integrate other theories such as Diffusion of innovation theory, transactional cost theory, and structurational theory of technology use, and proposes a holistic research model in order to investigate the antecedent conditions that are likely to influence the assimilation of public e-procurement.

The second section of this book focuses on country level analysis. Three developing countries, India, Turkey, and Slovenia, are analyzed by different authors. Chapter III is an excellent contribution by Podlogar, who focuses on e-procurement success factors from a small country's perspective. This chapter introduces e-procurement as a strategic tool for an organization's competitive position in the new information economy. It argues that e-procurement is significantly changing the ways businesses operate, and new business models are needed. E-procurement success factors that have to be considered are: cost factors, time factors, process simplification factors, and the volume of e-transactions factors. By gaining understanding of the most important e-procurement factors, organizations have to organize themselves in a way that ensures success. Furthermore, the author hopes that with knowing such factors, organizations will be able to better prepare for e-procurement and thus operate successfully and be able to compete in the global market.

In Chapter IV, Somasundaram has explained the concept of e-government procurement (e-GP), as it is being implemented in India. Furthermore, a set of six challenges encountered during implementation of e-procurement is discussed in depth. The six challenges discussed in the chapter are: lack of skilled personnel; multi-departmental implementation; inadequate IT and networking infrastructure; challenges in implementation of a state-wide system; the need to regulate e-procurement market; and replicating best practices in federal-state setup. A practitioner's perspective is adopted to write this chapter. While this chapter deals specifically with e-GP in India, certain aspects of it can be generalized to e-GP implementations elsewhere in the world. Such generalization is possible since government procurement is driven by the same set of principles such as efficiency and transparency.

In the fifth chapter, Yamamoto and Karaman have argued that e-procurement practice is not well established in emerging countries. There are barriers in terms of transportation, financial, telecommunication, and legal infrastructures. Also, a lack of a qualified workforce, cultural barriers, and security problems hinder the development of e-procurement activities. These are not such significant problems in the developed countries. The authors have analyzed macroeconomic data and Internet penetration data, and have presented a picture of the current situation of Turkey. They then discuss how these barriers can be overcome in Turkey. Finally, the authors have predicted how e-procurement may alter the situation and its potential for the Turkish market.

Section III analyzes various facades of e-procurement adoption. It contains chapters on cultural issues in buyer-supplier relation, digital divide, and game theoretic analysis of e-procurement adoption efforts. Chapter VI, by Xu and Nandhakumar, investigates the dynamics of the formation and transformation of electronic supply relationships (e-supply relationships) in the Chinese cultural, technological, and industrial network context. It focuses on a newly-formed large Chinese telecom company. The aim is to provide better insights into inter-organizational relationships (IORs) enabled by the application of newer types of Internet technology in different contexts, and to develop a new conceptual framework of e-supply relationships. In this research, the conceptualization of the transformation process of e-supply relationships represents circuits of interactions between managerial actions and social structures, as well as the particular cultural and technological context within which the interactions take place.

Chapter VII, by Serrecchia, Serrecchia, and Martinelli, analyzes the digital divide in Italy and the factors contributing to this situation, both at the regional and provincial levels. To do this, they used the registration of Internet domains under the ".it" country code top level domain as a proxy. In particular, they analyzed domain names registered by firms. This analysis has produced interesting results: The distribution of domains registered by firms in Italian provinces is more concentrated than the distribution related to income and the number of firms, suggesting a diffusive effect. Furthermore, in order to analyze the factors that may contribute to the presence of a digital divide at the regional level, a regression analysis was performed using demographic, social, economic, and infrastructure indicators. The results show that Internet technology, far from being an "equalizer", follows and possibly intensifies existing differences in economic opportunity in industrialized countries like Italy.

E-procurement adoption effort is analyzed in Chapter VIII. It includes a case study that looks into the evolution of various e-procurement systems at an Indian steel manufacturer, Tata Steel. This chapter argues that rather than sticking to one system, organizations need to manage a portfolio of e-procurement systems to realize the full potential of the Internet. Further, these systems evolve over a period of time, thus necessitating dynamic instead of static analysis. Prior research has analyzed e-procurement and its predecessor, EDI-based IOIS, as a static game with adoption and subsidy being the key issues. However, with e-procurement increasingly being a competitive necessity, the issue is not "if to adopt e-procurement" but "how to adopt e-procurement." This chapter analyzes e-procurement adoption efforts in a dynamic game setting. First, e-procurement adoption effort is analyzed in a "without subsidy" scenario and then in a "with subsidy" scenario. Results show that e-procurement adoption efforts are likely to be more if the buyer and suppliers are not myopic, and the rate of decay in strategic benefits from the dyadic relationship is low. Further, the buyer can induce more effort from the supplier by offering him subsidies. The buyer will offer subsidy only if he can take away more than half of the total e-procurement benefits. The level of subsidy depends on the effectiveness of the supplier's e-procurement adoption effort. Results for the game theoretic model are corroborated with the case study.

Section IV offers a technical perspective to e-procurement. It is dominated by the discussion on Web services. Chapter IX, contributed by Patra, argues that globalization has evoked rethinking in organizing the business processes of many enterprises in order to keep pace with the competition and dynamic nature of the market. There has been continuing research for suitable paradigms and technologies that can facilitate efficient and yet less expensive solutions, a feature that is so important for small and medium sized enterprises (SMEs). Towards this end, this chapter presents a service-oriented framework that is based on the notion of Internet-accessible services to represent applications and to integrate business processes. This model propounds a metadata-driven approach to dynamically publish, discover, and select services in heterogeneous settings while engaging in business transactions such as e-procurement across organizational boundaries. The concept of software agents is also employed as a means to automate the activities relating to a procurement cycle. The central theme of this chapter is to motivate the adoption of a service-oriented agent-based framework which can provide effective and efficient solutions to e-procurement.

Chapter X, contributed by Oliver and Maringanti, highlights the importance of e-procurement and the barriers affecting widespread adoption of it in the context of small and medium enterprises. This chapter takes a technical perspective and critically analyses the importance of information systems in the procurement domain and the integration challenges faced by SMEs in today's digitally networked economy. Next, the role of XML-based Web services in solving the integration challenges faced by SMEs is discussed. Subsequently, a procurement transformation framework enabled by Web services, which provides a clear methodology of the way in which information systems should be introduced in the procurement domain, is discussed. The chapter concludes by a discussion of the measures that must be undertaken by various stakeholders like the government and universities in increasing the awareness levels of SMEs to the latest e-business mechanisms.

The last chapter, contributed by Shrivastava, Gupta, and Mohapatra, examines the features of reverse auction sites. Twenty-five features of 38 reverse auction sites have been studied. These features are divided into core and complementary features. These sites are broadly divided into B2B/B2G and B2C/C2C groups. They have shown the differences that exist in the site design of these two groups insofar as the inclusion of these features are concerned. Weights are derived, signifying the importance which the site designs have assigned to various complementary features. These weights are used in two ways: (1) to provide benchmarks to evaluate the design of the Web sites, and (2) to find out the site evaluation index of any Web site for comparison with the benchmark. Using their complementary features, weights are derived for the features and develop site evaluation index for them.

Thus, this book has covered a vast landscape focusing on emerging economies. To our best knowledge, no book has ever looked into e-procurement in emerging economies. Further literature in this area is rather scarce and scattered. We hope this book can fill this gap by providing a platform for creation, contribution, and assimilation. We have looked at both managerial and technical challenges faced by organizations in emerging economies. We have also looked at the solution approaches to various infrastructural problems faced in these economies. We hope this book will be useful for both academicians and practitioners. It can serve as a reference for the students to understand how socio-economic context affects usage of a particular technology.

References

Agtmael, A. W. V. (1984). *Emerging securities markets: Investment banking opportunities in the developing world*. London: Euromoney Publications

Hempel, P. S., & Kwong, Y. K. (2001). B2B e-commerce in emerging economies: I-metal.com's non-ferrous metals exchange in China. *Journal of Strategic Information Systems, 10*(4), 335-355.

Pani, A. K., & Agrahari, A. (2004). E-market in emerging economy: A case study from Indian steel industry. *Journal of E-Commerce in Organization, 2*(4), 116-126.

Rayport, J., & Jaworski, B. (2002). *Introduction to e-commerce*. New York: McGraw-Hill.

Subramani, M. R. (1999). Linking IT use to benefits in inter-organizational networks: The mediating role of relationship-specific intangible investments. In *Proceedings of the 20th International Conference on Information Systems,* Charlotte (pp. 358-363).

Disclaimer

Acknowledgments

Compiling acknowledgements is the most fulfilling part of any work. It gives us a chance to say "Thank You" to those who helped at various stages of our work. Being an edited work, this book was not at all possible without generous cooperation from others. First and foremost, the editors would like to acknowledge the help and support provided by the staff at Idea Group Inc. Their excellent support from inception to final publication is unparalleled. Special thanks go to the publishing team at Idea Group Inc. In particular, we would like to thank our development editor, Kristin Roth, for her e-mails that kept us on track and helped in making this book happen.

We would like to acknowledge the staff at Sir Jehangir Gandhi Library, XLRI, for providing us with all possible resources and procuring it fast if we needed anything special. A special note of thanks goes to the technical support team at XLRI for ensuring that we did not miss any e-mails or lose any data.

In closing, we wish to thank chapter authors for their insights and excellent contributions to this book. We also want to thank reviewers for assisting us in the review process. In addition, we are thankful to Mehdi Khosrow-Pour and Jan Travers at Idea Group Inc., for ongoing professional support.

Section I

E-Procurement: Theoretical Underpinnings

Chapter I

Perspectives from IOIS, EDI, and Channel Management:
Research Issues in E-Procurement

Ashis K. Pani, XLRI, India

Abstract

Over the last couple of years, e-procurement has received tremendous attention from researchers and practitioners alike. However, research on e-procurement is still scarce and scattered. This chapter looks into prior research on inter-organizational information systems (IOIS), electronic data interchange (EDI), channel management, and procurement to develop a research framework and identify research issues in e-procurement. It is argued that supply market characteristics and product characteristics can explain the emergence of various e-procurement systems. Further, these e-procurement systems have different impacts on inter-organizational relationships and value generated from e-procurement. However, these impacts are moderated by adoption and implementation risks. Though this model provides us with a holistic view to e-procurement, it is not yet empirically validated, owing to low e-procurement penetration.

Introduction

Before the advent of the Internet, organizations were using electronic data interchange- (EDI) based inter-organizational information systems (IOIS) to share data with trading partners. Venkatraman and Zaheer (1990) defined EDI as the technical platform rooted in the set of standards, which enables informational exchange among participants in a marketplace. Inter-organizational information systems (IOIS) build on these common EDI standards (when necessary) to design and deploy different functionalities that interconnect multiple organizations. Therefore we can view e-procurement as Internet-enabled IOIS used for procurement.

Johnston and Mak (2000) argued that commercial availability of the Internet does more than simply provide a cheaper alternative document transmission channel. By upsetting the balance among the contextual factors, it allows the emergence of a new vision of supply chain featuring a backbone any-to-any network of EDI-compliant technologically-sophisticated trading partners, with Internet-based sub-networks, centered on large players or third parties using proprietary software, development tools, and message formatting to provide connection to unsophisticated players. They also observed that in traditional EDI systems, only 20% of suppliers, by number, who account for 80% of transaction value, participate and thus a large proportion of suppliers, usually small to medium-sized enterprises (SMEs), remain outside the EDI.

Interest in inter-organizational information systems (IOIS) can be traced back to Kaufman's (1966) prediction that computer networks would improve coordination between organizations and radically alter traditional billing and payment procedures. The term IOIS was born in the early 1980s, as Barrett and Konsynski (1982) used the term "inter-organizational information sharing system" for the first time, and Cash and Konsynski (1985) first coined the term "inter-organizational system." They defined IOIS as automated information systems shared by two or more companies. A number of studies on IOIS, theoretical as well as empirical, have been carried out during the last two decades. A survey of articles published in the area of e-commerce revealed that around 33% of articles were related to application area, and among them 36% were related to IOIS (Ngai & Wat, 2002). However, rapid growth and innovations in data standards, format, network technology, and computer science made management of IOIS a challenging task. The recent emergence of Internet technologies and e-commerce posed some new managerial challenges. The objective of this chapter is to review literature on IOIS,

EDI, channel management, and e-procurement to develop a framework that can enhance our understanding of e-procurement, and help us in exploring research issues in e-procurement.

Research on inter-organizational information systems can focus on the semantic or syntactic aspects of business-to-business linkage (Riggins & Rhee, 1999). The semantic aspect refers to the meaning of information and the way it might be used more effectively. The syntactic aspect concerns issues such as standards and protocols, adoption risk and benefits from the system, and so forth. This chapter looks at both aspects of the IOIS research, but will not touch upon technical issues such as data format standards and protocols. This chapter argues that supply market characteristics and product characteristics can explain the emergence of various e-procurement systems. Further, these e-procurement systems have different impacts on inter-organizational relationships and value generated by the system. However, these impacts are moderated by adoption and implementation risks (Figure 1). The chapter looks at various typologies, followed by a section which analyzes various ownership patterns. Next, the chapter looks at various product and supply market characteristics, which can explain "why organizations choose a specific kind of e-procurement." Effects on inter-organizational relationships are discussed followed by a section that looks at the values generated. Finally, the chapter looks at apportionment of the value generated and talks about adoption and implementation risks. This chapter is concluded with a discussion on directions for future research.

Figure 1. E-procurement space framework

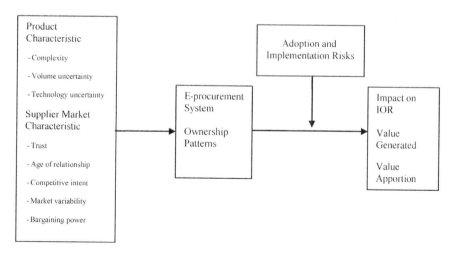

Analyzing Typology

IOIS have been analyzed using various lenses such as transaction costs, value chain, and inter-organizational interdependencies, and so forth. Analyzing e-procurement systems using these lenses will help us in understanding the emergence and nature of various e-procurement systems. A number of frameworks have been developed to classify IOIS. However, there is no widely-accepted typology in literature. The next section explains some of the prominent IOIS classifications.

Barrett and Konsynski (1982) developed five levels of IOIS based on the intensity of an organization's participation. Cash and Konsynski (1985) also used similar dimensions to develop three levels of IOIS. Bakos (1987) looked at IOIS from the value chain perspective. He used two dimensions, namely functional structure, describing the interconnection between system participants, and the location of the value-adding process, which transforms input into outputs. Malone, Benjamin, and Yates (1987) used transaction cost economics to identify two IOIS configurations corresponding to the two major governance structures. Transaction cost economics suggests market and hierarchy as two mechanisms of coordination, and any middle-range solution was considered to be inferior. Over the years, transaction cost economics has been revised to reflect the empirical reality that middle-range solutions could be actually more effective (Williamson, 1991). Choudhury (1997) enhanced the Malone, Yates, and Benjamin (1987) model, and proposed three kinds of IOIS design, namely electronic monopolies, electronic dyad, and multilateral IOIS. Using competitive advantage and innovation, Johnston and Vitale (1988) developed a three-dimensional model to classify IOIS. These dimensions are business function, relationships between IOIS and their sponsors, and information functions performed by the IOIS. Benjamin, deLong, and Scott Morton (1990) have identified four types of IOIS based on two dimensions: e-market versus e-hierarchies, as suggested by Malone et al. (1987), and routine transaction versus task support. Kumar and van Dissel (1996) classified IOIS on the basis of the type of interdependencies that exists between participating organizations. They proposed networked IOIS (supporting reciprocal interdependencies); pooled information resource IOIS (supporting pooled interdependencies); and value/supply-chain IOIS (supporting sequential interdependencies). Hong (2002) developed a classification scheme based on two dimensions, namely role linkage (vertical or horizontal) and system support level (operational support or strategic support). He suggested four basic types of IOIS: resource pooling (to compete with large organizations), operational cooperation (to share information for common interest), operational coordination (to increase operational efficiencies), and complementary cooperation (to integrate the value chain). Using level of information shared as the classification criteria, Riggins and Rhee (1998) proposed Intronets and Supranet as two types of IOIS. In Intronets, external trading partners receive controlled access behind the initiator's firewall and into the initiator's intranet, whereas Supranet is a consortium-sponsored and -controlled inter-organizational network providing seamless communication service between member organizations across multiple types of applications.

Existing literature on e-procurement has widely used transaction cost economics because of its mathematical tools and techniques. However, e-procurement is not analyzed using the value chain or interdependency perspective. Unlike EDI-based IOIS, e-procurement has greater reach and can fundamentally change the way organizations generate and add value. For example, Cisco and Dell have used the Internet to enable drop shipping, where the supplier

Table 1. IOIS classification

Author(s)	Classification Criteria	Typology
Barrett and Konsynski (1982)	Intensity of organization's participation	Remote I/O node; application processing node; multi-participant exchange node; network control node; integrating network node
Bakos (1987)	Value chain perspective	Two dimensions: functional structure and location of value-adding process
Malone, Benjamin, and Yates (1987)	Transaction cost economics	E-market and e-hierarchy
Choudhury (1997)	Transaction cost economics	E-monopolies, e-dyad, and multilateral IOIS
Johnston and Vitale (1988)	Competitive advantage and innovation	Dimensions are: business purpose; relationship between the sponsoring organizations and other participants; and information functions performed by the IOIS.
Benjamin, deLong, and Scott Morton (1990)	Transaction cost economics	Two dimensions: e-market versus e-hierarchies and routine transaction versus task support
Kumar and van Dissel (1996)	Interdependence among organizations	Networked IOIS, pooled information resource IOIS, and value/supply-chain IOIS
Hong (2002)	Role linkage and system support level	Resource pooling, operational cooperation, operational coordination, and complementary cooperation
Riggins and Rhee (1998)	Level of information shared	Intronets and Supranet

directly sends products to the end users. Thus changing the way that the focal organization adds value. Similarly, one also needs to analyze e-procurement using inter-organizational interdependencies. For example, consortium-sponsored e-markets such as Covisint.com generate pooled interdependencies among participating organizations. Analyzing e-procurement using interdependencies can better explain the emergence of these e-markets.

Analyzing Ownership Patterns

Unlike any other information systems, e-procurement includes two or more organizations. Hence organizations have to make a choice: Should the system be proprietary in nature or should it be open to all? Choudhury (1997) proposed that organizations could develop IOIS competitively or cooperatively, that is, with the involvement of other organizations at the same level of the value chain. The choice depends on the strategic significance of the IOIS and the size and bargaining power of the initiating organizations. When the strategic significance of the IOIS is high, a single user or a consortium of users (if bargaining power is low) will develop the IOIS based on a proprietary format. In the case of low strategic significance, the IOIS will be developed on a standard format. Volkoff, Chan, and Newson (1999) argued that in a collaborative IOIS, which is built to support reciprocal interdependencies, there is no obvious focal point for leadership and strategic drive, since no organization have enough power to become initiator and provide leadership. They argued that for a successful collaborative IOIS, some tasks require a sponsor external to all partners, whereas other tasks need an executive sponsor within each organization. Bakos and Nault (1997) argued that in an electronic market, if one or more assets are essential to all network participants, then all the assets should be owned together. Further, if there exists a single network participant who is indispensable to an asset essential to all participants, then he should own all network assets. In the absence of an indispensable participant and as long as the cooperation of at least two participants is necessary to create value, sole ownership is never the best form of ownership for an electronic network. This later result implies that as the leading participants of electronic networks become more dispensable, we should see movement towards forms of joint ownership.

Unlike EDI-based IOIS, e-procurement systems are relatively inexpensive and easy to implement. Hence, organizations may choose more than one way to develop e-procurement systems. As evident from numerous industry examples (the U.S. automobile industry has consortium-sponsored e-markets, private e-markets, and online collaboration systems), rather than simply sticking to one system, organizations may develop a portfolio of e-procurement systems. Further research needs to explore how organizations can manage this portfolio resulting in the right "supplier relation/product procured/e-procurement system" mix.

Determining E-Procurement Systems: Product and Supply Market Characteristics

Typology and ownership pattern analysis raises an important question: Why should an organization choose a specific e-procurement system? Conversely, what factors determine the emergence of various e-procurement systems? Choudhury (1997) suggested that an organization's choice of IOIS depends on the fit between the benefits offered by the particular IOIS and the benefits most valuable to the organization given the characteristics of the transactions to be supported by IOIS. Malone et al. (1987) proposed three kinds of transaction cost efficiencies that IOIS can offer. They are: electronic brokerage (low search cost); electronic communication (faster and efficient transmission of information); and electronic integration (efficient dyadic relationships that go beyond exchange of routine information). They proposed that transactions for products with high asset specificity and/or complexity of description will be supported by electronic hierarchies, while transactions for other products will be supported by electronic market. They have also suggested that the increasing adoption of IT will lead to a greater degree of outsourcing and hence less vertically-integrated organizations. Moreover, since search costs are reduced, organizations will rely more on search, leading to the emergence of e-markets. However, in a study of the airline parts supply industry, Choudhury (1997) revealed that even in cases of low complexity, organizations were not going for e-markets. He proposed that the choice rather depends on technological and volume uncertainty of demand and market variability. An organization will implement multilateral IOIS (similar to e-markets) for products with high market variability and high technological uncertainty but low volume uncertainty. Electronic dyads are more suitable for low market variability. Similarly, electronic monopolies (similar to e-hierarchy) are more suitable for low market variability and high volume uncertainty. Clemons,

Reddi, and Row (1993) argued that factors such as transaction economy of scale, learning curve effects, and so forth, favor a move towards long-term relationships with a small set of suppliers. Rosenthal, Shah, and Xiao (1993) concluded that purchasing policy is a force that will drive organizations to use hierarchies as their coordination mechanism. They have argued that the issues of quality, material costs, and product differentiation impose constraints on purchasing decisions. Hence hierarchies will prevail over markets.

It can be seen that the impact of information technology on the choice of governance structure (e-market vs. e-hierarchy) is not very clear. Literature using transaction cost economics overlook issues such as trust, competitive intent, and social fabric that influence the decision regarding choice of IOIS. For example, Riggins and Rhee (1998) argued that although consortium-sponsored Supranet promises significant efficiency improvements and better inter-organizational team coordination, they might easily be copied by a competing ecosystem. What is more likely is that Intronets, where individual companies maintain proprietary access to a unique information product, are better candidates for achieving significant competitive advantage. Bensaou and Anderson (1999) found that buyers make more specific investments to increase coordination when the manufacturing task is complex, to buffer against technological uncertainty and to build close relations when the requisite production skills are scarce. They found more specific investment in supply arrangements that are embedded in a broader business relationship. They also found a lower specific investment in a Japanese context. Their finding related to technological uncertainty contradicts Choudhury's (1997) finding, who argued that organizations will use an e-market-like system to manage uncertainty. Future studies can explore the impact of socio-cultural context on e-procurement choice. Similar views were expressed by Hempel and Kwong (2001), who argued that there is a fundamental difficulty in applying the Western best practices in e-commerce to Asian economies because of differences in business and cultural assumptions. Since e-procurement increases the business scope and context, the social-cultural issues become yet more prominent in e-procurement research.

Based on the above discussion, we can classify determinants of e-procurement systems as supply market characteristics and product characteristics. Product characteristics include variables such as complexity of description, volume uncertainty, and technological uncertainty. Supply market characteristics include variables such as trust with the existing suppliers, the age of the relationship, competitive intent among suppliers, market variability, and the bargaining power of the initiator.

Effect on Inter-Organizational Relationships (IOR)

E-procurement provides a new communication medium between business partners and affects the relationship between participating organizations. In IOIS research, some studies have shown a positive impact of IOIS use on inter-organizational relationships, while others have shown a negative relation. Studies showing a positive relation argue that since IOIS provides more information to facilitate mutual understanding, hence it should have a positive impact on relationships. For example, Stern and Kaufmann (1985) found that IOIS provides higher satisfaction in the bargaining situations, because it provides more complete and accurate information. Vijayasarathy and Robey (1997) found that more IOIS use leads to higher channel cooperation through its effect on information exchange intensity and channel formalization. Stump and Sriram (1997) also reported that an increased percentage of transactions using IT increases the overall closeness of the buyer-supplier relationship.

However, some studies argue that since IOIS reduce information asymmetry and have an impact on an organization's bargaining power, it can have a negative impact on inter-organizational relationships. Hart and Saunders (1997) suggested that information sharing with trading partners increases an organization's vulnerability. Similarly Clemons and Row (1993) described the case of grocery retailers who lost their bargaining power because IOIS reduced information asymmetry with manufacturers. Iacovou, Benbasat, and Dexter (1995) argued that small organizations are coerced to adopt IOIS by bigger trading partners, hence putting them into a disadvantageous position. Nakayama (2003) found that the retailers perceive less cooperation as the IOIS use increases, whereas their suppliers perceive reduction in conflict as IOIS use increases. At the operational level, retailers do perceive an increase in knowledge about partners as IOIS use increases, whereas suppliers does not perceive the same. However, both of them perceive that IOIS does increase joint decision-making.

The above studies were conducted on proprietary EDI-based IOIS. Unlike them, Internet-based e-procurement is much more pervasive, and transaction cost is significantly lower. Hence their impacts on IOR seem to be even greater. Further, except for Nakayama (2003), other studies have either taken only the suppliers' or buyers' perspective. Studying both partners in dyadic relation can offer a more complete and accurate picture, since their perceptions about IOIS differ significantly. Various measures such as cooperation,

Table 2. Research on IOIS and IOR

Author(s)	Relationship Measure	Results
Stern and Kaufmann (1985)	Satisfaction	Positive relation
Vijayasarathy and Robey (1997)	Channel Cooperation	Positive relation
Stump and Sriram (1997)	Overall Closeness	Positive relation
Hart and Saunders (1997)	Vulnerability	Positive relation
Clemons and Row (1993)	Bargaining Power	Negative relation
Nayakama (2003)	Cooperation	Negative (for retailers)
	Conflict	Negative (for suppliers)

satisfaction, conflict, overall closeness, and so forth, have been used to measure relationships. Individually, these variables cover only one aspect of IOR. Hence there is a need for a comprehensive study, including a few of these variables. Relationship quality is one such comprehensive measure. It can measure the extent to which a relationship is transactional or relational in nature. It is basically a three-dimensional measure, which includes trust, commitment, and satisfaction.

How Does E-Procurement Generate Value?

Subramaniam and Shaw (2002) proposed process quality, total procurement cost, user satisfaction, and system responsiveness as the performance measures for an e-procurement system. They also proposed that from the buying organization's point of view, use of a Web-based system affects four major categories of B2B operations: search, order processing, monitoring and control, and coordination. Lederer, Mirchandani, and Sims (2001) proposed that an organization could use the World Wide Web to create strategic advantage through improved customer relationships resulting from greater business efficiency and better information access and flexibility. Bakos (1991) argued that lower search costs, due to e-markets, enable buyers to search more suppliers and thus reduction in prices. Similarly, e-hierarchy provides functions ranging from simple order entry and invoicing, to product promotion, to document and data sharing, to joint product development and knowledge transfer (Chatfield & Yetton, 2000; Riggins & Rhee, 1998). E-hierarchies also enable collaborative forecast and efficient scheduling. It also saves expenses on order entry and improves customer services. (Mukhopadhyay, Kekre, & Kalathur, 1995; Riggins & Mukhopadhyay, 1994). Access to the buyer's inventory, sales, and product information also enables the participating supplier to accumulate expertise about market demand product features, which usually will lead to product innovation and market expansion (Riggins & Rhee, 1998; Subramani, 1999). Riggins and Rhee (1999) proposed that extranets could be used to create new knowledge through socialization, combination, externalization, and internalization. However, knowledge creation depends on media richness. Bakos and Brynjolfsson (1993a, 1993b) have argued that tightly-coupled operations supported by IT require increased investments by suppliers in non-contractible resources, such as quality, innovation, and information sharing. Bakos and Brynjolfsson (1993b) found that there are specific investments from the suppliers that benefit the buyer in terms of responsiveness, higher quality, innovation, and technology adoption. Benefits from IOIS is a function of number of suppliers participated. Treleven and Schweikhart (1988) argued that decisions regarding the number of suppliers can have a significant impact on total costs and can restrict the benefits from technology. Using Shapley value analysis, Raupp and Schober (2000) argued that when the number of suppliers increases, the value that any one supplier could obtain from the buyer-supplier relationship decreases.

Table 3 summarized the benefits proposed by IOIS. There is a need of empirical investigation on how initiators and adopters are benefited from e-procurement systems. We need to understand how the number of suppliers and the level of adoption efforts affect the value generated by the systems. Researches on IOIS have identified the supplier's specific investment in technology as having strategic benefit to the buyer. Present e-procurement systems require minimal specific investment from suppliers. Further, these investments can be redeployed in other relationships using middleware and imparting specialized training. Hence it raises another question about how e-procurement can generate strategic benefits for the organization.

How Does Value Get Apportioned?

Though e-procurement can definitely create value for an organization, the distribution of these benefits is a critical question. If the initiator takes all of

Table 3. Benefits from procurement IOIS

Benefits Identified	Authors
Process quality	Subramaniam and Shaw (2002)
Reduced procurement cost	Bakos (1991), Subramaniam and Shaw (2002), Mukhopadhayay, Kekre, and Kalathur (1995)
User satisfaction	Subramaniam and Shaw (2002)
Increased responsiveness	Bakos and Brynjolfsson (1993b), Subramaniam and Shaw (2002)
Improved customer service	Lederer, Mirchandani, and Sims (2001), Mukhopadhyay, Kekre, and Kalathur (1995), Riggins and Mukhopadhyay (1994)
Product innovation	Subramani (1999), Riggins and Rhee (1998), Bakos and Brynjolfsson (1993a, 1993b)
Market expansion	Subramani (1999)

the benefits, then what is the motivation for the adopters? Seidmann and Sundararajan (1997) used game theory to demonstrate that, although the supplier creates more value, the buyer (or initiator, who has the channel power) takes all outcomes. This is true irrespective of the levels of information shared by the organizations. Similarly, Drew (2003) argued that the Internet might not be an unmitigated blessing for small and medium enterprises (SMEs). The degree to which SMEs experience the Internet, as a threat or an opportunity, will depend on their market structure, industry structure, and macro environment. However, Lee, Clark, and Tam (1999) claimed that EDI adopters, who do not have channel power, can achieve significant benefits from EDI implementation if it is merged with changes in inter-organizational processes and policies. Analyzing the daily data on inventory level and stock-outs of 31 retail chains, they demonstrated that adopter organizations can also achieve dramatic performance improvements. Venkatraman and Zaheer (1990) also reported that insurance agents who were electronically interfaced with the focal carrier increased new business policies, but not the effectiveness or operating efficiencies. Crook and Kumar (1998) proposed a framework for understanding EDI use. They suggest that organizational (size, capabilities, management support) and environmental (industry experience with technology, suppliers, and customer's nature) context, together with casual conditions, affects the EDI use. They have also suggested that strategies (coercion, support, and collaboration) affect the consequence of EDI use. Bergeron and Raymond (1997) have found that while imposing EDI is associated with lower advantage in the short run, it does not have such an effect in the long run. Tuunainen (1999) suggested that small businesses could benefit in many ways from EDI. It is possible through more extensive business integration with a supplier's own and their partner's value chain or an expanded customer base. Kalwani and Narayandas (1995) suggested that suppliers that engage in a long-term relationship appear to suffer on some dimensions, namely margins. However, they profit on other dimensions, such as inventory holding costs. On the whole, the suppliers that invest in long-term relationships make profits by being able to grow their overall business and by improving their return on investment.

However, how suppliers are benefited by e-procurement systems has yet to be studied. Future studies can evaluate the impact of online bidding systems on suppliers' overall performance. Web-based bidding systems offer broader geographic coverage, which puts extreme pressure on suppliers' margins. The question is not whether suppliers should participate in e-procurement or not. The question to be asked is: How should they participate in e-procurement systems, so that they can also derive benefits?

Adoption and Implementation Risks

Like its predecessors, benefits from e-procurement can be hindered because of adoption and implementation risks. Riggins and Mukhopadhyay (1999) identified two areas where the inter-organizational system inherently carries more risk than ordinary information technology projects. These are adoption (whether business partners will join the system or not) and implementation risk (whether business partners will be able to implement the system optimally). Subsidies such as training, free software, and so forth, can be used to overcome these risks. This raises the question about how to provide subsidy, and to whom it should be provided. Reggins, Kriebel, and Mukhopadhyay (1995) proposed that as the cost to adopt the technology decreases at some steady rate over time, the buyer would hold off from offering any subsidy to join. Then, at some predetermined appropriate time, the buyer will offer a subsidy aimed at achieving full supplier participation. Riggins and Mukhopadhyay (1999) have suggested that the initiator should carry out an IOIS-readiness audit of their partners. When the initiator is able to target "ready" suppliers, they may not need to subsidize certain late laggards who may view adoption as a competitive necessity. Iacovou et al. (1995) identified perceived benefits, organizational readiness, and external pressure as explanatory factors for EDI adoption by small organizations. Their empirical finding suggests that external pressure from trading partners is a major reason for EDI adoption by small companies. Gebauer and Buxmann (2000) identified trust as a major hindrance for high IOIS growth rate. They divided costs of adoption into two dimensions, namely frequency of occurrence (one-time setup cost, current costs) and specificity (general system-related costs, partner-related costs). Chircu and Kauffman (2000) developed an intermediation-disintermediation-reintermediation (IDR) framework to look at the traditional intermediate's role in e-procurement. They asserted that reintermediation, especially by organizations with long-term commitments to their marketplaces, is likely to occur in the long run. They proposed three conditions for reintermediation to occur, namely imitation and weak appropriability of e-commerce innovations, ownership of co-specialized assets, and economies of scale. Davila, Gupat, and Palmer (2003) identified aggressive and conservative adopters of e-procurement technologies, and argued that these technologies will become an important part of supply chain management and that the rate of adoption will accelerate as aggressive adopters share their experience.

Conclusion

This chapter looked into prior research on IOIS, EDI, channel management, and procurement to identify future research issues in e-procurement. It is argued that research in e-procurement inherits some research issues from EDI-based IOIS. For example, though the IOIS classification proposed by Malone et al. (1987) and later augmented by Choudhury (1997) seem to prevail over other typology, one important question remains unanswered: How do organizations choose a specific IOIS? Prior work did not look at issues such as supply market characteristic, relationships with existing suppliers, knowledge creation, and product development. Prior works have taken transaction, organization, and industry level variables (complexity, uncertainty, etc.) as the units of analysis; however, there is no research available where relation (a unique tuple of buyer-supplier-product) was taken as the unit of analysis. An analysis of supplier-buyer relation and e-procurement can enable us to look at the impact of socio-cultural variables on the choice of an e-procurement system.

There are some areas where e-procurement systems differ significantly from its predecessors. For example, there is no literature available on the effect of e-procurement on inter-organizational relationships. Prior research has been carried out mostly on proprietary EDI. Unlike its predecessors, e-procurement is far more pervasive and hence capable of putting extreme pressures on suppliers' margins. The impact of a buyer consortium, which creates a virtual monopoly on suppliers' performance, calls for a detailed research. Except for Nakayama (2003), prior researches have not taken both sides of the buyer-supplier dyad into consideration. An empirical investigation on e-procurement can study both partners of the dyadic relation to understand its effect on the entire supply chain. Relationship quality is proposed as a measure to understand the impact of e-procurement on IOR. Similarly, strategic benefits from e-procurement need to be explored further. Organizations are using e-procurement mainly for indirect procurement, thus aiming at operational benefits. The Web-based functions and services used in e-procurement are easily replicable and do not call for much specific investment. So what is the source of strategic benefit from e-procurement, and how does it get apportioned? Answering these questions will definitely enhance our understanding about e-procurement.

References

Bakos, J. Y. (1987). *Inter-organizational information systems: Strategic implications for competition and cooperation.* Doctoral thesis, MIT Sloan School of Management, Cambridge, MA.

Bakos, J. Y. (1991). A strategic analysis of electronic marketplaces. *MIS Quarterly, 15*(3), 295-310.

Bakos, J. Y., & Brynjolfsson, E. (1993a). Why information technology hasn't increased the optimal number of suppliers. In *Proceedings of the 26th Hawaii International Conference on System Sciences* (pp. 799-808).

Bakos, J. Y., & Brynjolfsson, E. (1993b). Information technology, incentives, and the optimal number of suppliers. *Journal of Management Information Systems, 10*(2), 37-54.

Bakos, J. Y., & Nault, B. R. (1997). Ownership and investment in electronic networks. *Information Systems Research, 8*(4), 321-341.

Barrett, S., & Konsynski, B. R. (1982). Inter-organization information systems. *MIS Quarterly, 6*(4), 93-105.

Benjamin, R. I., deLong, D. W., & Scott Morton, M. S. (1990). Electronic data interchange: How much competitive advantage? *Long Range Planning, 23*(1), 29-40.

Bensaou, M., & Anderson, E. (1999). Buyer-supplier relations in industrial markets: When do buyers risk making idiosyncratic investments? *Organisation Science, 10*(4), 460-481.

Bergeron, F., & Raymond, L. (1997). Managing EDI for corporate advantage: A longitudinal study. *Information and Management, 31*(6), 319-333.

Cash, Jr., J. I., & Konsynski, B. R. (1985). IS redraws competitive boundaries. *Harvard Business Review, 63*(2), 134-142

Chatfield, A. K., & Yetton, P. (2000). Strategic payoff from EDI as a function of EDI embeddedness. *Journal of Management Information Systems, 16*(4), 195-224.

Chircu, A. M., & Kauffman, R. J. (2000). Reintermediation strategies in business-to-business electronic commerce. *International Journal of Electronic Commerce, 4*(4), 7-42.

Choudhury, V. (1997). Strategic choices in the development of inter-organisational information systems. *Information Systems Research, 8*(1), 1-24.

Clemons, E. K., Reddi, S. P., & Row, M. C. (1993). The impact of information technology on the organization of economic activity: The "move to the middle" hypothesis. *Journal of Management Information Systems, 10*(2), 9-35.

Clemons, E. K., & Row, M. C. (1993). Limits to interfirm coordination through information technology: Results of a field study in consumer packaged goods distribution. *Journal of Management Information Systems, 10*(1), 73-95.

Crook, C. W., & Kumar, R. L. (1998). Electronic data interchange: A multi-industry investigation using grounded theory. *Information and Management, 34*(2), 75-89.

Davila, A., Gupat, M., & Palmer, R. (2003). Moving procurement systems to the Internet: The adoption and use of e-procurement technology models. *European Management Journal, 21*(1), 11-23.

Drew, S. (2003). Strategic use of e-commerce by SMEs in the east of England. *European Management Journal, 21*(1), 79-88.

Gebauer, J., & Buxmann, P. (2000). Assessing the value of inter-organizational systems to support business transactions. *International Journal of Electronic Commerce, 4*(4), 61-82.

Hart, P., & Saunders, C. (1997). Power and trust: Critical factors in the adoption and use of electronic data interchange. *Organization Science, 8*(1), 23-42.

Hempel, P. S., & Kwong, Y. K. (2001). B2B e-commerce in emerging economies: I-metal.com's non-ferrous metals exchange in China. *Journal of Strategic Information Systems, 10*(4), 335-355.

Hong, I. B. (2002). A new framework for interorganizational systems based on the linkage of the participant's roles. *Information and Management, 39*(4), 261-270.

Iacovou, C. L., Benbasat, I., & Dexter, A. S. (1995). Electronic data interchange and small organizations: Adoption and impact of technology. *MIS Quarterly, 19*(4), 465-485.

Johnston, H. R., & Vitale, M. R. (1988). Creating competitive advantage with inter-organisational information systems. *MIS Quarterly, 12*(2), 153-166.

Johnston, R. B., & Mak, H. C. (2000). An emerging vision of Internet-enabled supply chain electronic commerce. *International Journal of Electronic Commerce, 4*(4), 43-59.

Kalwani, M., & Narayandas, N. (1995). Long term manufacture-supplier relationships: Do they pay off for supplier firms? *Journal of Marketing, 59*(January), 1-16.

Kaufman, F. (1966). Data systems that cross company boundaries. *Harvard Business Review, 44*(1), 141-152.

Kumar, K., & van Dissel, H. G. (1996). Sustainable collaboration: Managing conflict and cooperation in inter-organizational systems. *MIS Quarterly, 20*(3), 279-300.

Lederer, A. L., Mirchandani, D. A., & Sims, K. (2001). The search for strategic advantage from the World Wide Web. *International Journal of Electronic Commerce, 5*(4), 117-133.

Lee, H. G., Clark, T., & Tam, K. Y. (1999). Can EDI benefit adopters? *Information Systems Research, 10*(2), 186-197.

Malone, T. W., Yates, J., & Benjamin, R. I. (1987). Electronic markets and electronic hierarchies. *Communications of ACM, 30*(6), 484-497.

Mukhopadhyay, T., Kekre, S., & Kalathur, S. (1995). Business value of information technology: A study of electronic data interchange. *MIS Quarterly, 19*(2), 137-156.

Nakayama, M. (2003). An assessment of EDI use and other channel communications on trading behavior and trading partner knowledge. *Information and Management, 40*(6), 563-580.

Neef, D. (2002). *E-procurement from strategy to implementation.* NJ: Prentice Hall PTR.

Ngai, E. W. T., & Wat, F. K. T. (2002). A literature review and classification of electronic commerce research. *Information and Management, 39*(5), 415-429.

Rayport, J., & Jaworski, B. (2002). *Introduction to e-commerce.* New York: McGraw-Hill.

Riggins, F. J., & Mukhopadhyay, T. (1994). Interdependent benefits from inter-organizational systems: Opportunities for business partner reengineering. *Journal of Management Information Systems, 11*(2), 37-57.

Riggins, F. J., & Mukhopadhyay, T. (1999). Overcoming adoption and implementation risks of EDI. *International Journal of Electronic Commerce, 3*(4), 103-115.

Riggins, F. J., Mukhopadhyay, T., & Kriebel, C. H. (1995). Optimal policies for subsidizing supplier interorganizational system adoption. *Journal of Organizational Computing, 5*(3), 195-326.

Riggins, F. J., & Rhee, H. S. (1998). Towards a unified of electronic commerce. *Communications of the ACM, 41*(10), 88-95.

Riggins, F. J., & Rhee, H. S. (1999). Developing the learning network using extranet. *International Journal of Electronic Commerce, 4*(1), 65-83.

Rosenthal, D., Shah, S. K., & Xiao, B. (1993). The impact of purchasing policy on electronic markets and electronic hierarchies. *Information and Management, 25*(2), 105-117.

Schober, F., & Raupp, M. (2000, January 4-7). Why buyer-supplier chains differ: A strategic framework for electronic network organizations. In *Proceedings of the 33rd Hawaii International Conference on System Sciences,* (CD-ROM). Computer Society Press.

Seidmann, A., & Sundararajan, A. (1997). Building and sustaining inter-organizational information sharing relationships: The competitive impact of interfacing supply chain operations with marketing strategy. In K. Kumar & J. I. DeGross (Eds.), *Proceedings of the International Conference of Information System,* Atlanta (pp. 205-222).

Stern, L. W., & Kaufmann, P. J. (1985). Electronic data interchange in selected consumer goods industries: An inter-organisational perspective. In R. Buzzel (Ed.), *Marketing in an electronic age* (pp. 52-74). Boston: Harvard Business School Press.

Stump, R. L., & Sriram, V. (1997). Employing information technology in purchasing: Buyer-supplier relationship and the size of supplier base. *Industrial Marketing Management, 26*(2), 127-136.

Subramani, M. R. (1999). Linking IT use to benefits in interorganizational networks: The mediating role of relationship-specific intangible investments. In *Proceedings of the 20th International Conference on Information Systems (ICIS-99),* Charlotte, NC (pp. 358-363).

Subramaniam, C., & Shaw, M. J. (2002). A study of the value and impact of B2B e-commerce: The case of Web-based procurement. *International Journal of Electronic Commerce, 6*(4), 19-40.

Treleven, M., & Schweikhart, S. B. (1988). A risk/benefit analysis of sourcing strategies: Single vs. multiple sourcing. *Journal of Operations Management, 7*(4), 93-114.

Tuunainen, V. P. (1999). Opportunities of effective integration of EDI for small businesses in the automotive industry. *Information and Management, 34*(6), 361-375.

Venkatraman, N., & Zaheer, A. (1990). Electronic integration and strategic advantage: A quasi-experimental study in the insurance industry. *Information Systems Research, 1*(4), 377-393.

Vijayasarathy, L. R., & Robey, D. (1997). The effect of EDI on marketing channel relationships in retailing. *Information and Management, 33*(2), 73-86.

Volkoff, O., Chan, Y. E., & Newson, E. F. P. (1999). Leading the development and implementation of collaborative inter-organisational systems. *Information and Management, 35*(2), 63-75.

Williamson, O. E. (1991, June). Comparative economic organization: The analysis of discrete structural alternatives. *Administrative Science Quarterly, 36*, 269-296.

Chapter II

Organizational Assimilation of E-Procurement:
An Institutional Perspective and the Research Model

Kishor Vaidya, University of New England, Australia

Abstract

The focus of the majority of research on e-procurement has been on the possible impact of e-procurement adoption on the buyer's interaction with the suppliers, whereas very little has been discussed about e-procurement assimilation. This chapter looks beyond the decision of adoption of the technology, investigating the environmental conditions that may influence the successful assimilation of e-procurement in the public sector organizations. Using institutional theory and building on prior research on the theories of technology assimilation, this chapter investigates the institutional factors that enable higher levels of e-procurement assimilation in the public sector and also argues that the e-procurement benefits greatly depend on the operational and strategic organizational assimilation of e-procurement with different levels of success. This chapter also discusses the need to integrate other theories such as diffusion of innovation theory, transactional cost theory, and structurational theory of technology use, and proposes a holistic research model in order to investigate the antecedent conditions that are likely to influence the assimilation of public e-procurement.

Introduction and Background

Procurement encompasses a range of activities such as information search, requisition request, approval, purchase order, delivery receiving, and payment (operational activities), and identifying sourcing opportunities, negotiation, and contract (strategic activities) (Gebauer & Segev, 2001). Electronic procurement (e-procurement), for the purpose of this chapter, has been defined as the use of Internet-based information and communication technologies (ICTs) in order to carry out one or more transactional or strategic procurement activities. While there is no consistency in defining the terms procurement process and e-procurement in the existing literature (Vaidya, Yu, Soar, & Turner, 2003), this chapter considers various transactional and strategic procurement activities as the standard procurement process which can be conducted by using e-procurement technologies, including e-tendering, e-auctions, e-catalogues, e-marketplace, and integrated in-house or third-party e-procurement software (e-procurement system).

Over the last several years, the implementation of e-procurement has experienced explosive growth in some organizations, while others have resisted its assimilation. It has been suggested that if e-procurement were to be fully assimilated, it could save governments up to 5% on expenditure and up to 50-80% on transaction costs (Commissions of the European Communities [CEC], 2004). According to the recent e-procurement benchmark report by the Aberdeen Group, (Minhan, 2004), organizations have been able to reduce off-contract spending by 64%, requisition-to-order cycles by 66%, and requisition-to-order costs by 58%. IDC predicts that e-procurement will grow from US$225 billion in 2002 to about US$1.5 trillion by 2006 (Hamblen, 2002). Greater estimates have been made for the emerging economies. However, despite the growth of e-procurement and the potential benefits provided by the technology, organizations differ in the speed with which they assimilate e-procurement. Needless to say, the contribution of new technologies such as e-procurement to the improved procurement performance of an organization can only be realized when and if the procurement innovations are widely assimilated.

E-procurement has been on the political agenda in a number of countries as part of their e-government initiatives (Henriksen & Andersen, 2003). Of the entire multitude of developments that constitute the emergence of e-government, e-procurement is perhaps the most complex. While there are a variety of paths to implementation, comprehensive e-procurement across the public sector is inevitably large, involving hundreds or even thousands of buyers and suppliers. International experience is that, much more often than not, an assimilation gap (Fichman & Kemerer, 1997) will occur between adoption and implementation. In other words, regardless of the widespread initial adoption, an innovation may still not be thoroughly deployed among the organizations that acquire the innovation. As such, it is important to note that theories of technology assimilation (Cooper & Zmud, 1990; Fichman & Kemerer, 1997; Tornatzky & Klein, 1982) distinguish assimilation from the concept of adoption. Adoption is a dichotomous variable and indicates whether the organization has reached a decision of whether or not to utilize e-procurement, whereas assimilation is the extent of collective results of various antecedent conditions, the focus of this chapter being the discussion of the conditions that may influence the assimilation of e-procurement from the environmental perspective. While there has been much research on the issues of technology adoption, there has been very little research on assimilation issues.

From the theoretical arguments in the theories of technical assimilation, Purvis, Sambamurthy, and Zmud (2001) defined assimilation as the extent to which the use of the technology diffuses across the organizational projects or work processes and becomes routine in the activities of those projects and processes. In line with this definition, e-procurement assimilation, for the purpose of this chapter, is defined as the extent to which the organizational use of e-procurement technologies, including the e-procurement software, e-tendering, and e-marketplace diffuses across the procurement process and becomes standard business practice in facilitating transactional and strategic procurement activities associated with that process.

The objective of this chapter is to identify the environmental antecedent conditions that may influence the assimilation of public e-procurement. Published research and studies in the disciplines of information systems (IS)/inter-organizational information systems (IOS), electronic commerce (e-commerce) and supply chain management (SCM) have developed integrated models to define constructs relating to the environmental factors that impact innovation adoption. However, limited research has been focused on the relationship between innovation assimilation and the environmental factors in the public procurement context. The lack of research has also been noted by Qu and Pinsonneault (2004), who believe that the environmental factor is a key contingency for the success of e-procurement, since the industrial context can influence an organization's strategic decision. Due to word limitations on this chapter, an extensive discussion on institutionalization will not be provided; for a better understanding, only its relevance to the environmental factors associated with e-procurement assimilation will be considered.

The research method for this chapter is based on reviewing existing theory and applying it to other settings or issues to arrive at a new conceptual idea (Maxwell, 1996). The basis for reviewing theory is by identifying existing literature and noting any relevancies. The relevancies serve as the foundation for the development of new concepts. The literature review for this chapter was focused on various IS/IOS, organizational change models, and change management literature. The result of this exercise will be a conceptual theoretical framework (a research model) stated in qualitative terms.

The chapter is structured as follows. In the next section, the dependent variable, the intensity of e-procurement assimilation, has been conceptualized, followed by the discussion of the public procurement and the institutional theory, and the institutional pressures relevant for the greater assimilation of e-procurement have been identified. Following this, a literature review of environmental factors impacting IOS and Web-based IOS has been presented in order to identify the associated antecedent conditions that are likely to influence the assimilation of e-procurement. The chapter also discusses the three influential theories: diffusion of innovation theory (Rogers, 1983, 1995), transaction cost theory (Williamson, 1985), and structurational theory of technology use (Orlikowski, Yates, Okamura, & Fujimoto, 1995) that provide the theoretical foundation for the proposed research. The final sections of the chapter briefly discuss the future research plans and present a holistic research model that can help understand the relationships between the antecedent conditions and the e-procurement assimilation, and in turn, its impact on the overall procurement performance.

Intensity of E-Procurement Assimilation

As e-procurement comes in various forms, assessing the intensity of e-procurement assimilation can help identify what the public sector agencies are doing with e-procurement, which steps of the procurement process have been automated with e-procurement technologies, and how intensively each step of the operational and strategic procurement process have been "e-enabled." By differentiating the intensity of e-procurement assimilation across the procurement process, it can be possible to link each domain of assimilation with its resulting dimension of procurement performance. As such, the main dependent variable, the intensity of e-procurement assimilation, is conceptualized as an aggregate measure of three different but related dimensions: a set of e-procurement technologies which are utilized, common factors that have influence in the assimilation stages (Fichman & Kemerer, 1997), and the extent of each e-procurement technology's penetration across the procurement process. The assimilation process that includes adoption, implementation, and routinization (Kwon & Zmud, 1987; Prescott & Conger, 1995) has been modelled as containing the five stages: (1) intention to implement; (2) evaluation or pilot use; (3) commitment; (4) limited deployment; and (5) generalized deployment (Fichman & Kemerer, 1997). However, the participants of our pilot study indicated that they had to reject a few e-procurement initiatives once they were partly deployed in their organizations. This necessitated us to include the sixth stage of "rejection" in the assimilation process. This sort of approach is in line with Ramiller and Swanson (2003) who argue that the implementation of an innovation cannot be considered successful even if it survives through the deployment stage, as the innovation may ultimately be rejected by its users. Together, these three dimensions mentioned above provide an e-procurement intensity index that signifies how many e-procurement technologies are being used in an organization, to what extent these technologies are being assimilated, and in which stage of the procurement process. An aggregate strategy has been chosen to represent these three dimensions in order for the findings to be more robust and generalizable as our study favors aggregation of innovative technologies, identified by Fichman and Kemerer (2001).

Public Procurement

Public procurement establishes a contractual relationship between the government and the private sector (suppliers). Unlike the procurement in the private sector whose sole goal is to maximize profit, the government has various economic, political, and social goals on top of improving efficiency and effectiveness in procurement (Tether, 1977). In addition, the government is subject to institutional pressures that are unique to the public sector; it is publicly accountable to the taxpayers' money and as such, it must maintain transparency in its procurement processes. Furthermore, the government must develop unique strategies, guidelines, and policies in order to satisfy these requirements and thus address various problems associated with public procurement.

E-procurement can be expected to minimize discretion and personal favors from the decision-making process in public procurement as the Internet-based technology minimizes the chances of physical contacts with the potential suppliers. This can greatly help safeguard accountability in the procurement process. Similarly, transparency is another central characteristic of a sound and efficient public procurement system. Transparency in public procurement requires the disclosure of information sufficient to allow the involved stakeholders to know how the system is intended to work, and all potential suppliers have the same information about procurement opportunities, award criteria, and decisions (Organisation for Economic Cooperation and Development [OECD], 2003).

E-procurement can also be expected to provide real-time information on the various steps involved in the procurement process to enable potential suppliers to make informed decisions about whether to bid and how to improve the relevance of their bids by better addressing the government's needs and priorities. E-procurement promotes transparency in public purchases so that citizens can see quotations through the Internet in a universal and democratic way. It allows the public sector agencies to buy products and services directly from registered suppliers. The technology also makes it easy to find or track information about any purchase at any time. Further, because transactional information flows through the e-procurement systems, it is possible to easily monitor and extract information about orders, goods receipts, invoices, and vendor information such as price history, quantity, reliability, compliance, and quality; this all greatly contributes to transparency.

Given the transparency and accountability requirements of the governments and the opportunities provided by e-procurement to address the requirements in the public procurement process, it is important to understand which institutional (environmental) factors are likely to influence the assimilation of e-procurement. The section below reviews the Institutional Theory and derives the relevant factors from the theory.

Institutional Theory

The concept of institutions as "rules of the game in a society or, more formally, as the humanly devised constraints that shape human interaction… they structure incentives in human exchange, whether political, social or economic" (North, 1990, p. 3) is relevant to this chapter. Also, analyzing institutional change within public e-procurement can be expected to reveal how several adjustments in the "rules of the game" affect the behavior of agents.

Institutional forces guide strategic changes in the organizations. Institutional theory suggests organizations adopt rules and practices that may not necessarily increase technical efficiency, but do increase legitimacy in external stakeholders' view (DiMaggio & Powell, 1983). According to the authors, an increase in the number of organizations that adopt and implement an innovation creates pressure on the remaining organizations and trading partners and manipulates their decisions. Organizational legitimacy is the central element in institutional theory. It refers to the acceptance of an organization by its external environment (Deephouse, 1996; DiMaggio & Powell, 1983). Organizations achieve this legitimacy through adopting processes, structures, and strategies that others have already taken (Deephouse, 1996; DiMaggio & Powell, 1983). Organizational legitimacy in the case of IT adoption depends upon the pressure exerted by trading partners and stakeholders (Abrahamson & Rosenkopf, 1993). As such, organizations may concede to the pressure exerted by trading partners and stakeholders to obtain legitimacy, and this also may hold true in the case of e-procurement assimilation.

DiMaggio and Powell (1983) posit that managers have limited predictive capability; hence the adoption decision taken at other organizations becomes critical to make a decision. Adoption by other organizations may provide indications that the concerned technology is beneficial. If a significant proportion of an organization's stakeholders, such as buyers, suppliers, competitors, and other trading partners in the industry, adopt a technology, then the organization may feel pressure to expedite its assimilation. In line with these studies, institutional pressures seem to play a greater role in the assimilation of e-procurement by government organizations. In short, from an institutional theory perspective, the intensity of e-procurement assimilation depends on the government organizations' legitimization needs and resulting isomorphic pressures (DiMaggio & Powell, 1983). DiMaggio and Powell later classified this institutional isomorphism into three categories: coercive, mimetic, and normative.

Although prior studies of IOS adoption (e.g., EDI) using the institutional theory (e.g., Teo, Wei, & Benbasat, 2003) have included the three categories of isomorphic pressures, this chapter has excluded the coercive pressures that are likely to impact the assimilation of e-procurement. Since EDI is proprietary in nature and mainly used to support trading activities between existing buyers and suppliers, coercive pressures were significant for Teo et al.'s (2003) studies. But in the case of open IOS such as Internet-based e-procurement, the buyers may have new suppliers. And because suppliers only need simple Internet-based systems to participate in the e-procurement, coercive pressures may not be significant. But if we look at e-procurement from the supplier's perspective rather from the buyer's perspective, the coercive pressures can be significant because the supplier's well-being depends on the relationship with the buyer.

Mimetic Pressures

Mimetic isomorphism occurs when organizations copy the actions of others (DiMaggio & Powell, 1983). As this type of isomorphism mainly occurs in highly uncertain situations, an argument could be made that many of the e-procurement activities of public sector organizations are due to their imitation of other leader organizations. From a mimetic isomorphic point of view, government organizations model themselves after their parent organizations or similar organizations which they perceive to be more legitimate and successful. By imitating these other organizations, which have already implemented e-procurement initiatives successfully, they enhance their legitimacy by demonstrating that at least the organization is trying to improve the procurement performance. In the emerging economies, mimetic pressures occur by imitating the e-government initiatives in the advanced economies.

This line of reasoning has been supported by Yildiz (2004) who contends that some of the e-government projects are initiated partly because of legitimacy concerns such as keeping up with other organizations, being on the cutting edge of technology, as well as the value propositions including increasing effectiveness, efficiency, accountability, and so forth. According to the author, certain formal and informal groups, policy issue networks, within and/or across government agencies and e-government projects are influential in the making of critical decisions about setting the agenda. Because of such acquired legitimacy concerns, some government ICT projects are kept alive irrespective of whether or not they deliver their promised technical value (Avgerou, 2000) or even if they are not financially feasible in the short-run (Cohen & Eimicke, 2001).

Normative Pressures

Another type of isomorphism, normative isomorphism, deals with the pressures that organizations can feel from professional bodies to comply to established standards or norms (DiMaggio & Powell, 1983). Some organizations might feel the need to conform to procurement norms in order to fit into professional organizations. From a normative isomorphic standpoint, government organizations use e-procurement because of the newly emerging professional norms of public service (e.g., information economy, e-government, etc.). In addition, as contended by Abrahamson and Rosenkopf (1993), the assimilation of e-procurement also depends upon the pressure exerted by business partners and stakeholders. Normative pressures also arise from the threat of lost legitimacy. When normative pressures increase, Abrahamson and Rosenkopf (1993) argue that organizations adopt innovations on the basis of an institutional pressure caused by the trading partners and competitors that have already implemented the innovation.

Literature Review of Environmental Factors Impacting IOS Diffusion

Although the theory of innovation diffusion (Rogers, 1983, 1995) is widely used to study the adoption and use of an innovation, institutional theories have also been used to discuss information systems (IS) and diffusion of innovations more recently. The background for this chapter is derived from various literature on the adoption and use of technological innovations such as IOS/EDI, Web-based IOS, and the Internet. Previous research has examined several environmental factors in various industries using the survey and case studies as the main research methods. For example, competitive pressure has been found to be the main source of external pressure influencing the diffusion of innovation (Premkumar & King, 1995; Premkumar & Ramamurthy, 1995; Premkumar, Ramamurthy, & Crum, 1997). Iacovou, Benbasat, and Dexter (1995) proposed that greater pressure will be on the organization to follow them as more competitors adopt technological innovations. Wang (1997) goes further ahead and notes that failing to adopt electronic commerce technologies can mean bankruptcy. The changing environment is forcing organizations to change and innovate new ways of value creation. For example, participating in the Electronic Marketplaces, an advanced form of e-procurement, is one of the ways that can allow organizations to survive in new conditions. External pressure was found to be the predominant environmental factor in many studies (Barua & Lee, 1997; O'Callaghan, Kaufmann, & Konsynski, 1992; Premkumar et al., 1997). Supplier demand can also be one of the external pressures because suppliers may favor the buying organizations that participate in the e-marketplaces. Partner-dependence was presented as one of the factors in a study by Van Over and Kavan (1993) and was later empirically studied and found to be positively linked to EDI adoption (Premkumar et al., 1997) and EDI use (Hart & Saunders, 1997).

Studies in the field of IS have shown the importance of the often-underestimated critical role which "politics" play in the implementation of new technology (Avgerou, 2000) which can easily overpower the rational and planned economic and technical efforts made during the introduction of technology in an organization. Similarly, pressures from the government and industry, and legitimacy concerns have been identified in a field survey by Kuan and Chau (2001) and Grewal, Corner, and Mehta (2001). Table 1 lists the issues and the research methods for each source.

In the context of e-procurement, normative pressures are particularly relevant because the early growth stage of e-procurement was characterized by the popular hype of cost efficiency and process effectiveness. Normative pressures can potentially hasten e-procurement assimilation across the transactional and strategic procurement processes, depending on the specific kinds of pressures exercised by entities within the business environment. For example, as argued by Grewal et al. (2001), institutional pressures play a role in inducing upstream suppliers and downstream channel members to embrace socially-accepted norms and behaviors. This results in pressures on the procurement organization to conform in terms of adopting e-business initiatives in procurement processes with other parties.

Table 1. Environmental factors impacting IOS adoption and use

Source	Issue(s)	Method
Barua and Lee (1997)	External pressure	Economic model of a vertical market involving one manufacturer and two suppliers
Hart and Saunders (1997)	Supplier dependence; customer power	Field study of two companies and their suppliers
Iacovou, Benbasat, and Dexter (1995)	External pressure to adopt EDI	Seven case studies of small businesses
O'Callaghan, Kaufmann, and Konsynski (1992)	External pressure	Survey of 1,242 insurance agents
Premkumar, Ramamurthy, and Crum (1997)	Competitive pressure; dependence	Survey of 201 firms
Premkumar and King (1995)	Exercised power; competitive pressure	Field survey of 249 senior IS executives
Premkumar and Ramamurthy (1995)	Competitive pressure	Survey with 201 firm responses
Premkumar and King (1995)	Exercised power; competitive pressure	Field survey of 249 senior IS executives
Grewal et al. (2001)	Deemphasizing legitimacy motivations	Survey of 306 participants in the Polygon marketplace
Iacovou et al. (1995)	External pressure to adoption	7 case studies
Kuan and Chau (2001)	Government pressure and industry pressure	Conceptual model/Survey
Premkumar and Ramamurthy (1995)	Competitive pressure and exercised power	Survey

Future Research and the Proposed Research Model

Based on the literature review of the impact of environmental factors on the IS/IOS adoption and implementation, a set of five environmental conditions within the normative and mimetic pressures has been identified that are likely to influence the assimilation of e-procurement, namely: (1) the trading partners benefited from the adoption and use of e-procurement (trading partners benefited); (2) trading partners perceived favorably by the suppliers (supplier-favored trading partners); (3) demand from suppliers to use e-procurement (supplier demand); (4) significant pressure by a parent organization to participate in the e-procurement (parent organization's pressure); and (5) participation of the organization in industry/government associations that

Figure 1. The four perspectives of e-procurement assimilation

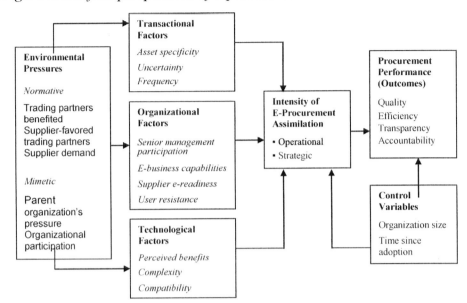

promote adoption and use of e-procurement (organizational participation). The overall conceptual model is presented in Figure 1. The model also shows the expected relationship with the intensity of e-procurement assimilation and in turn, the impact of e-procurement assimilation on the procurement performance. The proposed model will identify the antecedent conditions from other perspectives such as transactional, organizational, and technological. The corresponding factors for these perspectives have respectively been derived from the transaction cost theory (Williamson, 1985), the structurational theory of IT use (Orlikowski et al., 1995), and diffusion of innovation theory (Rogers, 1983, 1995). The following sections briefly discuss these perspectives and the relevant factors.

Transaction Cost Theory and the Transactional Factors

The actual intensity of e-procurement assimilation also depends on the specific transactional circumstances. As such, transaction cost theory is concerned with how organizations might best be organized to reduce transaction-related costs. Williamson (1985) suggests that three transaction characteristics are critical: frequency, uncertainty, and asset specificity. The transaction costs theory explains why governments would want to engage in e-procurement in order to reduce the cost of doing business and save budgetary resources (Reddick, 2004). While asset specificity refers to the extent of specific trans-actions and the uniqueness of the asset for specific transactions, uncertainty is related to technological change and contract complexity, among others. The assimilation of e-procurement in an organization is likely to be greater when products transacted using e-procurement technologies are character-ized as low in asset specificity. Furthermore, low uncertainty also leads to efficiency gains due to the reduction of direct procurement costs through shifting procurement activities from several decentralized layers of public hierarchies toward a transparent central marketplace for procurement (Henrik-sen, Mahnke, & Hansen, 2004). According to the transaction cost approach, a higher transaction frequency provides higher incentives for both buyers and sellers to improve their coordination. As such, e-procurement can be used to decrease transaction costs and increase potential benefits.

Structurational Theory of Technology Use and the Organizational Factors

In their study of Web technologies, Chatterjee, Grewal, and Sambamurthy (2002) see the need to learn from a range of experiences with the assimilation of such technologies and investigate how organizations can encourage their activities in order to further enhance the levels of technology assimilation. Drawing upon the ideas in the structurational theory of IT use (Orlikowski et al., 1995), Chatterjee et al. (2002) propose that the organizational assimilation of Web technologies in e-commerce initiatives is a cumulative consequence of the actions of managers and departments across the organization, and these actions are stimulated by an organizational milieu of norms, values, and rules. According to Orlikowski et al. (1995), individual cognition and behaviors are influenced by the three institutional structures of signification, legitimization, and domination, and individuals utilize these structures to make sense of the technology and undertake the improvisational actions (referred to as "structur-ing actions"). Chatterjee et al. (2002, p. 69) argue that "by mandating rules and policies about the assimilation of a technology, senior management can alter the prevailing structures of domination and either encourage or deter individual structuring actions." Furthermore, the institutional structures can be manipulated by the senior management, who influence the structuring actions indirectly (referred to as "meta-structuring actions") (Orlikowski et al., 1995; Purvis et al., 2001). The meta-structuring actions of particular interest for the proposed study are senior management participation, e-business capabilities, supplier e-readiness, and user resistance because they define institutional norms and values regarding which organizational factors the organization should take into account in order to participate in structuring actions related to e-procurement technologies. Drawing upon these ideas in the structurational theory of IT use (Chatterjee et al., 2002; Orlikowski et al., 1995; Purvis et al., 2001), these organizational factors are anticipated to impact the intensity of e-procurement assimilation through its influence on the institutional structures of signification, legitimization, and domination.

Diffusion of Innovation Theory and the Technological Factors

The assimilation of e-procurement initiative is surely an issue of technology diffusion and adoption of procurement innovation. Obviously, innovation diffusion theory (IDT) (Rogers, 1983, 1995) can be used to understand e-procurement assimilation as the theory has also been extensively used recently as a fundamental theoretical base of innovation adoption research in the field of IS/IOS. As the adoption of e-procurement as an innovation generates uncertainty, the procurement organization must be aware of the relative advantage and risk of implementing such innovation. Although the attributes suggested by IDT include relative advantage, compatibility, complexity, trialability, and observability (Rogers, 1983, 1995), only two variables, relative advantage (i.e., the degree to which an innovation is perceived as being better than the idea it supersedes) and compatibility (of an innovation with existing practices and values) have been consistently found to be positively related; only one variable, complexity (i.e., the degree to which an innovation is perceived as relatively difficult to understand and use) has been consistently found to be negatively related to adoption of innovation (Tornatzky & Klein, 1982). As the different public sector agencies with different intensities of assimilation can perceive the characteristics of the e-procurement technologies differently, Downs and Mohr (1976) suggest taking perception-based characteristics of innovation into account rather than the inherent characteristics of the technology that do not vary across settings and organizations.

Future Research

As the model in Figure 1 shows, changes in the environment cause environmental pressures, which influence the efficiency-oriented (transactional), organizational, and technological factors which, in turn, influence the intensity of operational and strategic assimilation of e-procurement. The outcome of the assimilation has been proposed to be measured in terms of quality, efficiency (cost efficiency and process efficiency), transparency, and accountability associated with the overall procurement performance. Similarly, constructs for the organizational factors include senior management participation, e-business capabilities, supplier e-readiness, and user resistance. While transaction cost theory (Williamson, 1985) gives us the constructs (asset specificity, uncertainty, and frequency) to study transactional factors, constructs for the technological factors (perceived benefits, complexity, and compatibility) have been derived from the diffusion of innovation theory (Rogers, 1983, 1995). Similarly, structurational theory of IT use (Chatterjee et al., 2002; Orlikowski et al., 1995; Purvis et al., 2001) has been utilized to help derive the constructs for the organizational factors. Control variables include the size of the organization, measured in terms of the organization's annual direct and indirect procurement expenditure for the last financial year, and assimilation gap, which can be measured by asking the respondents when their organizations first adopted e-procurement.

Our future research will focus on several research streams to compile knowledge as a foundation to predict the intensity of e-procurement assimilation in public procurement environment. Since no research to date has investigated into the antecedent conditions that influence the organizational assimilation of e-procurement, our future research will result in the validation of our proposed model through the integration of several theoretical frameworks as discussed above. Our future research will thus hypothesize the relationships between the environmental factors and other factors as depicted in the research model. In order to appropriately capture the antecedent conditions for e-procurement assimilation, a survey instrument will be designed to gather the appropriate data from the procurement/e-procurement professionals within the public sector agencies in order to test the proposed model as shown in the Figure above. It will be then possible to complete the necessary statistical analysis and communicate the validated findings of the research.

Conclusion

This chapter highlighted the need to assess the environmental factors existing in the institutionalized environment for the successful assimilation of e-procurement. Drawing upon the institutional theory, this chapter provided the theoretical support to understand how various environmental factors may impact the operational and strategic assimilation of e-procurement. The study presented in this chapter was motivated to identify and examine a set of environmental factors rather than to comprehensively list every potential antecedent conditions of organizational assimilation of e-procurement. Given the scope of the chapter, the impact of assimilation antecedents on the procurement performance has not been examined in greater detail. The chapter also did not examine how the environmental factors associated with e-procurement assimilation affect the organizational performance.

Academically, this chapter proposed a model in order to establish an empirical basis for examining the institutional theory to assimilation of e-procurement. Also, an understanding of the key environmental factors associated to organizational e-procurement assimilation will put practitioners in a better position to design and implement appropriate strategies to cope with the e-procurement implementation. The proposed model is also expected to provide a basis for managerial thinking about the types of e-procurement assimilations as operational and strategic. It has been anticipated that the research data on the environmental factors and the association between the two types of assimilation will stimulate further research into this area. However, DiMaggio and Powell (1983) and Tolbert and Zucker (1984) recognized that institutional forces are not always primary, noting the tendency for early adoption to be driven by technical, as opposed to legitimacy considerations. Furthermore, institutional theory has often been integrated with other theoretical frameworks to overcome its over-socialized perspective (Sherer & Lee, 2002). As such, our future research efforts will be directed towards validating the integrated model of e-procurement assimilation antecedent conditions, including from the transactional, technological, and organizational perspectives.

The aims of this chapter were to provide a concise review of literature on IT assimilation and the institutional theory, and the impact of environmental factors on the IOS assimilation. In line with the aims of this chapter, it has not been attempted to present the tested and validated environmental factors that can influence the assimilation of e-procurement, but this chapter has instead identified the more pertinent issues of assimilating e-procurement within the public sector. In effect, it has identified several streams of further research and presented a holistic model of e-procurement assimilation, in light of which, the procurement professionals can manage their e-procurement initiatives.

References

Abrahamson, E., & Rosenkopf, L. (1993). Institutional and competitive bandwagons: Using mathematical modeling as a tool to explore innovation diffusion. *Academy of Management Review, 18*(3), 487-517.

Avgerou, C. (2000). IT and organizational change: An institutional perspective. *Information Technology & People, 13*(4), 234-262.

Barua, A., & Lee, B. (1997, December). An economic analysis of the introduction of an electronic data interchange system. *Information Systems Research, 8*(4), 398-423.

Chatterjee, D., Grewal, R., & Sambamurthy, V. (2002). Shaping up for e-commerce: Institutional enablers of the organisational assimilation of Web technologies. *MIS Quarterly, 26*(2), 65-89.

Cohen, S., & Eimicke, W. (2001). The use of Internet in government service delivery. In M. Abramson & G. E. Means (Eds.), *E-government, 2001. The PricewaterhouseCoopers endowment for the business of government* (pp. 9-43). Oxford: Rowman and Littlefield Publishers, Inc.

Commissions of the European Communities (CEC). (2004, December). *Action plan for the implementation of the legal framework for electronic public procurement.* Brussels: CEC.

Cooper, R., & Zmud, R. (1990). Information technology implementation research: A technological diffusion approach. *Management Science, 36*(2), 123-139

Deephouse, D. L. (1996). Does isomorphism legitimate? *Academy of Management Journal, 39*(4), 1024-1039.

DiMaggio, P., & Powell, W. (1983). The iron cage revisited: Institutional isomorphism and collective rationality in organizational fields. *American Sociological Review, 48*, 147-160.

Downs, G. W., & Mohr, L. B. (1976). Conceptual issues in the study of innovation. *Administration Science Quarterly, 21*, 700-714.

Fichman, R. G., & Kemerer, C. F. (1997). The assimilation of software process innovations: An organisational learning perspective. *Management Science, 43*(10), 1345-1363.

Fichman, R. G., & Kemerer, C. F. (2001). Incentive compatibility and systematic software reuse. *Journal of Systems and Software, 57*(1), 45-60.

Gebauer, J., & Segev, A. (2001). *Changing shapes of supply chains—how the Internet could lead to a more integrated procurement function* (Working Paper 01-WP-1041). University of California, Fisher Centre.

Grewal, R., Corner, J. M., & Mehta, R. (2001, July). An investigation into the antecedents of organizational participation in business-to-business electronic markets. *Journal of Marketing, 65*, 17-33.

Hamblen, M. (2002). After the hype. *Computerworld, 36*(52), 33-34.

Hart, P., & Saunders, C. (1997). Power and trust: Critical factors in the adoption and use of electronic data interchange. *Organization Science, 8*(1), 23-42.

Henriksen, H. Z., & Andersen, K. V. (2003). E-procurement adoption: Theory and practice. In R. Traunmuller (Ed.), *EGOV* (LNCS 2739, pp. 121-124). Berlin: Springer-Verlag.

Henriksen, H. Z., Mahnke, V., & Hansen, J. M. (2004). Public e-procurement adoption: Economic and political rationality. In *Proceedings of the 37th Hawaii International Conference on System Sciences*. IEEE.

Iacovou, C. L., Benbasat, I., & Dexter, A. S. (1995). Electronic data interchange and small organizations: Adoption and impact of technology. *MIS Quarterly, 19*(4), 465-485.

Kuan, K. K. Y., & Chau, P. Y. K. (2001). A perception-based model for EDI adoption in small business using a technology-organizational-environment framework. *Information & Management, 38*(8), 507-521.

Kwon, T. H., & Zmud, R. W. (1987). Unifying the fragmented models of information systems implementation. In J. R. Boland & R. A. Hirschheim (Eds.), *Critical issues in information systems research* (pp. 227-251). New York: John Wiley.

Maxwell, J. A. (1996). *Qualitative research design: An interactive approach.* Thousand Oaks, CA: Sage.

Minhan, T. (2005). *The e-procurement benchmark report: Less hype, more results*. Aberdeen Group.

North, D. (1990). *Institutions, institutional change, and economic performance*. Cambridge, MA: Cambridge University Press.

O'Callaghan, R., Kaufmann, P. J., & Konsynski, B. R. (1992). Adoption correlates and share effects of electronic data interchange systems in marketing channels. *Journal of Marketing, 56*(2), 45-56.

Organisation for Economic Cooperation and Development (OECD). (2003, April 14). *Transparency in government procurement: The benefits of efficient governance and orientations for achieving it.* Working Party of the Trade Committee.

Orlikowski, W. J., Yates, J., Okamura, K., & Fujimoto, M. (1995, July/August). Shaping electronic communication: The metastructuring of technology in the context of use. *Organization Science, 6*, 423-444.

Premkumar, G., & King, W. R. (1994). Organizational characteristics and information systems planning: An empirical study. *Information Systems Research, 5*(2), 75-109.

Premkumar, G., & Ramamurthy, K. (1995). The role of inter-organizational and organizational factors on the decision mode for adoption of inter-organizational systems. *Decision Sciences, 26*(3), 303-337.

Premkumar, G., Ramamurthy, K., & Crum, M. (1997). Determinants of EDI adoption in the transportation industry. *European Journal of Information Systems, 6*, 107-121.

Prescott, M. B., & Conger, S. A. (1995). Information technology innovations—a classification by IT locus of impact and research approach. *Data Base for Advances in Information Systems, 26*(2-3), 20-41.

Purvis, R. L., Sambamurthy, V., & Zmud, R. W. (2001). The assimilation of knowledge platforms in organizations: An empirical investigation. *Organization Science, 12*(2), 117-135.

Qu, W. G., & Pinsonneault, A. (2004). Linking industrial innovation dynamics to e-procurement governance. In *Proceedings of the 10th Americas Conference on Information Systems*, New York.

Ramiller, N. C., & Swanson, E. B. (2003). *Whether, when, and how to innovate with information technology: What do empirical studies tell us?* (Working Paper 2-03). The Anderson School at UCLA, Information Systems.

Reddick, C. (2004). The growth of e-procurement in American state governments: A model and empirical evidence. *Journal of Public Procurement, 4*(2), 151-176.

Rogers, E. M. (1983). *Diffusion of innovation*. New York: The Free Press.

Rogers, E. M. (1995). *Diffusion of innovation*. New York: The Free Press.

Sherer, P. D., & Lee, K. (2002). Institutional change in large law firms: A resource dependency and institutional perspective. *Academy of Management Journal, 45*(1), 47-60.

Teo, H. H., Wei, K. K., & Benbasat, I. (2003). Predicting intention to adopt inter-organizational linkages: An institutional perspective. *MIS Quarterly, 27*(1), 19-49.

Tether, I. (1977). *Government procurement and operations*. Cambridge, MA: Ballinger Publishing Company.

Tolbert, P. S., & Zucker, L. G. (1996). The institutionalization of institutional theory. In S. R. Clegg, C. Hardy, & W. R. Nord (Eds.), *Handbook of organizational studies* (pp. 175-190). Sage.

Tornatzky, L. G., & Klein, K. (1982). Innovation characteristics and innovation implementation: A meta-analysis of findings. *IEEE Transactions on Engineering Management, 29*(1), 28-45.

Vaidya, K., Yu, P., Soar, J., & Turner, T. (2003). Measuring the performance of e-procurement implementation in the Australian public sector: Results of a preliminary investigation. In N. Cerpa & P. Bro (Eds.), *Building the society with e-commerce: E-business, e-government, and e-education* (pp. 47-61). University of Talca, Chile.

Van Over, D., & Kavan, B. C. (1993). Adopting EDI: When and why. *Information Strategy, 9*(4), 50-53.

Wang, S. (1997). Impact of information technology on organizations. *Human Systems Management, 16*, 83-90.

Williamson, O. E. (1985). *The economics institutions of capitalism*. New York: Free Press.

Yildiz, M. (2004). *Examining the motivations for e-government from an institutional theory perspective: Evidence from Turkey*. Bloomington: Indiana University.

Section II

Country Level Analysis

Chapter III

E-Procurement Success Factors:
Challenges and Opportunities for a Small Developing Country

Mateja Podlogar, University of Maribor, Slovenia

Abstract

This chapter introduces e-procurement as a strategic tool for organizations' competitive position in the new information economy. It argues that that e-procurement is significantly changing the ways businesses operate and thus new business models are needed. E-procurement success factors that have to be considered are: cost factors, time factors, process simplification factors and the volume of e-transactions factors. By gaining understanding of the most important e-procurement factors, organizations have to organize themselves in a way that ensures success. Furthermore, author hopes that with knowing such factors, organizations will be able to better prepare for e-procurement and thus operate successfully and thus be able to compete in the global market.

Definition of E-Procurement

E-procurement deals with the linking and integration of inter-organizational business processes and systems, and commences with the automation of the requisitioning, the approval purchase order management, and accounting processes through an Internet-based protocol. To understand e-procurement, it is also important to achieve common understanding of some other terms, scopes, and relationships. Relationships between the most important terms used in the field of e-procurement are shown in Figure 1.

Purchasing process is a narrowly defined process within the procurement process and refers to the actual buying of materials and those activities associated with the buying process (Kalakota & Robinson, 1999). An extensive term relating to the procurement process is a supply chain. A *supply chain* includes business partners (suppliers, manufacturers, distributors, retail outlets, and customers) that use transactions to purchase, convert/manufacture, assemble, or distribute products and services to the customers or end users (Komp Leonard, 1999). A supply chain consists of the paths reaching out to all of the suppliers of parts and services to an organization. A supply chain consists of an organization's suppliers and its suppliers' suppliers as well (Haag, Cummings, & McCubbrey, 2002).

Buyer and *supplier* are business partners in the e-procurement with cardinality of 1: n, which means that one buyer may have several suppliers (Shaw, Blanning, Strader, & Whinston, 2000). Conversely, the relationship among

Figure 1. Relationships between the most important terms used in the field of e-procurement

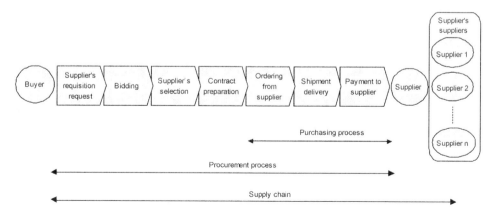

them could be m: n, which means that several buyers may have several suppliers via e-markets (Pucihar, 2002).

E-Procurement Process and
Business Model

The procurement process is a closed loop process (supplier's requisition request, bidding, and supplier's selection, contract preparation, ordering from supplier, shipment delivery, and payment to supplier) between buyers and suppliers, which begins with the requisition and ends with the payment (Dai & Kauffman, 2001; Gebauer, Beam, & Segev, 1998; Gebauer & Segev, 2001; Kalakota & Robinson, 1999; Podlogar, 2002; Shaw et al., 2000).

The e-procurement process is somewhat different from classical procurement. An e-procurement model (Figure 2) and its processes could be shortly described as follows (Gebauer & Shaw, 2002; Poirer & Bauer, 2001). We can observe that the buyer has a new electronic system at his or her disposal. Communications between buyers and suppliers, coming over the Internet access system, are linked together in the new procurement network. Through this access, the buyer can select, from product catalogs, the items needed to meet manufacturing or delivery demands. The approval is received online, significantly cutting the cycle time, and the workflow proceeds through the network (Gebauer & Shaw, 2002; Poirer & Bauer, 2001). Buyers can input their needs using the e-catalog included in the e-procurement program. Needs are input represented as "requests for procurement." The automation of the process involves all approvals needed to purchase goods. In the automation process, different requests for procurement are merged into one order that is passed to the supplier electronically. The entire process is totally automated through the electronic interchange. The position of a classical procurement officer is no longer necessary because copying the paper request for procurement to the electronic one is no longer needed. In the new environment, the procurement officer tries to understand the supplier's needs, and assesses the efficiency and the optimum procurement conditions for their organization (Vaupot, 2001).

The approval is accomplished online, thus significantly cutting the cycle time, and the workflow proceeds through the network. The purchase ordering process is automated and feeds directly into the organization's enterprise resource

Figure 2. An e-procurement business model (Source: Gebauer & Shaw, 2002)

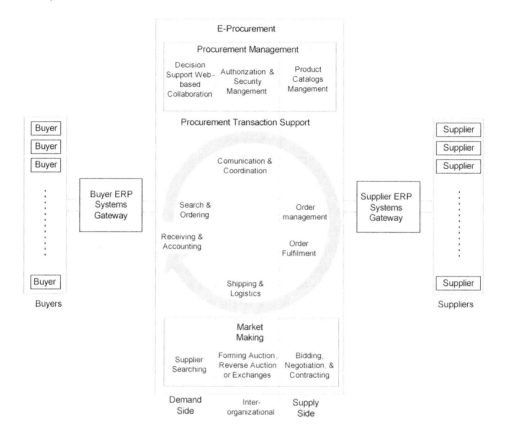

planning (ERP) system for retention, payables, and any reconciliation that may be necessary. Financial services (for credit and payment) and logistics services (for pooled shipments and cross-docking) can be accessed online, speeding those processes (Gebauer & Shaw, 2002; Poirer & Bauer, 2001).

ERP E-Procurement Integration

For an organization, it is also very important to achieve the ERP and e-procurement integration. While implementing new technologies such as an ERP, a lot of changes in business processes have to be done. ERP implementation and e-procurement integration is impossible without process reengineering. With implementing e-procurement, organizations want to improve business process effectiveness based on close relationship between all business partners (Podlogar, 2002). ERP will support or even automate the whole procurement process in the organization. For achieving business partners' collaboration, collaborative processes are established. We can say that collaborative processes are a synonym for ERP. These systems reduce costs and enhance effectiveness through business process integration and through cooperation along the whole procurement process. Geographical differences will be reduced, and organizations will procure goods from suppliers located anywhere in the world. For e-procurement, the Web-based ERPs are becoming more appropriate technology, especially for the reason of growing communication and rising importance of the information.

E-procurement begins with the automation of the requisition, the approval purchase order management, and accounting processes through an Internet-based protocol. The key elements of this automation include the following:

- A Web-based user interface
- Utilization of standard internet communication and security protocols
- A software that supports the requisition process, including approval, work flow, and product catalog maintenance such as an ERP

Organizations can be competitive only by very well-organized internal and external processes with all business partners. It is important to have, on one side, buyers that are able to create orders online and, on the other side, suppliers that are able to deliver goods in a timely manner in cooperation with external logistics partners that are able to deliver ordered goods on time at the right place (Lesničar, 2002; Poirer & Bauer, 2001).

Initially, ERP implementation is necessary along with business process optimization inside and outside the organization border. Higher control of all procurement processes is very important (European Commission, 2000). If we want to implement e-procurement successfully, an ERP of one organization has to be connected with the ERPs of other business partners. E-procurement cannot be limited to only one organization. By using reliable, open and Web-based information infrastructure of ERPs, which support business processes and also enable organizations to be flexible, we can optimize the entire procurement process and achieve successful e-procurement implementation.

With ERP implementation, organizations reach a higher level of e-procurement through the interchange of standardized documents with business partners. The research in Slovenia shows that organizations need to direct to standard interchange of purchase order, payment order, order acknowledgment, and invoice. In accordance with the above directions, the Slovenian Chamber of Commerce along with a group of major Slovene companies is undertaking a project called ESlog in order to introduce e-business to Slovene companies. Since e-business interoperability is a key issue, the project delivered XML documents for payment order, payment cancellation, credit advice, debit advice, banking status, and financial statement to enable organizations to use e-commerce (eEurope, 2003).

Organizations Savings and Added Value of E-Procurement Use

For the purpose of designing the e-procurement model and the standard for e-commerce on the Internet, open buying on the Internet (henceforth OBI) standard was formed. OBI is an open, flexible frame for e-commerce's business-to-business programs. It is designed for the organizations having a large number of transactions with a low-money value. These transactions represent 80% of all transactions of large organizations. With regard to the e-procurement, the benefits of OBI standard are as follows:

- Buyers want to have a choice of suppliers depending on a business value such as price, quality, and so forth.
- Implementation of the e-procurement needs to be independent of the technology which is used.
- Buyers want a solution based on a fair price without any influence from the system and from suppliers previously used.
- Time is decreased for the entire procurement process from days to minutes.

Organizations (Poirer & Bauer, 2001) divide the initial savings into three areas:

- Better purchasing information for improved contract negotiation and management results in 7% to 27% reduction in cost.
- Improved information handling results in cost reduction for transactions, from as high as $100 per transaction to less than $4 per transaction.
- The cycle time for completing transactions is reduced between 30% and 50%, from order to delivery.

Added value of e-procurement is as follows (Van Weele, 1998):

- Effective development of the procurement process between buyer and supplier
- Verification of supplier's order acknowledgment
- Development and implementation of computer-based different methods for order and control fulfillment
- Development of computer-supported database about critical items of procurement process and suppliers
- Development of a well-defined process for order-handling
- Successful problem solving, when necessary.

Problem Definition

If organizations want to maintain a sustainable competitive position in the new information economy, then they have to do business electronically. Examples of major e-business process categories include procurement, selling, production management, internal communication, and support services (Mesenbourg, 2002). Today a greater number of organizations are aware of how e-commerce solutions can lead to integration along the entire supply chain, especially in the procurement process, which is the topic which this chapter addresses. In the information age, e-procurement is an important topic. Why? Arguably, because it is of a strategic importance to organizations, and presents a central part of any changes, which have to be executed for Web strategy support. With e-procurement, buyers and suppliers try to reduce costs and time, achieve error reductions while executing business quality improvements. It is suggested that there are key opportunities for effective and efficient e-procurement to bring about improvements in business processes. E-procurement promises great opportunities for closer relationships between buyers and suppliers (Archer & Gebauer, 2001; Ilijaš & Grum; 2001; Lefebvre, Cassivi, & Lefebvre, 2001) and enables business processes to take directions between buyers and suppliers (Berg, 1995; Esichaikul & Chavananon, 2001).

Review of the literature identifies many advantages and opportunities from the field of e-procurement. In the commercial arena, an organization will procure goods in an electronic way only if it will see enough benefits that might be gained with value-added services resulting from e-procurement. In any case, an organization must take very careful steps to prepare business processes for successful implementation of e-procurement. By gaining understanding of the most important e-procurement factors, organizations have to organize themselves in a way that ensures success. With knowing such factors, organizations will be able to better prepare for e-procurement and thus operate successfully and be able to compete in the global market. For successful e-procurement implementation, organizations have to investigate these factors in detail.

Today, organizations do not ask why they should adopt e-procurement; in fact, it is just the opposite. Instead, they ask how to do it in a way to get the maximum benefits that they can. We argue that e-procurement is significantly changing the ways businesses operate; new business models are needed, and pose many challenges to existing and future measurement of such changes.

With the changing classical business model to the electronic one, the processes have changed. These changes are most important for successful operation of e-procurement, and require the following groups of success factors: time and cost, processes reengineering, processes simplifying, and the volume of e-transactions. For that reason, such e-procurement factors were investigated in this research that was conducted among 133 large organizations in Slovenia. The importance of these factors is presented further in the chapter.

Background: Prior Research

On the basis of prior published research results and interviews with industry experts, we identified four groups of factors that organizations need to consider when making decisions regarding successful e-procurement use in their business:

- Process reengineering factors
- Process simplifying factors
- Time and cost factors
- Volume of e-transactions factors

Process Reengineering Factors

Awareness of Technology Opportunities with an Emphasis on Technology and Process Complexity and Compatibility

Literature indicates that many organizations' e-procurement processes with their suppliers are organized in numerous arrangements. First, these processes have to be reengineered, uniformed, and incorporated to collaborative processes, which will then enable successful e-procurement and, in turn, give access to all data at the time when all business partners will need them (ActivMedia Research, 2000; Athabasca University, 2002; Chan & Swatman, 1999; European Commission, 2000; Kalakota & Robinson, 1999; Lindemann & Schmit, 1998; Ody, 2001a, 2001b; Podlogar, Hribar, & Gričar, 2001; Pucihar, 1999; RIS, 2001; Segev, Gebauer, & Beam, 1998; Sterle, 2001). Growing technology opportunities, with an emphasis on technology, process complexity, and compatibility, are the most important issues in organizing e-procurement (Chan & Swatman, 1999). Organizations that are healthier in a sense of information technology also have a better organized e-procurement (Segev et al., 1998).

Ability to Achieve Process Effectiveness

It is important to achieve better control and process tracking of the whole procurement process (European Commission, 2000). Organizations spend billions of dollars of additional costs annually to improve e-procurement ef-fectiveness (Kalakota & Robinson, 1999; Ody, 2001a, 2001b). Implementing process reengineering requires removing processes that contribute no added value. It is also important to choose software and hardware that would offer effective support to enhanced business processes (Lesničar, 2002; Sterle, 2001).

Readiness for E-Procurement Collaboration

Organizations want to have e-procurement, because they can improve process effectiveness by collaborating closely with all supply chain business partners. Collaboration is improved by reviewing an organization's internal and exter-nal processes. Implementing collaborative e-processes requires methods to increase inputs and to improve organization and business development.

Process Simplifying Factors

Satisfaction and Positive E-Procurement Experiences Sharing

If the e-procurement system provides quality customer service, the buyer will take the view that the experience was positive and simple to use. Benefits and simple e-procurement contribute to a positive perception of e-procure-ment, which will gradually lead to actual use (Chen, 2000). Successful organizations in practice are the ones that succeed in process simplification with the help of suppliers. It is also important to share savings that result from improvements with suppliers, creating a win-win situation. This kind of business leads to closer and longer connections with business partners (Komp Leonard, 1999).

Environment Changing Response

Process simplification leads to a great deal of e-procurement opportunities, especially because organizations have to react quickly to a changing envi-ronment (such as demand variability) as well as goods and process changes (European Commission, 2000).

E-Procurement Process Type

For the buyer, it is most important to simplify the following processes: goods availability (goods need to be at hand when a buyer needs them), order cycle, data retrieval, order adaptability, goods receiving, order mistakes dismissing, damaged goods returning, reserved parts availability, and technical support (Komp Leonard, 1999).

E-Procurement Participants and Its Accessibility

E-procurement processes allow participants to easily change rules and eliminate some business partners through the whole supply chain by, for example, undertaking direct e-procurement from the supplier without other partners, thereby simplifying the whole e-procurement. Generally speaking, however, it is difficult to say if the total number of participants in the whole supply chain will decrease (Mesenbourg, 2001). Those who satisfy with buyers' needs and offer software suitability created added value become successful and stay in the marketplace (Kordež & Jelovčan, 2001; Zupančič & Sedej, 2000).

Time and Costs Factors

Ability to Deliver Goods at the Right Moment

The greatest opportunity to decrease time is present in quick and reliable receiving, and quick-response to orders submitted. It is necessary to implement delivery at the right moment, meaning at the time when the buyer wants selected goods (Cao, 2001).

Ability to Setup and Maintain E-Catalog

Very well organized e-catalogs can decrease costs in e-procurement. E-catalogs that enable the provision of quality and adequate data to all business partners make it possible to decrease costs of searching, and offers extra possibilities, such as e-ordering and immediate order tracking for all business partners. Very well organized e-catalogs (effective data exchange and good communication between business partners) means a decrease in the transaction cost, which is an important part of the total price of goods (Kordež & Jelovčan, 2001; Lindemann & Schmit, 1998).

Ability to Reach Internal E-Procurement Excellence

It is essential for an organization to reach internal excellence before it can proceed to the first stage of e-procurement. Savings can be significant as the organization completes this stage. Research shows typical savings of 8% to 10% in purchasing and another 8% to 10% in logistics, while inventory will decrease by 25% to 30% without hurting fill rates or on time deliveries (Poirer & Bauer, 2001). However, industry leaders surpass these percentages. E-procurement solution analysis shows a potential decrease in the amount from 10% to 20% in all procurement costs (Vaupot, 2001).

Awareness of Savings with Respect to Different Organization Type

With respect to trade organizations, we can get the biggest cost savings with lower inventory levels, shorter ordering, and higher trade availability (at least on items in stock). With respect to manufacturers, we can get the biggest savings with shorter ordering, lower costs of production, and lower inventory levels (Poirer & Bauer, 2001).

Existence of Buyers' and Suppliers' Collaboration

In the case of e-procurement when large organizations want to decrease costs, they also use pressure suppliers to reduce costs, or alternatively they try to find new suppliers who are offering goods at lower costs (European Commission, 2000; Sitarski, 2001). The research shows that e-procurement in Canadian organizations see the biggest opportunities for cost and time decrease in a joint access to suppliers' and buyers' inventory data (Athabasca University, 2002).

Use of E-Commerce Between Business Partners in the Whole Supply Chain

Possibilities for time and cost decrease of process are shown, as well as e-data processing in the supply chain, because organizations become more and more effective and have to fulfill conditions for good collaboration with their business partners. E-commerce is already widespread, but it will be even more widespread in the future. At least 20% of all organizations present on the Internet need to exchange data electronically with business partners (suppliers, mediators, etc.). In a supply chain, we need to exchange data with all business partners in the supply chain very quickly and reliably. Non-readiness for e-procurement between business partners leads to lengthening of the time needed to react on business opportunities when they appear, or to a lost opportunity (European Commission, 2000; Lesničar, 2002; Sitarski, 2001; Tung, 2001).

Volume of E-Transactions Factors

The Frequency of E-Procurement Use

About half of all online B2B marketers (52%) currently established e-procurement. Some large manufactures require their vendors to implement e-procurement as a requirement for doing business. About half of all B2B sites currently perform some of the specified e-procurement functions online. We can anticipate that 70% of the organizations will have one or more procurement processes on the Internet in the next few years (ActivMedia Research, 2000).

The Level of E-Procurement Subprocess Frequency Use

Bidding is the subprocess of the procurement process that is most frequently carried out by using e-procurement. A number of organizations (15%) expect to add this capability within the next years. With the exception of bidding, far fewer B2B e-marketers will implement any other procurement process (ActivMedia Research, 2000). Research in the United States showed that 50% of the participants already used e-catalogs to acquire data about goods in the year 1998 (Segev et al., 1998). Shipment schedules (56%), order status (56%), and inventory status (45%) are the most commonly stated types of information currently being shared with respondents' customers and suppliers in Canada. This same type of information is indicated to be shared in the next five years, however, by larger proportions of respondents (66%, 66%, and 61% respectively) (Athabasca University, 2002).

Use of E-Procurement in Developing Country

E-procurement in Slovenia is not, as yet, very widespread. However, there are some indices from various organizations, showing an increasing interest. Since Slovenia has joined the European Union, in the future many Slovenian organizations will have the opportunity to operate and compete in the common European market.

Results from the Slovenian research that has been done between all sizes of organizations (from micro-organizations to large establishments) (Pucihar & Gričar, 2004) shows that the number of organizations that have procured goods online in Slovenia is 28.0%. The percentage of different e-procurement processes that have been already used is as follows: e-catalog in 48.0%, pricelists in 38.0%, catalog searching in 25.0%, ordering in 20.0%, and payments in only 2.0%. Most of the organizations do not have online connections with at least one supplier (76.0%) or with at least one buyer (66.0%).

While considering e-procurement use, organizations are also concerned with:

- ERP use
- Defining e-commerce strategy
- Having a director/manager of e-commerce

Based on the research (Podlogar, 2002) we can conclude that Slovenian large organizations are very well equipped with information technology. It is interesting that the majority of these organizations (75.2%) already use enterprise resource planning (ERP) systems. However, we can attribute the high percentage to the type of the research, because large organizations that took part in the research were very well equipped with information technology and have better connections with their suppliers. On the other hand, talks to different experts and organizations show that organizations in Slovenia have already implemented ERPs into their internal business processes. Many organizations have short-term plans to connect their ERPs to the ERPs of their business partners. With this accession, these organizations will have better chances to do e-procurement with all their partners. The most frequently applied programs are: own solution (18.3%), SAP (15.1%), Baan (6%) and Microsoft Business Solutions—Navision (6%). Due to the high level of information technology use in Slovenia, we can expect a correspondingly large dissemination of e-procurement among organizations as well.

The situation in Slovenian organizations for the existing or future plans for e-commerce strategy varies greatly. However, respondents' opinions are heterogeneous. Most of the Slovenian organizations had already defined e-commerce strategy (25.6%). Almost a quarter (22.6%) of them answered that the e-commerce strategy is going to be defined in the near future. Respondents listed different document names, by which their e-commerce strategy is defined. The most frequently used documents are: "strategic plan," "enterprise resource planning system development strategy" and "electronic commerce strategy."

Research results showed that more than half of Slovenian large organizations (54.1%) do not have a director/manager of e-commerce. Conversely, 29.3% of respondents indicated that their organization has a person in such a position. This information is very interesting because organizations need to have a director/manager of e-commerce who stimulates the implementation and development of e-commerce in the organization.

If we look for connections between the existence of the director/manager of e-commerce and e-commerce strategy and between the existence of director/manager of e-commerce and the use of the ERP, into detail we can find strong connections. Based on e-commerce strategy, organizations need to implement ERPs for their internal and external business and they need an executive responsible for e-commerce developing and operating.

E-Procurement Success Factors:
Case of Slovenia

Research Methodology and Data Analysis

The research was carried out in 133 large organizations that had the highest revenues and also Web page in Slovenia during spring, 2002. To be qualified as a large organization, it has to fulfill at least two of the following conditions based on the 51st article of the organizations' act:

*   More than 250 employees
*   Annual revenue more that 4 billions Slovene tolars (SIT)
*   Average asset value of more than 2 billions Slovene tolars (SIT)

The main reason for making such choices lies in the assumption that e-procurement is associated with extra expenses and extra investments in new

Figure 3. Research model

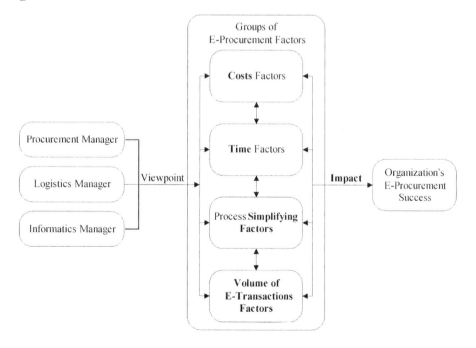

knowledge, business processes reengineering, and new technologies, and it is expected that large organizations have available more resources for that purpose. The second reason was that large organizations have better IT equipment and that they have closer relationships with suppliers. Both presumptions were proved correct in our research.

The questionnaire was designed on the basis of a research model that was derived from theoretical knowledge derived prior to the research, and the use of case studies. Opinions of experienced experts (procurement, logistics, and informatics managers) in this field were also considered. The research model consists of costs factors, time factors, process simplifying factors, and volume of e-transactions factors that an organization needs to achieve e-procurement success. The research model is shown in Figure 3.

Each group of e-procurement factors represents one section in the questionnaire. Each section in the questionnaire was defined with regard to processes that are necessary for the execution of the entire e-procurement. They were as follows:

- Possible supplier's requisition request
- Replacement of supplier
- Bidding
- Access to suppliers' goods or services catalogs
- Access to suppliers' inventory data
- Suppliers' access to buyer's inventory
- Ordering from supplier
- Payment to supplier
- Order tracking
- Search for transporters
- Transport ordering
- Receiving of shipment announcement
- Shipment delivery
- Reclamation solving
- Inventory turnover

Figure 4. The model of an organization's e-procurement success factors

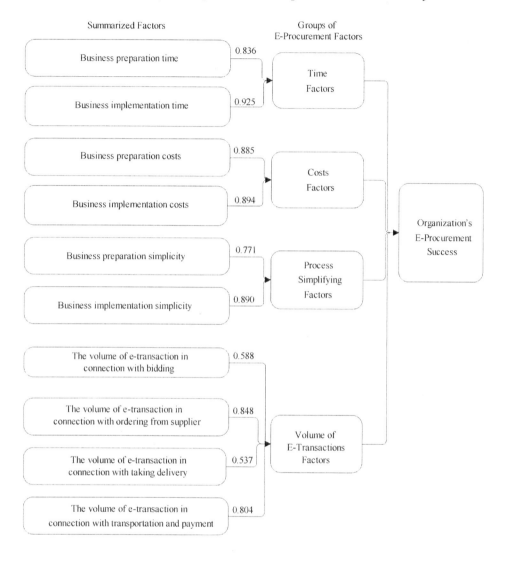

In order to ensure that the responses reflect the situation in each organization, letters with the questionnaires were sent directly to the general manager of 250 organizations with the request to hand over the questionnaire to the procurement manager, logistics manager, and informatics manager of their organizations. These managers represent the actual procurement process participants. We received 143 responses, of which 133 were used for further analysis.

The data analysis was done by using principal component analysis as the extraction method and Varimax with Kaiser Normalization as a technique of rotation. It was found (Podlogar, 2002) that for each group of factors of time, costs, and simplifying, specifying two summarized factors produced the most interpretable results. These factors were interpreted as "business process preparation factors" and "business process operation factors." For the group of factors regarding volume of e-transaction, specifying four sum-marized factors produced the most interpretable results. These factors were interpreted as "volume of e-transactions in connection with: bidding, order-ing from supplier, taking delivery, and transportation and payment." Based on the loadings of the fifteen items of each summarized factor (for a factor loading greater than 0.50), the model of an organization's e-procurement success factors was developed, and is depicted in Figure 4.

Each e-procurement success factors analysis which resulted from this research is explained in more detail in the following sections.

Time as an E-Procurement Success Factor

In all statements that are connected to e-procurement time factors, respon-dents, on average, agree that e-procurement decreases time spent on each separate subprocess of e-procurement.

Most respondents from the survey indicated the highest possibilities to de-crease time by e-procurement in the following procurement subprocesses:

- Ordering from supplier (88.60%)
- Access to suppliers' goods or catalogs (83.40%)
- Bidding (81.20%)
- Possible supplier's requisition request (74.20%)
- Payment to supplier (70.70%)

In contrast, "replacement of supplier" (45.1%) and "search for transporters" (47.4%) are e-procurement subprocesses where fewer respondents see pos-sibilities to decrease time.

The importance of all researched time factors for successful e-procurement is shown in Table 1. Part of the model of time factors is depicted in Figure 5.

Table 1. Time factors importance

Time Factors	The level of importance of factors in %						Average value
	Significant decrease				Significant increase	No answer	
	1	2	3	4	5	0	
Ordering from supplier time	49.2	39.4	0	6.1	1.5	3.8	4.23
Access to suppliers' goods or catalogs time	43.6	39.8	9	0.8	1.5	5.3	4.08
Bidding time	43.6	37.6	11.3	2.3	1.5	3.8	4.08
Possible supplier's requisition request time	33.8	44.4	9.8	2.3	1.5	8.3	3.82
Payment to supplier time	42.1	28.6	12	1.5	1.5	14.3	3.65
Order tracking time	42.1	27.8	16.5	0.8	2.3	10.5	3.75
Access to suppliers' inventory data time	40.6	29.3	12.8	2.3	1.5	13.5	3.65
Receiving the shipment announcement time	36.1	33.1	16.5	0.8	0.8	12.8	3.65
Reclamation solving time	18.8	45.1	18	4.5	1.5	12	3.39
Inventory turnover time	28.6	33.8	15.8	3.8	0.8	17.3	3.34
Transport ordering time	27.8	29.3	21.1	5.3	0.8	15.8	3.31
Shipment delivery time	24.1	32.3	25.6	5.3	0.8	12	3.38
Suppliers' access to buyer's inventory time	30.8	22.6	15	5.3	3.8	22.6	3.04
Search for transporters time	22.6	24.8	28.6	5.3	1.5	17.3	3.10
Replacement of supplier time	11.3	33.8	45.1	3	1.5	5.3	3.35

Figure 5. The model of time factors

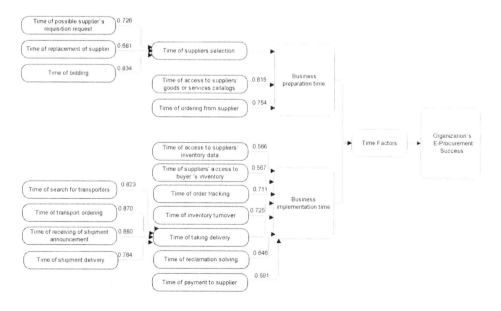

Costs as an E-Procurement Success Factor

In all respondent statements that are associated with e-procurement factors, with reference to business processing costs, respondents on average agree that e-procurement decreases costs spent on the each separate subprocess of e-procurement. The one exception is the subprocess "suppliers' access to buyers' inventory," where respondents expressed that costs could be increased by e-procurement implementation into this subprocess.

Most respondents from the survey indicated the highest possibilities to decrease costs by e-procurement in the following procurement subprocesses:

- Ordering from supplier (81.20%)
- Bidding (77.40%)
- Access to suppliers' goods or catalogs (76.70%)
- Possible supplier's requisition request (74.50%)
- Order tracking (73.60%)

On the contrary, we have the subprocess "replacement of supplier" where a lesser percent of respondents (36.8%) means that e-procurement could decrease costs.

The importance of all researched costs factors for successful e-procurement is shown in Table 2. Part of the model of costs factors is depicted in Figure 6.

Process Simplifying Factors as an E-Procurement Success Factor

In all statements that are connected to e-procurement factors, with reference to business processing simplifying, respondents on average, agree that e-procurement simplifies each separate subprocess of e-procurement.

Most respondents from the survey indicated the highest possibilities to simplify e-procurement in the following procurement subprocesses:

- Possible supplier's requisition request (85.70%)
- Bidding (85.70%)

Table 2. Costs factors importance

Costs Factors	The level of importance of factors in %						Average value
	Significant decrease				Significant increase	No answer	
	1	2	3	4	5	0	
Access to suppliers' inventory data costs	36.1	35.3	16.5	1.5	0	10.5	3.74
Ordering from supplier costs	36.8	44.4	11.3	0	0	7.5	3.95
Bidding costs	30.1	47.4	14.3	1.5	0	6.8	3.86
Access to suppliers' goods or catalogs costs	34.6	42.1	15	1.8	1.8	6.8	3.89
Possible supplier's requisition request costs	28.6	45.9	17.3	1.5	0	6.8	3.81
Order tracking costs	33.8	39.8	15	0.8	0	10.5	3.75
Receiving of shipment announcement costs	28.6	36.1	18	2.3	0	15	3.46
Payment to supplier costs	37.6	27.1	18	3	0	14.3	3.56
Inventory warehousing costs	25.6	36.1	18.8	2.3	0	17.3	3.33
Reclamation solving costs	22.6	34.6	28.6	3.8	0	10.5	3.44
Transport ordering costs	22.6	33.8	21.1	4.5	0	18	3.58
Shipment delivery costs	18.9	36.4	27.3	5.3	0	12.1	3.33
Searching for transporters costs	19.5	35.3	21.8	6.8	0	16.5	3.18
Suppliers' access to buyers' inventory costs	21.8	21.1	28.6	6.8	0	21.8	2.92
Replacement of supplier costs	10.5	26.3	51.1	3	0	9	3.17

Figure 6. The model of costs factors

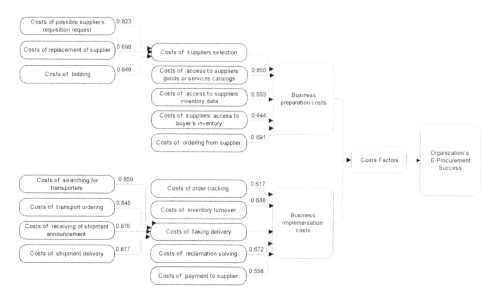

- Access to suppliers' goods or catalogs (85%)
- Ordering from supplier (84.20%)
- Order tracking (80.50%)

In contrast, "replacement of supplier" (45.8%) is the e-procurement subprocess where fewer respondents see possibilities to simplify it.

The importance of all researched process simplifying factors for successful e-procurement is shown in Table 3. Part of the model of process simplifying factors is depicted in Figure 7.

Table 3. Process simplifying factors importance

Process Simplifying Factors	The level of importance of factors in %						
	Significantly simplifies				Does not significantly simplify	No answer	Average value
	1	2	3	4	5	0	
Possible supplier's requisition request simplifying	34.6	51.1	7.5	0.8	0	6.0	4.02
Bidding simplifying	42.9	42.9	9	0	0.8	4.5	4.14
Access to suppliers' goods or catalogs simplifying	47.4	37.6	7.5	0.8	0.8	6.0	4.12
Ordering from supplier simplifying	45.9	38.3	6.0	1.5	1.5	6.8	4.05
Order tracking simplifying	48.9	31.6	11.3	0	0	8.3	4.05
Receiving of shipment announcement simplifying	34.6	39.8	12.8	0.8	0.8	11.3	3.73
Access to suppliers' inventory data simplifying	44.4	29.3	13.5	1.5	0	11.3	3.83
Payment to supplier simplifying	45.1	21.8	15.8	3.0	0	14.3	3.66
Shipment delivery simplifying	27.1	33.1	27.8	2.3	0.8	9.0	3.56
Inventory management simplifying	30.8	34.6	17.3	2.3	0.8	14.3	3.50
Transport ordering simplifying	24.8	35.3	18.0	5.3	0	16.5	3.30
Suppliers' access to buyer's inventory simplifying	30.1	27.8	15.0	7.5	0.8	18.8	3.23
Search for transporters simplifying	21.1	36.1	21.8	3	1.5	16.5	3.23
Reclamation solving simplifying	22.6	32.3	29.3	4.5	0	11.3	3.39
Replacement of supplier simplifying	13.5	32.3	39.8	6.0	0	8.3	3.29

Figure 7. The model of process simplifying factors

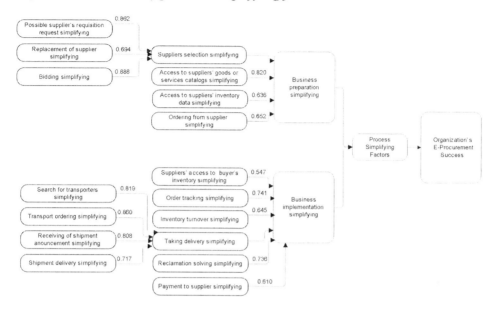

Volume of E-Transaction Factors as an E-Procurement Success Factor

"Payment to supplier" is a subprocess that is most frequently carried out by using e-procurement. Less than half (46.6%) of the respondents frequently pay their supplier electronically. The following processes are practiced to a very similar extent: "a possible supplier's requisition request" (35.30%), "bidding" (36.10%), and "ordering from supplier" (29.30%).

"Order acknowledgment" is a document, which is designed in the procurement process, and whose importance is growing along with the progress of the e-procurement itself. The same percentages of respondents (27.1%) who have electronic "access to suppliers' goods or catalogs" also "receive order acknowledgment from supplier" electronically. This is very stimulating because "order acknowledgment" was barely used prior to the use of the e-procurement.

In contrast, "access to suppliers' inventory data" (3%); "search for transporters" (3.8%) and "transport ordering" (9%) are subprocesses where e-procurement is less expanded.

Table 4. Volume of e-transaction factors importance

Volume of E-Transaction Factors	The level of importance of factors in %						
	The most frequently used				The least frequently used	No answer	Do not use at all
	1	2	3	4	5	0	
Payment to supplier	36.1	10.5	4.5	7.5	4.5	1.3	25.6
Possible supplier's requisition request	15.0	20.3	38.3	11.3	8.3	3.0	3.8
Bidding	15.0	21.1	32.3	13.5	6.8	4.5	6.8
Ordering from supplier	9.0	20.3	31.6	10.5	6.0	6.8	15.8
Access to suppliers' goods or catalogs	8.3	18.8	33.1	18.8	11.3	5.3	4.5
Receiving of order acknowledgment from supplier	8.3	18.8	27.8	12.8	12.8	7.5	12.0
Order tracking	6.0	8.3	12.8	18.0	16.5	7.5	30.8
Receiving of invoice from supplier	3.8	3.0	7.5	13.5	24.1	8.3	39.8
Receiving of shipment delivery data	3.8	4.5	17.3	15.8	23.3	7.5	27.8
Receiving of supply order from supplier	3.0	5.3	10.5	15.8	25.6	7.5	32.3
Suppliers' access to buyer's inventory	1.5	2.3	4.5	6.0	27.8	9.8	48.1
Transport ordering	1.5	7.5	9.8	13.5	19.5	8.3	39.8
Search for transporters	0.8	3.0	12.0	17.3	21.8	8.3	36.8
Access to suppliers' inventory data	0	3.0	12.8	19.5	27.1	7.5	30.1

The importance of all researched volume of e-transaction factors for successful e-procurement is shown in Table 4. Part of the model of volume of e-transaction factors is depicted in Figure 8.

Comparison of E-Procurement Success Factors Between Slovenian and Canadian Organizations

Generally, a comparison of factors between our research and "supply chain management issues study" from Athabasca University (2002) did not show significant differences. We can expose only one exception, in the volume of e-transactions in e-procurement in Canadian organizations. We can conclude that in Canadian organizations, e-procurement is better implemented in the following processes: "receiving of delivery data announcement," "order tracking," "access to suppliers' inventory data" and "access to suppliers' goods or catalogs," than it is in Slovenia (Table 5). The comparison of findings of Slovenian research with Canadian research regarding the volume of

Figure 8. The model of volume of e-transaction factors

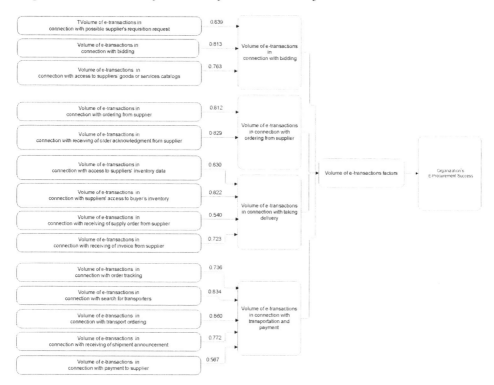

Table 5. Differences of the volume of e-transaction between the most used e-procurement subprocesses in Slovenia and in Canada

E-Procurement Subprocess	Canada	Slovenia
Receiving of delivery data announcement	56%	8.3%
Order tracking	56%	14.3%
Access to suppliers' inventory	45%	3%
Access to suppliers' goods or catalogs	50%	27.1%

e-transactions in the process of "bidding" displays a similarity which finds bidding to be the most frequently used electronically implemented e-procurement subprocess in Slovenia as well as abroad.

Another difference was shown in the comparison of the possibilities for costs decreasing in the e-procurement subprocess "suppliers' access to buyer inventory." The supply chain ,anagement issues study from Athabasca University (2002) shows that e-procurement could also decrease costs of this subprocess, while Slovenian respondents expressed that costs could be increased by e-procurement implementation into this subprocess. The reason for this could be, in the opinion of Slovenian organizations, that buyers first need to have access to suppliers' inventory data, and after that it is the suppliers' turn.

E-Procurement Factors Model Discussion

The challenges and opportunities of e-procurement for a small developing country such as Slovenia lies in the following factors: costs factors, time factors, process simplifying factors, and the volume of e-transactions factors. Of importance in e-procurement introduction is to pay attention to the reengineering of those processes, which are the basis of providing greater benefit from e-procurement (Table 6).

Based on statements from respondents, we conclude that organizations which endeavor to have a success in doing e-procurement, should simplify and decrease time and costs in most of the following subprocesses: ordering from supplier, bidding, and access to suppliers' goods or catalogs. These three processes are procurement subprocesses where e-procurement could bring the highest benefits in process simplifying and time and costs decreasing of business data processing.

For organizations, it is important also to decrease costs and simplify the process "possible supplier's requisition request." "Order tracking" is an

Table 6. Cross-section of the most important e-procurement success factors

E-Procurement Subprocess	Time Factors	Costs Factors	Process Simplifying Factors	Volume of E-Transactions Factors
Possible suppliers' requisition request		√	√	√
Bidding	√	√	√	√
Access to suppliers' goods or catalogs	√	√	√	
Ordering from supplier	√	√	√	
Order tracking			√	
Payment to supplier				√

e-procurement subprocess which has to be added to the group of the most important process simplifying factors, because the chances for simplifying this process are also high.

Payment to supplier, a possible supplier's requisition request, and bidding are the most frequently carried out by using e-procurement. The e-procurement opportunities to enlarge the volume of e-transactions in these processes are high.

Suggestions for Future Research

Research execution between organizations that have already defined the position of electronic commerce executive: When considering only those organizations that have already adopted a director/manager of e-commerce, we facilitated perceptions from the chief procurement officer, chief logistic officer, and chief information officer as well as director/manager, to elicit points of view from the holders of these positions of increasing importance over the last few years.

Research execution between organizations that have already adopted e-procurement: Large organizations were included in the research. Based on data collected using questionnaires, we established a database for further research. In compliance with these data, we could expand the future research only to those organizations that have been already used e-procurement. With this, we can capture the organizations which have a responsible person for e-procurement and a lot of useful experience in this field, and who would be able to answer our questions clearly and easily.

Factors of expansion from e-procurement to the e-supply chain: With this expansion, we would capture all business partners (suppliers, manufacturers, distributors, retail outlets, and buyers) that use transactions to purchase, convert/manufacture, assemble, or distribute goods and services to the buyers or end users. This would enable us to collect different supply chain participants' points of view; for example, besides the direct supplier, it would also include the suppliers' supplier's point of view.

Factors expansion to the possibility of benefits estimation resulting from completing e-procurement: One of the results of our research was identification of four independent factor groups. For further research, we would suggest taking into consideration the factor group's dependence, and thus will enable an estimation of work performed.

Research expansion to small and medium organizations: Our research includes large organizations, where we presume that large organizations have better IT equipment and that they have closer relationships with suppliers. It would be interesting and useful to compare collected statements derived from other small and medium organizations, which are not so well equipped with IT.

Regional research expansion: E-procurement research interest is very large between European countries and all other larger countries that border on Slovenia. With research expansion on neighbored countries such as Italy, Croatia, and Austria, we would get a model of e-procurement factors from regional connected countries' point of view. This would signify large added-value for all collaborated organizations and also to organizations that would not be included in the research.

Empirical research stimulating on the field of e-procurement: Empirical research on the e-procurement field has not been widespread. It is important to stimulate researchers to do empirical research on the e-procurement field and get an exhaustive research of the researched subject.

Recommendations: Six Useful Actions

Based on the experiences gained in doing e-procurement research, the following factors should be taken into consideration for higher success of e-procurement operations.

First, when introducing e-procurement into business processes, it is important to pay attention to the reengineering of those processes, which are the basis of providing benefit from e-procurement. Data shows that organizations have different organized processes with their business partners (suppliers). Above all, it is necessary to reengineer processes, make them uniform, incorporate them into common processes that will make it possible to operate processes electronically by all business partners, as well as to access all data that are needed, at the time it is needed.

Second, implementing e-procurement indicates benefits in costs and decreasing time, process simplifying, and by increasing the volume of e-transactions. For this reason, organizations should advance into these fields, thereby gaining savings as a result of e-procurement.

A third issue of importance in e-procurement introduction to business is to pay attention to the reengineering of those processes, which are the basis of providing greater benefit from e-procurement. In the first group of factors, time decreasing, these processes are: "ordering from supplier," "bidding," and "access to suppliers' goods or catalogs." In the second group, costs decreasing, the same processes are those which demand organizations' attention as are those in the time-decreasing factors group, together with one subprocess more: "possible supplier's requisition request." In the third group, process simplifying, organizations which endeavor to have a success in doing business electronically, should simplify subprocesses, namely: "bidding," "access to suppliers' goods or catalogs," "ordering from supplier," "order tracking" and "possible suppliers' requisition request." These five processes are subprocesses where e-procurement could bring the highest benefits in process simplifying. In the fourth group, volume of transactions, procurement, logistics, and informatics managers need to assure a higher volume of e-transactions in the following subprocesses: "payment to supplier," "possible suppliers' requisition request," and "bidding." These subprocesses include transactions that offer the greatest opportunity to be interchanged electronically.

Fourth, other than providing an e-procurement, it is very important for organizations to reach a higher level of e-procurement through the interchange of standardized documents with business partners. The research in Slovenia shows that organizations need to standardize interchange of the documents as follows: "purchase order," "payment order," "order acknowledgment," and "invoice." These documents are nowadays the most frequently interchanged in a standardized way.

Fifth, organizations have to undertake linkages between e-procurement factors groups. The research shows following important linkages which have to be considered by organizations: costs decreasing leads to time decreasing, and process simplifying leads to time and costs decreasing.

Sixth, the processes are changing with e-procurement, and it is also important that these changes are monitored and measured. It is necessary that organizations estimate benefits resulting from carrying out the procurement process electronically.

To sum up, it is apparent that organizations which have already designed an e-commerce strategy, appointed a director/manager of e-commerce, and introduced enterprise resource management systems, are more ready to successfully implement e-procurement.

Conclusion

The research provides a clear idea about e-procurement success factors, especially from a developing country's point of view. With e-procurement's successful implementing, such countries will be able to operate and compete equivalently in the common market.

The research shows that the e-procurement success factors that have to be considered are: cost factors, time factors, process simplification factors, and the volume of e-transactions factors. Most important for e-procurement introduction is to pay attention to the reengineering of those processes, which is the basis of providing greater benefits from e-procurement.

If an organization wants to implement e-procurement successfully, it is very important also to clearly define e-commerce strategy. Top management has to support the e-procurement implementation into their business. When the top executive level advocates electronic commerce, an organization can elevate the importance of e-procurement for the organization.

References

ActivMedia Research. (2000). *Business-to-business online, 2000.* Report. Retrieved from http://www.bitpipe.com

Archer, N., & Gebauer, J. (2001). Business-to-business applications to support business transactions: Overview and management considerations. In M. Warkentin (Ed.), *Business-to-business electronic commerce.* Hershey, PA: Idea Group Publishing.

Athabasca University (2002, May). Supply chain management issues study. *Media release, Centre for Innovative Management.* Retrieved from http://www.athabascaau.ca/scm

Berg, T. (1995, September). *The business value of electronic commerce* (Strategic Analysis Report, R-617-121). GartnerGroup.

Cao, Q. (2001). *Enhancing business performance in an electronic commerce setting: An empirical study.* Doctoral dissertation, University of Nebraska, Lincoln.

Chan, C., & Swatman, P. (1999). B-to-B e-commerce implementation: The case of BPH Steel. In *Proceedings of the European Conference on Information Systems (ECIS99)* (pp.70-83). Copenhagen Denmark: Copenhagen Business School.

Chen, L. (2000). *Consumer acceptance of virtual stores: A theoretical model and critical success factors for virtual stores.* Doctoral dissertation, The University of Memphis.

Dai, Q., & Kauffman, R. J. (2001, January 3-6). Business models for Internet-based e-procurement systems and B2B electronic markets: An exploratory assessment. *Thirty-Fourth Annual Hawaii International Conference on Systems Sciences (HICSS-34)*, Maui (Vol. 7, p. 10).

eEurope+2003. (2004). Progress report (pp. 1-48). Retrieved from http://ec.europa.eu/information_society/eeurope/plus/doc/progress_report.pdf.

Esichaikul, V., & Chavananon, S. (2001, June 26). Electronic commerce and electronic business implementation success factors. In B. O'Keefe, C. Loebbecke, J. Gričar, A. Pucihar, & G. Lenart (Eds.), *Proceedings of the 14th Bled Electronic Commerce Conference, E-Everything: E-Commerce, E-Government, E-Household, E-Democracy,* Bled, Slovenia, Kranj. *Moderna organizacija* (Vol 1., pp. 259-275).

European Commission (2000, July). EcaTT final report, electronic commerce, and telework trends: Benchmarking progress on new ways of working and new forms of business across Europe. *EMPIRICA, Project EcaTT98, EP29299.*

Gebauer, J., Beam, C., & Segev, A. (1998, February). *Impact of the Internet on procurement* (Fisher Center Paper). *Acquisition Review Quarterly,* 1-14.

Gebauer, J., & Segev, A. (2001). *Changing shapes of supply chains—How the Internet could lead to a more integrated procurement function* (Fisher Center Working Paper 01-WP-1041). Revue Internationale de l'Achat.

Gebauer, J., & Shaw, M. J. (2002, Summer). Introduction to the special section: Business-to-Business electronic commerce. *International Journal of Electronic Commerce, 6*(4), 7-17.

Haag, S., Cummings, M., & McCubbrey, D. J. (2002). *Management information systems for the information age* (3rd ed.). McGraw-Hill Irwin.

Ilijaš, T., & Grum, A. (2001, December). Why e-commerce? Goriška e-region, on the way to information society. In Š. Krapše (Ed.), *Mestna občina Nova gorica and Občina Šempeter-Vrtojba.*

Kalakota, R., & Robinson, M. (1999). *E-business, roadmap for success.* Reading, MA: Addison-Wesley Longman.

Komp Leonard, L. N. (1999). *Validating the electronic commerce success model through the supply chain management model.* Doctoral dissertation, University of Arkansas.

Kordež, B., & Jelovčan, M. (2001). E-commerce and wholesale. *Journal of Management, Informatics, and Human Resources, 34*(3), 150-152.

Lefebvre, L. A., Cassivi, L., & Lefebvre, E. (2001, January 3-6). Business-to-business e-commerce: A transition model. *Thirty-Fourth Annual Hawaii International Conference on Systems Sciences (HICSS-34),* Maui (Vol. 7, p.10).

Lesničar, T. (2002). *E-commerce influence on supply chains.* Master's thesis, University of Ljubljana, Faculty of Economics, Ljubljana.

Lindemann, M. A., & Schmid, B. F. (1998-99). Framework for specifying, building, and operating electronic markets. *International Journal of Electronic Commerce, 3*(2), 7-21.

Mesenbourg, T. L. (2002). *Measuring electronic business.* Retrieved from http://www.census.gov.

Ody, P. (2001a, December 5). Supply chain collaboration. *Financial Times, Twice-monthly review of Information and Communications Technology,* p. x.

Ody, P. (2001b, December 5). Winning idea masks hidden problems. *Financial Times, Twice–monthly review of Information and Communications Technology,* pp. x-xi.

Podlogar, M. (2002). *A model of electronic commerce critical success factors in procurement process.* Doctoral dissertation, University of Maribor, Faculty of Organizational Sciences, Kranj, Slovenia.

Podlogar, M., Hribar, U., & Gričar, J. (2001). IT use for e-commerce: Chief information officers' statements. *Journal of Management, Informatics, and Human Resources, 34*(3), 173-180.

Poirier, C. C., & Bauer, M. J. (2001). *E-supply chain: Using the Internet to revolutionize your business.* San Francisco: Berrett-Koehler Publishers.

Pucihar, A. (1999). *Opportunities and threats of e-commerce in organizations in Slovenia.* Master thesis, University of Maribor, Faculty of Organizational Sciences, Kranj, Slovenia.

Pucihar, A. (2002). *A model of factors influencing on organization's entering e-marketplace.* Doctoral dissertation, University of Maribor, Faculty of Organizational Sciences, Kranj, Slovenia.

Pucihar, A., & Gričar, J. (2004). Management, knowledge, and EU. *Proceedings of the 23rd International Conference on Organizational Science Development,* Slovenia, Portorož, Kranj. *Modern organization* (pp. 451-458).

RIS (May 2001). Slovene research on the Internet. *Report, University of Ljubljana, Faculty of Social Sciences, Slovenia.* Retrieved from http://www.ris.si

Segev, A., Gebauer, J., & Beam, C. (1998). *Procurement in the Internet age—Current practices and emerging trends (results from a field study)* (CMIT Working Paper WP-98-1033).

Shaw, M., Blanning, R., Strader, T., & Whinston, A. (2000). *Handbook on electronic commerce.* Berlin: Springer-Verlag.

Sitarski, E. (2001). Building a collaborative supply chain for the mid-sized company, supply chain management future. (July). Retrieved from http://www.ebizchronicle.com

Sterle, V. (2001). Electronic commerce in procurement process of Ministry of Defense (case of Department of Defense, United States of America). *Journal of Management, Informatics, and Human Resources, 34*(3), 143-149.

Tung, L. A. (2001). The role of trust in business-to-business electronic commerce in Singapore. *Conference Proceedings of the 14th Bled Electronic Commerce Conference, E-Everything: E-Commerce, E-Government, E-Household, E-Democracy* (Vol. 1) Bled, Slovenia. *Moderna organizacija.*

Van Weele, A. (1998). *Procurement management.* Ljubljana, Slovenia: Gospodarski vestnik.

Vaupot, Ž. (2001). E-marketplaces. *Journal of Management, Informatics, and Human Resources, 34*(3), 165-168.

Zupančič, B., & Sedej, M. (2000). Electronic commerce in the supply chain. *Journal of Management, Informatics, and Human Resources, 33*(3), 194-199.

Chapter IV

Challenges in Implementation of E-Procurement in the Indian Government

Ramanathan Somasundaram, National Institute for Smart Government, India

Abstract

In this chapter, the concept of e-government procurement (e-GP), as it is being implemented in India, is explained. Furthermore, a set of six challenges encountered during implementation of e-procurement is discussed in depth. The six challenges discussed in the chapter are: lack of skilled personnel; multi-departmental implementation; inadequate IT and networking infrastructure; challenges in implementation of state-wide system; the need to regulate e-procurement market; and replicating best practices in federal-state setup. A practitioner's perspective is adopted to write this chapter. While this chapter deals specifically with e-GP in India, certain aspects of it can be generalized to e-GP implementations elsewhere in the world. Such generalization is possible since government procurement is driven by the same set of principles such as efficiency and transparency.

Introduction

The uptake of e-procurement in the government sector is on the rise. Developed nations such as Australia, Denmark, Singapore, the USA, Korea, and a few South American nations such as Chile and Brazil were the forerunners in implementing e-procurement. The forerunners got into e-procurement during the late 1990s. In India, the State of Andhra Pradesh pioneered with the implementation of e-procurement during early 2000. Elsewhere in Asia, Philippines and Indonesia have embarked on implementing e-procurement recently. Multi-lateral bodies such as the World Bank, Asian Development Bank, and Inter-American Development Bank have joined hands together to constitute a body for implementing e-procurement all across the developing and less-developed nations. This body, named Multilateral Development Bank e-Government Procurement (MDB-e-GP), is actively promoting implementation of e-procurement.

Government procurement is a voluminous activity, and in developing countries such as India, it is fast-growing. As per a country assessment report prepared by the World Bank, the Indian government is estimated to buy for US$100 billion each year. Similarly, across the globe, governments spend significant sums of money in public procurement. It is estimated that public procurement accounts for about 10-15% of a nation's GDP. In a country, the government is typically the largest buying entity. Despite the significance, there have not been many analytical write-ups on implementation of e-government procurement (e-GP). The implementation of e-procurement in the government setup is quite a challenging activity; in order to effectively deal with the challenges, it is vital that the nature of challenges are well-understood, and that the means to address the challenges are analyzed and discussed.

In this chapter, challenges encountered in implementation of e-procurement in India are explained. The explanation is preceded by the following sections:

1. Functional Overview of E-Procurement
2. Benefits of E-Procurement
3. Public Procurement in India
4. State of E-Procurement Internationally
5. State of E-Procurement in India
6. Geographical Scope Discussed in the Chapter

This chapter is written from a practitioner's perspective, one who is attempting to tackle the challenges being explained. While this chapter deals specifically with e-GP in India, certain aspects of it can be generalized to e-GP implementations elsewhere in the world. Such generalization is possible since government procurement is driven by the same set of principles, that is, efficiency, transparency, and accountability.

This chapter is written based on practical exposure, which the author has gained while implementing e-procurement in two state governments in India. The author was involved in preparation of a request for proposal (RFP), based on which a private partner will be selected for implementing an end-to-end e-procurement system in both the states. As part of the effort, the author has had the opportunity to interact with end users in government departments who undertake procurement, application service providers (ASP) community and nodal officers initiating the implementation effort. Moreover, he has been an integral part of the decision-making process within the government. The rich experience gained during the implementation effort is relied upon to write this chapter.

Functional Overview of E-Procurement

E-procurement, as it is referred to in this chapter, is an integrated end-to-end application with the following modules:

1. Indent management (workflow system administering administrative and technical approval processes)
2. E-tendering (PKI-enabled electronic bid submission)
3. E-auctions (forward and reverse)
4. Contract management (preparation and verification of bills with respect of works and services contract)
5. Order management (for utilization of goods and services rate contracts)
6. Supplier enrollment
7. E-payments
8. MIS
9. Accounting

Figure 1. Functional overview of e-procurement

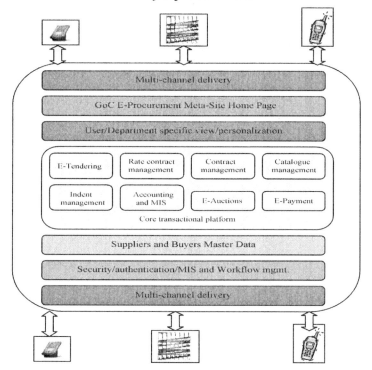

It is to be noted that in India, e-tendering is customarily referred to as e-procurement. It needs to be clarified that e-procurement is much more comprehensive than e-tendering. E-procurement includes many other modules such as contract management and order management, which are equally if not more significant than the e-tendering. For seamless procurement operations, the e-procurement system has to be integrated with inventory management, budgeting, treasury, and payment gateways.

Benefits of E-Procurement

The implementation of e-procurement in private enterprises, as it is claimed, has resulted in savings in the range of 10-15% of procurement value. It is logical to assume that government would likewise be able to save on a similar scale. Since government is typically the largest procurement agency in a country, the amount of savings in value terms is quite significant. If the Indian government can save 10% of its $100 billion a year procurement expenditure, then the resultant savings will be in the range of US$100 billion, or 4,500 billion Rupees (World Bank, 2003) (converting at US$1 = 45 Indian Rupees), an amount that will contribute significantly towards managing the fiscal deficit (Kaul, 2005).

Apart from efficiency, enhanced transparency is another important benefit resulting from e-procurement. Especially since the *"Right to Information"* Act (RTI Act), 2005, has come into force in India, the government is obligated to be transparent about its operations. Since procurement of works, goods, and services accounts for a major part of the operations, government agencies are flooded with queries about the procedure adopted for the award of contracts and the status of contracts (especially related to public works).[1] The amount of queries will increase in coming years when the RTI Act will come into full force, and as the number of works (e.g., roads, metro rail, and bridges) undertaken by the government will increase. Since e-procurement is implemented in the Internet environment, government agencies can voluntarily share with the public some information on tendering and contract management activities. Such information sharing will show the government in a good light and simultaneously minimize its workload.

In addition to efficiency and transparency, implementation of e-procurement results in many more benefits, a summary of which is provided below:

- Elimination of delays arising out of processing tenders manually and on paper
- Publication of tender notice/IFB in newspapers can be avoided, resulting in saving of time and money
- Cartel formation can be arrested, as any bidder interested will be able to participate with anonymity
- Fair, free, and fearless participation of tenderers becomes possible
- Improvement in work culture in the departments
- Database on goods, services, works, and contractors gets build up
- Economy of scale is achieved by aggregation of requirements
- Better access to procurement spend information and analytical reports

Public Procurement in India

Government procurement in India is a highly-dispersed activity. The estimated US$100 billion is spent by multiple offices across the country. Since procurement is essentially an expenditure activity, the locations and manner of expenditure depends on the allocation of funds and responsibility within the government. The procurement process is performed at multiple levels in government, and it is centralized as well as decentralized. Various methods employed in government procurement are explained in this section to give the reader an idea of the complexity involved in a move to e-procurement. The shift to e-procurement cannot be achieved if procurement, as explained below, is not handled electronically.

Rate Contract Negotiation

For rate contracts, a central agency empanels one (single rate contract) or more (parallel rate contract) suppliers to deliver a good/service for a price to all agencies within a given jurisdiction, which could be nation,[2] state,[3] department,[4] or office,[5] for a period of time.[6] The empanelment of suppliers is done based on a tendering process. An estimate of utilization, that is, the number of items which the government is expected to purchase, is provided based on the volume of procurement done in the previous years. In general, users on whose behalf the negotiation is done are not obligated to use the rate contracts. For example a government agency may choose to purchase an item such as furniture by using Directorate General of Supplies & Disposals (DGS&D's) rate contract or a contract negotiated by a state agency or by its own.

Rate Contract Ordering

There are two variations in rate contract ordering, which are: centrally-negotiated and decentrally-ordered; and centrally-negotiated and centrally-ordered:

- **Centrally-negotiated and decentrally-ordered:** The agencies negotiating rate contracts on behalf of the nation and a state hardly utilize the rate contracts which they have negotiated. Instead, ordering of items is done by agencies dispersed across the nation. The ordering is done in such a decentralized manner that the negotiating agencies are unaware of the extent to which the rate contracts are utilized. Likewise, rate contracts are centrally negotiated at the department level, for example, procurement of medicines and equipment by the Health Department. In case of departmental rate contracts, end users[7] in departments are typically obligated to order using the centrally-negotiated rate contracts.

- **Centrally-negotiated and centrally-ordered:** In some departments and offices, rate contract negotiation and rate contract ordering are done from a central location.[8] A bulk order is placed on suppliers using rate contracts, which is then distributed to various offices in the hierarchy as and when the need arises. The needed information is transmitted to the central location using requisitions.

ECV-Based Procurement

ECV is an abbreviation of estimated cost value. ECV is typically prepared for works procurement and for some types of services procurement. The basis for preparation of ECV is the schedule of rates (SOR), a price list maintained by departments. To do ECV-based procurement, Government agencies need to get two types of approvals: administrative and technical. While the administrative and technical approvals are given from the higher-ups in the hierarchy, the groundwork required for the preparation of the cost estimates is done by those lower in the hierarchy.[9] Typically, a project file moves back-and-forth in the hierarchy several times before the notice inviting tender (NIT) is issued. In line departments, such as the Public Works Department (PWD) and the Water Resources Department (WRD), the hierarchy is extensive, and it branches out from the secretariat at the top to subdivisional offices at the bottom. On the other hand, in boards and corporations, hierarchy tends to be short and, more importantly, the offices are co-located within a small geographical area and typically in the networked capital city.

Procurement in Line Departments, Boards and Institutions, and Urban Local Bodies

Procurement done by all the three agencies fall under rate contract-based procurement[10] and ECV-based procurement. However, the three agencies handle their procurement differently. Firstly, much of the procurement done by line departments falls under "*capital expenditure*," which results in the creation of assets (e.g., construction of highways and roads). The remaining part is spent on maintenance work, which in macroeconomics falls under "*revenue expenditure*." Since the value of capital expenditure tends to be high, multiples levels of authority have been created to develop and monitor the projects. Unless line departments have a "*Pay and Accounts*" office, payment for the work done by contractors is paid through the state's treasury department.

Boards and institutions are created specifically for a purpose, and they exist and operate with a high level of autonomy. Since government is engaged in many different activities, the purposes for which the boards and institutions are created vary significantly. For example, a board or an institution could be created specifically for the development of highways using World Bank loans,[11] for manufacturing of soaps and detergents,[12] for improving schooling infrastructure,[13] and for the development of metro rail.[14] Some of the organizations continue to exist perpetually, whereas others close down when the purpose is accomplished. Decision-making in these organizations is not as bureaucratic as that of the line departments; they operate in a focused manner and are therefore much more efficient. For reporting purposes, boards and institutions fall under one of the line departments.

Urban local bodies (ULB) comprises of zilla parishads (district-level committee), city and town corporations and taluk and gram panchayats (village-level committee). The administrative head of a ULB is Zilla Parishad (ZP), to which a sum of money is allocated each year as part of the budget. The ZP in turn allocates the money to "people-oriented" line departments reporting to it and panchayat organizations. The city and town corporations are typically autonomous bodies. They plough back the revenue earned and grants received to develop and maintain cities and towns. For implementation of development-oriented schemes, money is allocated to ZPs, in some cases, directly from the central government and alternatively through state government. In India, a move to decentralization is underway, and procurement handled by gram panchayats is expected to increase in future. So far, much of the procurement done at ULB falls under revenue expenditure. However, efforts are underway to increase the implementation of development-oriented projects through schemes funded by the central government.

Institutional Setup

In most of the Indian states, an institutional setup is not available to evolve procurement practices. In the country assessment report prepared by the World Bank, the lack of a policy-making department at the states and in the center is identified as a weakness of the regime. Some efforts are being taken by governments, either internally or using external agencies such as the World Bank and DFID, to study procurement practices. However, an organized approach is not adopted to internalize the best practices resulting from the study at the state level and promulgate the use of such practices across the nation. As of now, the reports generated by the committees and external agencies are not easily accessible, and best practices recommended in those reports often go unnoticed. Moreover, only two states in the country have institutionalized transparency in a Public Procurement act, which are Karnataka and Tamil Nadu. The legislation, as it is in the two states, needs to be amended to facilitate e-procurement. At the national level, there is a definite need to develop legislation on public procurement.

State of E-Procurement Internationally

E-procurement is being actively implemented in many countries in the World. A few countries such as Singapore and Korea have had good success in implementing an end-to-end solution as a national initiative. E-procurement is implemented at the state level in federal nations such as Australia, the United States, and Canada. Efforts are now underway in the European Union to cohesively advance implementation of e-procurement in the entire community. In December, 2004, the European Commission has published an action plan for implementation of the legal framework for electronic public procurement (European Union [EU], 2004). Moreover, the EU has prepared a model functional requirements specification (FRS) document, which is used as the scale for certifying e-procurement systems. The Union members could then call for an EU certified e-procurement system and not self-engage in preparation of FRS and in evaluation of a technical specifications document. International standards on e-procurement are emerging, such as UNCTAD have taken efforts to develop an e-tendering standard.

In most countries that are in the forefront of implementing e-procurement, e-catalogue-based procurement is typically associated with e-procurement. In those countries, a lot of emphasis is laid on enhancing efficiency in goods procurement. There, e-procurement is implemented to increase operational efficiency and to introduce strategic sourcing.

Elsewhere in Denmark (www.gatetrade.com) and in the state of North Carolina in the United States (http://www.ncgov.com/eprocurement/asp/section/ep_index.asp), private-public-partnership (PPP) models have been used for implementing e-procurement. The state of Philippines is implementing e-procurement using the build-operate-transfer (BOT) model. In Singapore, the state government has developed an e-procurement solution on its own.

The Korean e-procurement system (http://www.korean.go.kr) is widely regarded as the state-of-the-art. Some of the noticeable features in the Korean system are: auto-bid evaluation where both technical and commercial bids are evaluated in minutes;[15] linkages with 30 procurement-related agencies such as Ministry of Finance, supplier certification agencies, e-guarantee and e-payment systems; and payment automation[16] (World Bank, 2004).

Multilateral development banks (MDB), such as the World Bank, Asian Development Bank, and Inter-American Development Bank have joined hands together to develop an organization specifically to foster implementation of e-procurement across the world. The organization named MDB e-Government Procurement (e-GP) group is now providing consulting services and the funds required for implementing e-procurement to many developing and less-developed countries. Thus, e-procurement is being implemented all across the world and not just in economically well-developed nations.

State of E-Procurement in India

The concept of e-tendering is well publicized among government agencies in India. Except for a pioneering few, e-tendering is done in parallel with manual tendering, that is, bidders responding back to a tender could submit their bids online, or else submit the bids manually, or do both. The state of Andhra Pradesh is a pioneer in implementing a PKI-enabled e-tendering system that is used by government agencies all across the state. The government of Rajasthan has recently taken efforts to implement e-procurement at the state level. The efforts have fructified with the selection of an implementation agency, which is in the process of implementing the system across the state. Two other state governments, those of Karnataka and Chhattisgarh, are in the process of preparing a request for proposal (RFP) for implementation of a state-wide e-procurement system. While it is clear that the two state governments intend to adopt a private-public-partnership approach, the exact business model has not been decided as yet.

Typically, elsewhere in India, e-tendering systems are implemented at the departmental level. Departments individually take efforts to identify an e-procurement vendor, whose services they use. The business model adopted for funding these projects varies. For example, the payment could be made on a "fixed fee per tender" or "fixed fee per year" or "percentage of an ECV with cap" basis. In some of the states, departments place orders directly[17] to another government agency,[18] which in turn has a back-to-back agreement or a memorandum of understanding (MoU) with an e-procurement application service provider. In one of the states, having had the opportunity to study the contracts between government departments and another government agency to whom the order is placed, the author has learned that the payments are calculated in an arbitrary manner, not just in terms of the price quoted but in terms of the business model itself.

Apart from e-tendering, a system for administering the contract management aspects of e-procurement has been implemented in some of the public works departments. The system[19] is typically static in nature and implemented for the purposes of documentation and report generation. Such systems are prevalent in agencies that administer loans given by multi-lateral development banks. The business model typically adopted for procurement of the system is build-own-transfer (BOT). Many agencies have sunk in millions of rupees in deploying the systems and furthermore spending hundreds of thousand of rupees to upgrade and Web-enable the system. In this regard, it should be noted that implementation of the contract management module does not fully benefit government until it is integrated with the e-tendering module and supplier database. Only when the integration is done is it possible to automate technical-bid evaluation, a functionality that denotes an advanced state of e-procurement implementation.

The project management system implemented by the Karnataka State Police Housing Corporation (www.khspc.org) is a pioneering effort. As of now, more than 1,000 projects are managed using this system. Since the system is Web-based, information about the projects handled by the corporation is available on the net for the citizens to see. The drawback of the system, however, is that the project management module is a stand-alone system, and it is not integrated with the e-tendering module and supplier database.

Driven by business interests, e-procurement vendors have taken tremendous efforts to bring awareness about e-tendering in government agencies. Similarly, the success that the government of Andhra Pradesh has had in routing Rs. 36,000 crores[20] worth of procurement has publicized e-procurement across the country and elsewhere in the world too. The Central Vigilance Commission (CVC), on its part, has directed government agencies *"to eventually switch over to the process of e-procurement/e-sale wherever it is found to be feasible and practical"* (Central Vigilance Commission, p. 2).

In India, there are about 10 vendors operating in the e-procurement market. Most of them have a well-developed e-tendering product, which they have successfully implemented in several locations. A few of the vendors claim to have developed end-to-end e-procurement, as it is explained in the third section. The e-procurement market in India has good players, who have the capacity to implement large scale e-procurement projects.

There is a good amount of interest among Indian government agencies to implement e-procurement. So far, driven by self-propelled individuals, vendor marketing, and peer pressure, the e-procurement scene in India has emerged in an unorganized manner. In terms of capacity, e-procurement product vendors and the required workforce are available. Taking into account the state of development, interest, and capacity, the timing is just about right to initiate e-procurement implementation across the country in an organized manner and develop a technically sound, fully interoperable, end-to-end e-procurement system.

Geographical Scope Discussed in the Chapter

Two terms are used in this chapter to denote geographical scope, which are: state-wide e-procurement system; and national e-procurement system.

In a state-wide e-procurement system, all procurement-related information flows,[21] handled by line departments, boards and institutions, and urban local bodies, (located within the geographical boundaries of a state) will be routed through a single, fully-integrated, end-to-end e-procurement application in a legally valid manner. In this chapter, an end-to-end system developed for central government agencies is termed as a state-wide system. The state-wide system will be regarded as fully implemented only when the e-procurement application is integrated with payment gateways, budgeting, and treasury systems. An integral part of implementing the state-wide system will be the development of an ecosystem, a policy-making organization, that will incorporate the best procurement practices in the state.

Under the national e-procurement system, implementation of e-procurement in all 29 Indian states, 6 union territories, and central government agencies is planned. To implement the national e-procurement system, certain aspects of the many state-wide systems are to be centrally developed/integrated. For example, there is a need for a contractor database at the national level; MIS data generated by many state-wide systems could be integrated to generate real-time data on government procurement at the national level. As part of the system, a national policy-making organization and e-Government Procurement-specific legislation has to be developed.

It is important to realize that the challenges in implementing nationwide e-procurement systems are different from those in implementation of state-wide e-procurement systems. One or more departments in a state may choose to take the initiative in implementing an e-procurement system for needs specific to them. However, such a decentralized approach is not considered as good practice, reasons for which are explained in the following section. From a researcher's point of view, nation, state, and department are three different units of analyses. Furthermore, federal-state nations such as India, the USA, Australia, and the European Union have a complex administrative structure, whereas small-sized countries such as Singapore, Denmark, and South Korea follow simpler structure. Given the categorization, it is proper to compare the implementation of e-procurement in India with other federal-state nations such as the USA, Australia, and the European Union, and likewise the effort taken by the state of North Carolina in the USA with that of the state of Andhra Pradesh in India.

Challenges in Implementation of E-Procurement in India

One may get the initial impression that unavailability of financial resources is a barrier for implementing e-procurement in developing countries. From experience, the author has learned that India, despite being a developing country, has adequate financial resources for implementing e-procurement. For that matter, developing countries are able to get loans from donor agencies for implementing e-procurement. If a government chooses to adopt a PPP model and seek e-procurement as a service, then resource requirements are minimal. The private partner will need to implement the application and charge a service fee for transactions routed through the system. Since procurement is a commerce activity, the government can pay the private partner as per the usage and gradually purchase the application. For example, the government of Andhra Pradesh has implemented e-procurement quite successfully all across the state without making any upfront investment for setting up the e-procurement application.

The challenges in implementing e-procurement, as they are explained below, are mainly socio-political in nature. The deployment of e-procurement emerges as a key challenge since the system has to be deployed and accessed from a very large number of offices. Furthermore, the lack of skilled personnel is a critical challenge in the implementation of e-procurement. A set of six challenges is explained in detail below:

Challenge 1: Lack of Skilled Personnel

In a developing country such as India, the lack of an adequate number of skilled personnel in the government is probably the most significant challenge in implementing e-procurement. To implement e-procurement, government agencies will first need to specify things such as functional, technical, security, and service requirements, service level agreement (SLA) criteria, roll-out plan, and so forth. Furthermore, if e-procurement is implemented on a private-public-partnership (PPP) basis, then they have to decide on a business model and more importantly, customize the model to fit the e-procurement activity. The e-procurement project development is a comprehensive activity, and it requires skilled personnel to be on the job for a considerable period of time, usually between three and six months. Once the private partner is identified, then a team has to be deployed for a longer period of time to manage and monitor the implementation effort.

The implementation of state-wide e-procurement system is typically initiated by the department of IT/e-governance in tandem with public works departments. Employees in these departments typically lack the required skill sets to engage in the project development effort. Their understanding of e-procurement is obtained from vendors' marketing efforts and through hearsay. Such an understanding is inadequate to envision a state-wide end-to-end e-procurement system. Due to this inadequacy, government agencies implement e-tendering and often term it wrongly as end-to-end e-procurement.

As a remedy, government agencies look to hire external consultants to engage in the project development effort. Even for selecting the consultants, government agencies will need to prepare a terms of reference (ToR), for which they tend to lack the knowledge. If the government does prepare a ToR, then selecting an external consultant as per the laid-out procedural requirements is tedious. Except for the top management in the department of IT/e-governance and a few more employees, the rest in the department lack the capability to meaningfully engage in the project development effort. For the top management, e-procurement is only one of the many projects they have to handle, and hence efforts get diverted.

As it is often said in conferences and workshops, e-procurement, just like e-government, is not about "e" but about "procurement." Hence, one initiating the implementation of e-procurement needs to understand public procurement. In reality, however, only an exceptional few are aware of both the "e" and "procurement" attributes. If a project is implemented without proper understanding of both the attributes, then it is unlikely that the project will meet the desired objectives.

If the status quo has to change, then the government has to amend its human resource policies. Hiring of skilled personnel for a shorter duration of time has to be made simpler. Since salary structure is well-defined, government employees lack the incentive to initiate new projects. On the contrary, if an initiative taken by an employee does not fructify, then the employee becomes an easy target for criticism; thus the organization's own policies discourage personnel from taking initiatives. Furthermore, government personnel have to be trained at regular intervals. Unfortunately, government as it is lacks the institutional setup required for training its own employees. Unless skill sets of government employees are developed, implementation of e-procurement and, in a larger scale, e-government in a country as large as India will be difficult.

Challenge 2: Multi-Departmental Implementation

It is frequently mentioned that e-government cuts across departmental boundaries and mergers silos of operations within government. In a state-wide e-procurement system, procurement handled by multiple departments is routed through a single end-to-end application. Since a state-wide system is meant to be used by all departments in the state, the implementation authority has to consult with a wide range of stakeholders during project development and project implementation. Such a consultation process is fraught with difficulties because the department of IT, which typically is the implementation agency, lacks authority over other departments in the state. The lack of authority is typically overcome with several rounds of consultations, training, and negotiations. Unless one or more powerful authorities is fully involved in the implementation effort for a considerable period of time (ranging from three to six months), the project is unlikely to have the desired effect. The IT department may go ahead with project development on its own which, however, will have an adverse effect on uptake of the system. It definitely helps if a top ranking political or administrative authority in a state stamps his interest in the project.

Government agencies in India do not have information on procurement activities (procedures, spend break-up, etc.) in an easily retrievable manner. In order to prepare functional requirements and plan the system rollout, the implementation agency will need to gather procurement information from about 40 departments and around 100 government agencies. To undertake such a task, a high level of persistence is required.

Challenge 3:
Inadequacy of IT and Networking Infrastructure

To implement an end-to-end e-procurement, IT and networking infrastructure across government offices is a basic requirement. In India, government agencies have inadequate IT infrastructure and connectivity problems in district and taluka (town and village) levels.

So far in India, there has not been a coordinated effort to improve the IT infrastructure. Instead, government agencies have taken efforts independently to computerize their offices. Often, computers are purchased just to utilize the funds allocated to an agency before the budget period lapses. The computers which are purchased in such a manner are typically shelved and hardly put to use. Additionally, government agencies purchase computers as part of externally-aided programs funded by donor agencies such as the World Bank. Since an asset management system is not in use in Indian government agencies, we lack information on IT readiness at the departmental level. Before initiating e-procurement implementation, one will need to collate the availability of IT infrastructure in the government.

Thanks to the deregulation of the telecom industry in India, broadband connectivity is becoming pervasive. As of now, broadband is readily available in all major cities, and its coverage is spreading towards smaller cities and towns. The government, as part of its Rs. 12,500 crores National e-Government Plan (NeGP), is in the process of implementing State-Wide Area Network (SWAN), which will bring Internet connectivity all across the country.

IT and network connectivity requirements are different for many e-procurement modules. For example, an e-tendering module is typically used at the district level (cities) offices and above, whereas a contract management module is used at the subdivisional offices (in remote areas) where a work gets implemented. Given the state of IT and network readiness in government, it is easier to implement the e-tendering aspect of e-procurement, since offices which handle the tendering work have better IT and network infrastructure when compared with offices that engage in contract management. Such distinction has to be taken into consideration while planning the rollout of the application function-wise and geography-wise.

Challenge 4:
Implementation of State-Wide E-Procurement System

Given the awareness, peer pressure, and vendor marketing, many entities, departments and corporations, have independently taken the initiative to engage in e-procurement. Typically, the entities have implemented an e-tendering system, where tender information is uploaded/downloaded, and bid submissions are handled both manually and electronically in parallel. In a few exceptional cases, e-auctions are implemented, and 100% PKI-enabled e-bidding is put in place.

The independent efforts, while they have to be appreciated, typically have the following drawbacks:

1. A plan for scaling-up the initiative both function-wise and geography-wise is not envisaged.

2. Proper measures are not taken to secure data from e-procurement ASP in a restorable format, that is, if an ASP becomes dysfunctional, then the government may lose the past transactional data or, at the most, have it in a readable format.

3. Exit management strategy is not conceived.

4. Service level agreement (SLA) is not established with ASP.

5. Implementation of e-procurement is not looked at as an opportunity to reform processes, standardize formats, and make the necessary legislative amendments; hence, the manual system is at best handled in an electronic manner; the entities typically lack the mandate and the authority to implement reforms.

6. The business model adopted to remunerate ASPs for the service provided varies a lot; in some cases, ASPs are offered a fixed fee per tender and, in other cases, on an annuity basis; the rates quoted are quite varying and in the end, the government pays much more to ASPs than if they would have negotiated centrally as a single agency.

7. Often, a government agency is selected to implement e-procurement, which in turn has a back-to-back agreement with an ASP; the government agency charges a percentage of the fee, in the range of 10-15%, charged by an ASP for the services rendered; the process adopted by the government agency to select the ASP is often unclear, and contractual obligations between the two are not known to the entities using the system.

8. If there are any security loopholes in the e-procurement application, government agencies may be unaware of them since a security audit of the application is not typically done.

9. A set of suppliers will need to be trained to use multiple systems, to which they would resist.

10. To achieve a fully-integrated end-to-end system, an e-procurement application has to be integrated with external systems such as treasury systems, supplier database, and e-payment gateways; if multiple systems

are operating in a state, such integration has to be done many times; since integration is an expensive activity, it is advisable to keep it to the minimum; moreover, opening sensitive applications such as the treasury to multiple e-procurement applications is not advisable.

A few of the drawbacks explained above get addressed inherently when a state-wide system is implemented. For example, with a state-wide system, the supplier community will have access to government procurement opportunities in a single location, and consequently they will need to be trained in using a single application. Some of the drawbacks such as exit management, rollout plan, SLA criteria, process reforms, and business model are addressed during the project development effort. Furthermore, in an effort to think of procurement at the state-level, an ecosystem in the form of a procurement cell could be created as part of the project development effort. The cell would address project monitoring, system audit, system maintenance, and process reform requirements.

To implement e-tendering and especially contract management/project management module, agencies have to invest significant sums of money, in some cases ranging in tens of millions of rupees. Such investments are asset-specific in nature and hence could be considered as sunk-costs. In addition to paying for the system, the agencies would have to invest in complementary activities such as project development, training, and publicity. Government agencies, which have already made such investments, may tend to get attached with their own efforts and consequently resist adopting the state-wide system. With further delay in planning state-wide e-procurement systems, many more islands of overlapping systems will emerge. The emergence of such islands will make it increasingly harder to implement state-wide systems. Fortunately in India, there are not so many legacy systems. In other words, the slate is clean. Unless urgency is shown in the implementation of state-wide systems, the government may lose the opportunity to develop end-to-end e-procurement systems consistently across the nation.

Challenge 5:
The Need to Regulate E-Procurement Market

Procurement as an activity is done in a small or big way in almost all government offices in India. Government administration in India is the second largest in the world, and procurement done by the government is estimated at $100 billion each year. Moreover, if growth[22] in the Indian economy is taken into consideration along with investments made for infrastructure development,[23] the volume of government procurement will increase significantly in the years to come. If the government is to handle its geographically-widespread, voluminous, and fast-growing procurement electronically in an end-to-end manner, it will need to invest significantly in the implementation effort. The investment will be needed for planning, application deployment, training, hardware procurement, network installation, and purchase of security infrastructure. Apart from investing in implementation of e-procurement, the government will need to pay for maintenance, training, licenses, hardware, and software upgrades recurrently. Given the size of the market, its current state, and the effort required, business potential in the e-procurement market in the government sector is significant. The government has to outsource the implementation of e-procurement to external agencies in one form or the other. Thus it is no surprise that the market has more than 10 players showing active interest, including a few internationally-renowned firms.

Since the government represents the demand side of the supply-demand equation in the e-procurement market, it is not in a position to play the role of a regulator as it has done, for example, in the telecom industry. Despite the paradoxical situation, the need for regulation in the e-procurement market still remains. First and foremost, the process to be adopted for the selection of an ASP is not clear. In many cases, government agencies are selecting an e-procurement ASP without a tendering process. Such "back-door entry" creates distaste among the ASP community since equal opportunities were not given.

Second, a plan is not in place for e-procurement implementation in an organized manner all across the country. The implementation of such a plan should allow for experience sharing, and thus avoid reinvention of the wheel. Moreover, when a plan is in place, the ASPs will have clarity on the business that is available, which will cultivate healthy competition. For successful e-procurement implementation in the Indian government, it is vital that the ASPs work in harmony. Specifically for such, the government needs to regulate the e-procurement market.

Third, in the e-procurement market, a few of the ASPs are in dispute with one another, and consequently a couple of legal battles are ongoing. Especially in recent times, the disputes are getting spilled over and ASPs are resorting to trading accusations on the implementation efforts taken by the government and that too publicly. Citing the sensitive nature of procurement, government agencies are even threatened with public interest litigation (PIL) for the efforts they have taken in implementing e-procurement. Such behavior by the ASPs is destructive in nature, and it does not augur well to any of the stakeholders. Government agencies and, consequently, individuals in government are being accused by ASPs for the initiative they have taken to implement e-procurement. Such accusations will have a dampening effect in the uptake of e-procurement in the country. For the e-procurement scene to develop in an expeditious and harmonious manner, it is vital that ASPs are constructive and forthcoming. Disputes that ASPs have should be kept to themselves and not spilled over to the implementation locations. The need of the hour is a regulatory body that will monitor the market for destructive behavior and reprimand those who are found guilty.

Fourth, there is need to advocate the use of certain technology standards so that interoperability among the many e-procurement systems and with external systems will be possible. In this regard, the regulatory body will need to know the state of development of external systems such as treasury and budgeting systems across the nation. If the external systems are being developed in an unorganized manner, then integration with such systems will be difficult. When the regulatory body expresses its concern about the lack of standardization in a certain type of external system, then awareness will be created. Such awareness will catalyze the standardization of systems across many other national e-government initiatives.

Fifth, since government procurement is a sensitive activity, the use of certain security features is needed. In relation to this, there is need for an agency which will monitor advancement in technologies and advocate the use of the most advanced features.

Sixth, an e-procurement functional requirements specifications (FRS) standard needs to evolve to fit the procurement practices in the Indian government. The implementation of the FRS standard could be monitored through certification mechanisms. The European Union (EU) on its part has developed a FRS standard, which is accessible at the URL: http://europa.eu.int/idabc/en/document/4721/5874.

If the e-procurement market is not regulated at this juncture, then the e-procurement market would become fragmented, and islands of systems would emerge.

Challenge 6:
Replicating Best Practices in Federal-State Setup

In India, the state of Andhra Pradesh (AP) pioneered the implementation of a state-wide e-procurement system in the year 2003. The system gained widespread usage within the state, and as of September 2005, Rs. 36,000 Crores worth of tenders are now handled through the e-tendering module. The AP system was developed on a PPP basis, where the private partner's name we shall call as "Company X" from here on. Even though AP's initiative was regarded as a best practice, many government agencies all across the country selected their own partner instead of opting to use the proven AP system implemented in government. In other words, the wheel was reinvented.

It is advocated that a best practice shall be replicated all across the nation so that the entire government setup receives benefits. So, why is this contradiction? Why did not other state governments use AP's proven e-procurement system? Could the federal government not have identified the AP's effort as a best practice and issued an order to all the state governments asking them to utilize the system? One may say that, had the federal government issued the order, and assuming that the order was adhered to by all the states, then the e-GP market in India would have been monopolized by Company X, which is not a desirable development. Alternatively, the federal government could have at least asked the states to replicate the procedure and frameworks adopted by AP and implement state-wide e-procurement on a PPP model. The federal government has not made such a policy, due to which e-procurement in India is emerging in a disorganized manner. Why has not the federal government made such a policy recommendation?

The key to answering the question lies in understanding the federal-state dynamics. As per the constitution, the states are autonomous bodies. The extent of autonomy given to states differs from one setup to another. In the USA, the states enjoy much higher autonomy than the states in India and Canada. Even if the federal government identifies a best practice and informs/recommends/suggests to replicate a best practice all across the nation, the state governments have the right to disagree with the advice and act as per their wish. In practice, some state governments look up to the federal government for direction whereas others prefer and even insist on acting independently. In the e-procurement context, the two alternatives get played out as follows: The ones who look up to the federal government for direction query as to why a national effort on e-procurement has not been taken. The others who insist on acting independently engage in the development of a state-wide system or, with further decentralization, a department-level system. We have studied why these alternative perceptions occur in the Danish context. From the study, it was found that those who perceive the nation as a single, independent entity seek the development of a centralized system at the national level. On the contrary, those who perceive state or a department as a single, independent entity argue for development of decentralized systems. In other words, the centralization versus decentralization *"debates originate due to differences in perception about the extent to which government is a single organization"* (Ramanathan, 2004, p. 3). Such an explanation holds true in the Indian context as well.

Regardless of the differences in perception, it is important that key stakeholders come together and agree on an approach for replicating best practices across the nation. Only when a plan is in place will e-procurement diffuse across the nation in a consistent manner.

Concluding Remarks

In this chapter, the concept of e-government procurement, as it is being implemented in India, is explained. Furthermore, a set of six challenges encountered during implementation of e-procurement are discussed in depth. The six challenges are intertwined and hence they shall not be treated independently. Instead, a concerted approach is required to address the challenges. To develop the approach, key stakeholders from all across the government have to set aside their differences and agree on a way forward. Unless urgency is shown in planning the state-wide systems, there is a risk that numerous islands of legacy systems will emerge. The emergence of the islands of systems will make it harder to implement the preferred state-wide end-to-end e-procurement system.

Since public procurement is driven by the same set of principles everywhere, the rich descriptions and explanations in this chapter can be generalized to e-GP implementations in developing countries and in federal-state setup.

References

Central Vigilance Commission. (2003, December 18). No. 98/ORD/1. Retrieved from http://cvc.nic.in/98ord12k312.pdf

European Union (EU). (2004, December 13). Action plan for the implementation of the legal framework for electronic public procurement. *Commission of the European Communities*. Retrieved from http://ec.europa.eu/internal_market/publicprocurement/e-procurement_en.htm

Kaul, V. (2005). *All you wanted to know about fiscal deficit*. Retrieved February 6, 2006, from http://www.rediff.com/money/2005/apr/12fiscal.htm

Ramanathan, S. (2004). *Diffusion of electronic public procurement in Denmark*. PhD thesis, Aalborg University, Denmark.

World Bank. (2003, December 10). *Procurement Services: South Asian Region* (India Country Procurement Assessment Rep. No. 27859-IN). Retrieved from http://www-wds.worldbank.org/servlet/WDSContentServer/WDSP/IB/2004/04/02/000012009_20040402111746/Rendered/PDF/278590IN.pdf

World Bank. (2004, July). Korea's move to e-procurement (No. 90). *Prem Notes: Public Sector*. Retrieved from http://www1.worldbank.org/prem/PREMNotes/premnote90.pdf

Endnotes

[1] Recently, when roads in Mumbai went bad due to the incessant rains, many citizens groups had sought information about the efforts taken by the government to repair the roads. Such enquiries have become commonplace nowadays, and they get the media's attention too.

[2] For example, Director General of Supplies and Disposals (DGS&D) is an agency that negotiates rate contracts on behalf of government agencies in India.

[3] An example would be Chhattisgarh State Industrial Development Corporation (CSIDC), which is a state-specific rate contract negotiation agency.

[4] Typically, the health department in a state negotiates rate contracts to meet its requirements.

[5] City and town corporations, for instance, negotiate their own rate contracts for items such as street lights and phenyl.

6   Periods range from one to two years.

7   These end users are located in secretariat, district, and taluka levels.

8   The central location is typically the state capital.

9   Examples would include assistant engineer and assistant executive engineer, who are present at the district and taluka levels.

10   This can also be termed as non-ECV-based procurement.

11   Karnataka State Highways Improvement Project (K-SHIP)

12   Karnataka Soaps and Detergents Limited (KSDL), which manufactures the famous Mysore Sandal soap

13   Karnataka Residential Institutional Society (KRIS)

14   Delhi Metro Rail Corporation Limited (DMRCL)

15   The implementation of auto-bid evaluation functionality is one of the most challenging aspects of e-procurement. It can be done only when a supplier database is developed and linked with an evaluation engine. The logic underlying the evaluation engine has to be developed by the domain experts.

16   The Korean government makes payment to suppliers in less than 4 hours after the inventory inspection is done as against the regulatory requirements of 14 days. Due to such prompt payment, the number of suppliers bidding for government contracts has trebled.

17   This means without a tendering process.

18   Typically, it is an IT agency.

19   This system is also known as project finance management system (PFMS).

20   This was the exchange rate as of September 2005.

21   These include not just tendering, but also contract management, ordering, and workflow approvals, among others.

22   The Indian economy is growing at a rate of about 6-7% in the last few years. Given the steadfast buoyancy in the stock markets and the high expectations, it is likely that the current growth rate will at least be maintained in the next few years, if not enhanced.

23   The plan expenditure was estimated at 4.44% of the GDP in the year 2004-2005, and there is a strong lobby to increase the plan expenditure to 8% of the GDP so the economy would grow at the rate of 10-12% each year.

Chapter V

Barriers to E-Procurement Adoption:
The Turkish Case

Gonca Telli Yamamoto, Okan University, Turkey

Faruk Karaman, Okan University, Turkey

Abstract

E-procurement practice is not well-established in emerging countries. There are barriers in terms of transportation, financial, telecommunication, and legal infrastructures. Also, a lack of a qualified workforce, cultural barriers, and security problems hinder the development of e-procurement activities. These are not such significant problems in the developed countries. In this study, we examined the Turkish practice. We gave country background information including macroeconomic data and Internet penetration data, and we gave a picture of the current situation of Turkey. We then discussed how these barriers can be overcome in Turkey. Finally, we gave predictions about how m-procurement may alter the situation and its potential for the Turkish market.

Introduction

E-procurement is the use of electronic technologies to flow and enable the procurement activities of an organization. It is used particularly within the range of the operational, professional purchase. E-procurement is also defined as the business-to-business purchase and sale of supplies and services over the Internet. Typically, e-procurement Web sites allow qualified and registered users to look for buyers or sellers of goods and services.

E-procurement is a concept strongly related to concepts such as logistics, supply chain management (SCM), and even e-commerce. Although, some definitions are suggested to distinguish between these concepts, the problems faced are similar. They all require financial, transportation, legal, and communication infrastructures (Ohmae, 2000). If a country is weak in one or some of these infrastructures, then e-procurement activities are destined to fail. In addition to these four factors, education of the e-procurement personnel, security issues, societal readiness to use information and communication technologies (ICT), and the impact of the wireless technologies should also be considered.

In countries like Turkey, huge infrastructure investments are the norm. However, since these investments are heavily affected by short-term political concerns and voter influence, projects function most of the time at a suboptimal rate. A planned and systematic approach is rarely found. Even so, as the economy grows and international trade rises, Turkish companies are facing the pressure of global competition. To stay alive in this environment of fierce competition, efficient tools such as e-procurement are being introduced. However, this is an ongoing process, and fast improvements should not be expected. Problems are still paramount and can slow down the widespread adoption of the e-procurement practices.

In this study, we try to assess the e-procurement activities from a developing country's perspective, namely Turkey. Turkey's unique problems and strengths are also examined. In addition, given the widespread use of wireless technology in Turkey, we have also elaborated on the concepts of m-procurement. The role of ICT is well-documented in the literature, but the possible outcomes of the widespread use of wireless technology in procurement activities are rather an uncharted territory. These issues are discussed in the "Future Trends" section of this chapter.

Background

Changes and developments in technology and macro trends such as globalization also affect the micro world of enterprises and functions in the companies. In this respect, purchasing has morphed into procurement (Kotler, 2004). In the past, the purchasing function was seen as a way to execute a transaction between a buyer and a seller. Nowadays purchasing is a function that needs to be executed on a broader level. This means connecting different partners and helping them come up to the mark (Shah, 2002). Pride and Ferrel (1989) classified the three types of organizational purchases as new task, modified rebuy, and straight rebuy purchases.

Internet procurement has the potential to redesign and streamline procurement processes by shaping electronic markets that are tailored to reflect the contracts, purchasing rules, and business workflow of an individual buying organization (Aberdeen Group Profile, n.d.).

E-procurement has a multi-layered body and is connected to ancillary industries and distribution channels. For example, vehicle routing problems are part of the general purchasing system (Emel, Taskin, & Deniz, 2004). These problems are also part of e-procurement. Stanton and Stanton (2002) have created a model of Internet purchasing to show the link between personality, predisposition towards innovativeness, and adoption. However, there is not an adequate solution in the monetary value of face-to-face bargaining.

Tomkins (2000) proposed the supply chain synthesis (SCS) which he claimed to be the next step to SCM. If SCS can be implemented, procurement activities throughout the supply chain can be streamlined. Raisch (2001) saw the future of SCM and e-procurement as B2B marketplaces and stressed the importance of content management and community building. Bovet and Martha (2000) use the term "value net" as almost the equivalent of B2B e-marketplaces. Kuglin and Rosenbaum (2001) and Guinipero and Sawchuk (2000) are among others who have discussed how the Internet has revolutionized the supply chain and procurement process.

Croom (2000) recognized the operational and strategic benefits and their influences on Web-based procurement systems. There is also a global procurement bias not only for goods but for the service activities. Global procurement has received an increasing amount of managerial attention in recent years for service activities (Kotabe & Murray, 2004). Trends in global sourcing, emphasis on time to market, customer uncertainty, and the need to improve bottom line costs affects the procurement processes (Kalakota & Robinson, 2001), and this conveys e-procurement's very important role.

Vigoroso (1999) considered the pros and cons for buyers and sellers by migrating business onto the Internet. E-procurement pros include saving sourcing time, receiving accurate information, having new sources of supply and having the ability of comparing different sellers, lowering overall operating costs and prices paid, optimizing the supply base, and having more control over spending and inventory for sellers. However, lack of security is a major problem concerning e-procurement.

Generally, studies on e-procurement report large efficiencies regarding process and procurement costs (Gebauer & Segev, 1998). Puschmann and Alt (2005) discussed the use and success of e-procurement in supply chains.

According to Neef (2001), e-procurement becomes the catalyst that will allow companies to finally integrate their supply chains from end to end, from sales to supplier, with shared pricing, availability, and performance data that will allow buyers and suppliers to work to an optimum level with mutually-beneficial prices and schedules.

The UND (International Transportation Association of Turkey) officials state that logistics in general and procurement in particular is highly crucial for Turkey, given Turkey's heavy dependence on the textile sector and fast-growing international trade volume (E-mail correspondence of Dr. Yamamoto with UND officials, July 15, 2005).

It is stated that the sector representatives were aware of the Internet's potential; however, they were hesitant to make purchases over the Internet for the following reasons:

1.   Companies and state enterprises in Turkey are not ready to share data over the Internet or by classical means; they see data sharing as a threat to their competitive position in the industry.

2.   For large-scale purchases over the Internet, companies want legal protection; although e-signature regulations have recently been passed, there is still time for e-signature applications to mature.

3.   E-procurement requires a large-scale implementation of a network of companies with seamless integration of hardware, software, firm data, and legal, regulatory, and supervisory organizations; this means there needs to be a very serious dimensional integration in developing countries.

4. Companies do not want their procurement activities to stop because of electricity shortages, software or hardware problems, or viruses; purchasing everything online will make companies dependent on the Internet, and they will be much more vulnerable to its problems.

5. Especially for international procurement activities, there are numerous official documents in use, and they should be transferred to the electronic medium; such a study is under way in cooperation with the United Nations, and pilot work is currently being done for the Gemlik Industrial Zone of the Bursa province of Turkey.

There is a huge potential for e-procurement in Turkey; however, a turnkey solution is needed which would encompass the hardware and software needs, and those regulatory issues which are specific to Turkey. It can be concluded that Turkish companies are aware of e-procurement, but they are far from implementing it fully. However, they are likely to adopt e-procurement at a slow pace. The rate of its acceptance depends on the work that will be done by nongovernmental organizations (NGOs), state organizations, and private-sector unions.

Turkey: Basic Country Information

Turkey is a mid-sized developing country located between the Middle East and Asia. Turkey also meets the Slavic countries with the Arab world, and Caucasian countries with the Mediterranean countries. This highly strategic geographical position gives the country the role of a mediating bridge and a facilitator of regional trade. However, this fact also means that Turkey needs to spend heavily for its defense given the conflicts abundant in the region.

According to the State Institute of Statistics (SIS), the surface area of Turkey is 769,604 km^2. In the year 2000, the Turkish population was counted as 67.8 million. The population growth rate per year averages 1.8% and the life expectancy from birth is 70 years. The city population is 64.9% of the total population. The total literacy rate is 87.3%: The male literacy rate is 93.9%, and the female literacy rate is 80.6%. Higher education levels are still insufficient, however, given the total rate of 7.8%, with the male higher education rate of 10.2% and the female rate of 5.4%.

The SIS also reported that, in 2004, Turkey's gross national product (GNP) reached $299.5 billion. The gross domestic product (GDP) growth rate was calculated to be 9.9%, a record level for the last 10 years. Per capita GNP was reported as $4,172. Foreign debt at the end of 2004 was $161.8 billion, which was 54% of GNP.

In the year 2004, total exports were $63.1 billion, while imports reached $97.5 billion. These numbers translates into a trade deficit of $34.4 billion. Another problem is unemployment, which averaged 10.5% in the years 2003 and 2004 despite the high growth rate of GNP.

In brief, Turkey has a very dynamic young population eager to use new technologies and to take new approaches. The EU accession process gives a reliable road map for the infrastructure upgrade in technological-enabled procurement. Turkey's geographical position and its globally-integrated economy make it a country that needs great improvements in its procurement processes.

Issues and Problems Related to the Business Environment

These problems and issues have secondary or indirect effect over the process of e-procurement activities. However, in the long run, they are as important as the factors related to its infrastructure.

- EU accession and its implications over the procurement process
- The interrelationship of e-procurement and e-governance activities
- Small and medium-sized enterprises (SMEs)
- International procurement
- Organizational resistance
- Lack of qualified workforce
- Widespread use of mobile technology

EU Accession and Its Implications on the Procurement Process

Turkey has had a long history with the European integration process. She made her first application in July, 1959. At that time, EU was called the European Economic Community (EEC). As of the end of 2003, Turkey was EU's 7th biggest trading partner (up from 9th in 1990). It was also the 13th biggest exporter to the EU (up from 17th in 1990) (EU - Turkey relations, n.d.).

Turkey is a European Union (EU) candidate and despite skeptics, she has a great chance to gain accession by the year 2015. Thus the EU factor must be taken into account in any analysis made about Turkey. After the December 17, 2004, decisions of the EU, Turkey was categorized as a "converging country" rather than as an "emerging country." In the year 2005, the explosion in foreign direct investments (FDI) is a direct result of that changing outlook. Even so, membership has not been finalized yet, and Turkey still shows most of the traits of an emerging country; therefore, Turkish practice is valuable to understand business procurement activities in an emerging country.

Throughout the EU process, it is most likely that Turkey will be forced by the EU to upgrade her infrastructure to EU standards. At that point, professional e-procurement and m-procurement applications in the developed countries will be very relevant for Turkey. However, the greatest challenge is managing the fastened process of migration from an emerging country to an EU-country.

The Interrelationship of E-Procurement and E-Governance Activities

According to the UK Office of Government Commerce Manual (2005), e-procurement reduces paperwork and speeds up payment. This is especially important in government services, since it is known that these services are highly inefficient. It is also applicable to Turkey and other developing countries.

Although e-procurement is very essential in all sectors beginning with the public sector, its implementation is not so easy. The reasons are:

- **More efficient processes will mean less need for labor:** In Turkey, unemployment is a significant problem; it averaged around 10-11% after the 2001 crisis. The public sector was used as a vehicle to circumvent the unemployment problem by hiring unneeded employees. In spite of the fact that the International Monetary Fund (IMF) wants Turkey to shrink the government sector, little progress can be made. Therefore, efficiency tools such as e-procurement are hard to be accepted by the public sector workers in Turkey.

- **Public sector workers are undereducated:** The private sector in Turkey is very dynamic and competitive, and its workers are young, dynamic, and highly educated. The opposite is true for the public sector. In these enterprises, job security is very high, and it is hard for the government to lay off these workers. This makes it unnecessary for the public workers to retrain themselves in new technologies and management techniques. The public sector also faces the probable resistance to these new methods and technological developments in Turkey. Also, the recruitment process in the public sector is not efficient. The result is an undereducated, noncompetitive employee with outdated knowledge and skills. In other words, the human capital of the public sector is much lower and less valuable than that of the private sector. This is an obstacle for the effective implementation of e-procurement projects in the Turkish public sector in spite of the enthusiasm presented by some of the politicians.

Small and Medium-Sized Enterprises (SMEs)

Yanıklar (2003) states that 99.5% of the enterprises in Turkey are SMEs. They are the primary source of employment and the basic driver of economic growth. Yanıklar also adds that 23% of the Turkish SMEs use computers; however, only 2% have e-commerce activity. Recalling that e-commerce is a broader concept than e-procurement, we can deduct that e-procurement is practically nonexistent in Turkish SMEs.

These numbers are not so surprising since SMEs have weak financial resources to implement e-commerce or e-procurement projects. They cannot employ the talented workforce needed in these projects. The solution may come from a collaboration of such companies and establishment common e-commerce and e-procurement platforms.

The five forces of competition, as proposed by Michael Porter (1998), require SMEs to make collaborations to become competitive players in the global marketplace. Among the five forces, the bargaining power of suppliers and bargaining power of customers especially apply to SMEs. When SMEs come together, new and advanced management techniques including e-procurement can be afforded just as large companies. The Internet makes it easier and cheaper for the SMEs to cooperate.

International Procurement

International trade exploded after the fall of communism and the victory of the liberal economic system. In fact, such a high degree of globalization was also witnessed in the 19th century, but the 20th century witnessed a world divided into two camps. Even so, international trade is a very old phenomenon which gave rise to well-known business practices in this area. However, the developments in the ICT field and the widespread use of the Internet changed the whole paradigm, and old practices became out-of-date.

Previously, international trade could be performed by highly specialized professionals and agent firms. The profit margins and earnings were very high, and such professions were very prestigious. Today's Internet world dimmed their shiny outlook, and these professionals are struggling to survive by means of their dying profession. Their specialized expertise is becoming worthless in over the Internet. Even a teenager can order a product from abroad and pay for it.

In Turkey, the situation is even more dramatic in that such professions denied adopting the change for a long time, and now they face a much more accelerated and devastating situation in a short period of time. The understandable psychological reaction is total refusal of the merits of e-procurement in international procurement activities. They still dream about a world of published special legal documents, obscure trading regulations, clumsy transactions, and guru-like status stemming from their specialization in them.

Technology is known to be killing some professions and giving birth to new ones. The industrial revolution has made craftsmen unemployed, and that has given rise to the communism in the end. However, the information revolution occurred in a much shorter time period than the industrial revolution. People having classical occupations could not find time even to understand that they needed to retrain themselves in the new ways of doing business. In Turkey, the change was even more dramatic, in that Turkey marched into the information age without first being an industrial country. The effects on the personal lives of people are catastrophic. The solution is to retrain people. But first they must accept that they need to be retrained.

Organizational Resistance

Similar to international trade specialists, employees in the classical procurement function could not adapt to changes brought by the Internet. In other words, they resist against e-procurement. As for m-procurement, they have little idea about it and they cannot even visualize it.

Companies mistakenly delegate the transformation of e-procurement to the classical procurement personnel. Understandably, they resist against the establishment of the online purchasing infrastructure. They claim that technology is not yet ready to perform the purchasing activity that they used to do with the telephone and the personal contact.

A purchaser, just like salespeople, depends on his or her personal contacts in an organization. In other words, the social network he or she possesses is his or her most valuable asset. The Internet allows the establishment of such social networks in a different way. Online communities, e-mail groups, forums, and even friendship sites are places to develop such a network. Some of the classical purchasers and salespeople deny the value of such virtual networks. They claim that there is nothing that can match human contact. According to them, Turkish culture values personal communication. In this view, the Internet will never replace the human contact.

In fact, the Internet is still an evolving technology and is merging with other technologies such as voice and video technologies. Using voice over IP (VoIP), people can also talk to each other. Skype is the industry leader in this field; other Instant-Messenger (IM) applications such as Yahoo Messenger and MSN Messenger are also modifying their products in order to catch up. Internet contact will resemble classical human contact with growing broadband Internet access technologies such as video conferencing.

In Turkey, broadband came late but diffused fast. DSL membership increased in the last two years thanks to the subsidies offered by Turkish Telecom. This is due to the fact that the Turkish population is young and dynamic and ready to accept technological innovations. Of course, old workers are still skeptical about new technology and believe that technology is not adequate. This point is further analyzed in the next subsection.

Lack of Qualified Workforce

Since the professional implementation of procurement is rather a new concept in Turkey, employees do not have formal training in this field and are unaware of formal approaches. The rapid explosion in e-procurement activities has worsened the problem. Even though new schools are opened to address this issue, their full effect cannot be seen in the near future. Newly-established non-governmental organizations (NGOs) take a greater and greater role and try to speed up the learning curve by means of collaborating with all of the stakeholders.

Another important trend for Turkey is the proliferation of private universities, especially after the year 1990. Private universities have closer ties with the industry and respond to their needs in a faster manner. Logistics, procurement, and supply chain training programs are offered, and this will help alleviate the problem of the lack of a qualified workforce for procurement activities. As these more qualified employees replace the ones with no formal education, more sophisticated procurement systems can be established.

It is often stated that Turkey lacks the human capital in terms of specialized blue-collar workers. However, an even more severe problem is at the managerial level. Turkish companies are quite conservative and young managers, such as those seen in American companies, are rare. Thus, Turkey cannot make full use of its young, educated, and technologically-savvy population. Older people may not fully appreciate the impacts of new technologies and may even fear them. Thus they may postpone the adoption of new technologies. Therefore, even top management should be retrained in new technologies and new methods such as e-procurement.

Widespread Use of Mobile Technology

Wireless technology has already made great impacts, but in the near future that impact will largely be amplified (Gratton & Gratton, 2004). In fact, we are in the midst of the wireless revolution which extends to the boundaries of the Internet revolution. Since the Internet and mobile technologies are integrated and interrelated technologies, before analyzing the state of the wireless technology in Turkey, it will be helpful to look at the Internet penetration in selected countries.

Internet usage in the Middle East was reported to be 8.3%. Global penetration was given as 14.9%. Apparently the Middle East lags the world in terms of Internet usage. The reason may be closed societies and governments found in the region. Turkey's penetration was given as 9.9%. The highest rate of penetration was in Israel with 44.8%, and the lowest was Iraq with 0.1%. The highest penetration rates were given in Sweden (73.6%), Hong Kong (70.7%), Denmark (68.7%), and United States (68.5%). Given these rates, Turkey has a serious competitive disadvantage in terms of Internet usage (http://www.internetworldstats.com).

A World Bank study indicates that among 115 countries, Turkey is 50th in terms of Internet penetration, with 85 users in 1,000 in 2003. Similarly, the penetration of mobile phones and wired phones was 662 in 1,000 in Turkey in the year 2003. With this penetration rate, Turkey was 46th among 115 countries (Türkiye Cep Zengini, n.d.).

According to the State Institute of Statistics of Turkey, in the year 2004, 92.19% of the households of Turkey had TV sets, 53.64% had cell phones, 9.98% had personal computers, 5.86% had Internet connection, 2.85% had game consoles, 0.85% had laptops, and 0.13% had PDAs. Although laptops, PDAs, game consoles, and cell phones are all new products, Turkish people have heavily invested in one of them, namely the cell phones. We do not need these data to reach such a conclusion. By making a short trip in one of the big cities of Turkey, one can easily observe Turkish people's attraction to the cell phones. Of course, this phenomenon is not unique to Turkey; however, the change in Turkey is highly visible because of the late industrialization of the country.

In Turkey, mobile phones gained very favorable customer acceptance, and diffusion of mobile technology occurred much faster than that of the Internet. Therefore, we may conclude that with the advances in wireless technology, the mobile phone can become a primary Internet access tool for Turkish people. Thus, in Turkey, m-procurement has a better chance of success than e-procurement.

Countries like Turkey can attain the most recent technology advancement without following the same long path of the learning curve that developed countries have followed. For Turkey, this means that mobile technologies and m-commerce will become the most successful applications.

Thus for Turkey, directly developing m-procurement and m-business applications is much more reasonable than trying to transfer the e-procurement and e-business practices of the developed world. Other developing countries may also choose to jump directly to mobile technologies. However, in the Turkish case, this is a necessity rather than a means of choice, given the large established base of mobile users in Turkey.

Issues and Problems Related to Infrastructure

The previous section has analyzed the business environment in Turkey. We will now focus on the infrastructure-related issues and problems. These can be listed as: legal and regulatory environment; security issues; transportation infrastruture; financial infrastructure; and telecommunication infrastrucure.

Legal and Regulatory Environment

The legal and regulatory environment in developing countries is far behind technology. One major problem is that these countries lack human capital with expertise in diverse fields such as information and communication technologies (ICT), domestic law, international law, international trade, logistics, and procurement. Without such experts, the regulatory environment cannot cater to the new and sophisticated needs of the industry.

Although Turkey was slow in adopting a regulatory framework, the EU process, the exploding foreign trade, and foreign direct investment (FDI) through privatization activities speeded up the adoption of the legal infrastructure derived from the best practices around the world. According to the official e-government Web site of Turkey (Vatandaşın Sadece %3'ü e-devlet hizmetlerinden yararlanıyor, n.d.), e-signature is now formally accepted as a legal equivalent of the classical signature. This will positively affect the spread of e-procurement activities without doubt. However, security issues related to e-signature should be resolved before widespread use.

Security Issues

Security is a major issue for all kinds of e-business and m-business applications. In emerging countries like Turkey, this problem is exacerbated by the inefficient and out-of-date legal system and unknowledgeable technology users who can easily be victims of technology-related crime or fraud. Cases in the popular press make people hesitant to use technology.

Security complaints in Turkey are on the rise recently. This can be attributed the fact that cheap DSL Internet access by Turkish Telecom (TT) increased the number of Internet users is Turkey in a short time (ADSL Abone sayısı 900bini Geçti, n.d.). In 18 months, the number of subscribers rose from 56,000 to 901,000. New subscribers are less experienced over the Internet, but stay connected for a long duration due to the unlimited hours of access offered by DSL service. As a result, such users become easy victims of hacking, spying, and phishing activities.

There is no established insurance system to alleviate victims' problems and to foster trust on advanced technology. In Turkey, with the spread of technology, online and mobile crime exploded unexpectedly. Thus, the security issue will be among the most important issues in the years to come.

Transportation Infrastructure

Although e-procurement is a revolutionary step over classical procurement, goods purchased are still delivered by classical means. In other words, transportation and logistics services have not changed much. Of course, information content is added, and transported goods can now be tracked down to some degree. However, we authors still need a good transportation infrastructure, which is expensive and slow to build.

Emerging economies often face financial and economic difficulties in building their transportation infrastructures (TI). Such projects span many years, and weak governments cannot persuade society to make short-term sacrifices for long-term benefits. TI projects are often financed with high-interest foreign loans, and high sovereign debt levels of such countries put a limit on the opportunity to borrow additional debt.

TI can be divided to five categories:

1.   Surface transportation infrastructure (STI)
2.   Railroads transportation infrastructure (RTI)
3.   Marine transportation infrastructure (MTI)

4.   Airline transportation infrastructure (ATI)

5.   Transportation infrastructure integration and management (TIIM)

The first four categories are obvious. The fifth one, that is, the TIIM category, is a newly-developing meta-component that uses information and communication technologies (ICT). Transportation in Turkey is mainly conducted by trucks on motorways and highways. Railroads and marine transportation have not been fully exploited yet. Especially in the late 1980s, superhighways have been built throughout the country. Air transportation within Turkey has only been recently opened due to the competition from the private sector. Previously, the only carrier was the state-owned Turkish Airlines. The lack of an infrastructure in Turkey may seem like a handicap, but it is also an opportunity for both Turkey and its trading partners.

Financial Infrastructure

Banks have had a central role in trading or business activity in the past. This was due to the fact that processes of trading and commerce were inefficient, and businessmen needed trust supplied by banks. However, given the exploding security problems, banks are not as secure and trusted as before. Also, technology makes it possible for large companies to perform some of the functions of banks within their organizations. In the future, banks may even cease to exist in today's terms. There is one big central global bank which brings together all sides, and it is called the Internet.

In the year 2001, Turkey fell in a deep financial crisis due to the weaknesses of the banking sector. Since then, with the help of the IMF, the financial strength of Turkish banks improved with the help of foreign investments in the sector. Although it gave rise to some criticisms from globalization opponents in Turkey, the increasing share of foreign banks in the sector also means that banking services in Turkey will meet global standards.

Even before the entry of foreign banks, the Turkish banking sector was using the most advanced technology in its operations. However, these investments were not so efficient, and choosing the wrong technology was a common mistake. The development of the sector will no doubt enhance e-procurement activities in Turkey. However, in the future we will be able to use the development of the banking sector and the development of the Internet interchangeably. When the legal infrastructure and the use of e-signature applications advance, the banking services will also develop more in depth and breadth.

Telecommunication Infrastructure

The Turkish Telecom (TT) has been recently privatized after decades of debate. In those countries with privatization and deregulation, their telecommunications sectors are reported to have made great advances in ICT-related industries. Thus, for the development of e-procurement activities, this should be considered as positive news. Although the debate was still continuing when we were writing this chapter, we believe that the privatization of TT was finalized during this time after several years. But unfortunately, according to predicted analysis, its value will decrease substantially, and new technologies will erode much of the competitive power of TT.

Huge public companies are known to be slow to adapt to new technologies, and they are found to be irresponsive to the needs of the consumer. A private TT, therefore, will need to increase its investments in new technologies. One possible problem is that privatization does not always mean deregulation and more competition. If competing firms are allowed to enter into the arena, then the telecommunication infrastructure of Turkey may be upgraded in a few years. That will mean a friendlier atmosphere for e-commerce in general and e-procurement in particular. The widespread use of broadband applications will also be valuable.

Case Study:
Public Procurement Authority of Turkey

Until recent privatization efforts, the public sector has dominated the Turkish economy. Thus the best examples of e-procurement in Turkey are from the public sector. Also, more information is available for these enterprises as they are public. Thus we have taken Public Procurement Authority (PPA) of Turkey for our case study.

The procurement process in Turkey is shown in Figure 1 from the perspectives of both the public sector and the private sector. The public procurement process is more complicated than the private sector's procurement process.

Figure 1. Procurement/public procurement process in Turkey (Source: Elektronik İhale Forumu, n.d.)

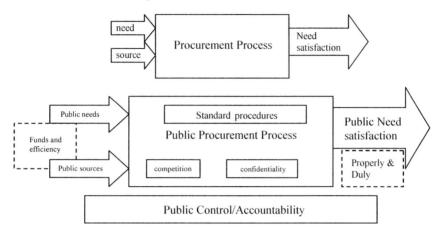

In the procurement process, first the needs are identified and then the available resources are determined. The ultimate goal is the satisfaction of each of the stakeholders throughout the process. For a successful public procurement process, the state authorities should treat all parties equally. The confidentality of trade secrets is also criticial.

The PPA is taking an active part in e-government activities in Turkey. The intention of PPA is to achieve the establishment of a clear, transparent system for public procurement. In the past, corruption in the public sector was one of the biggest problems. E-procurement will bring openness, accountability, and efficiency in this field.

As it can be seen in Figure 2, there is an electronic bid platform where government institutions, solicitors, citizens, and so forth, meet. In this electronic platform, buyers and sellers are able to make transactions in a faster, easier, and open manner. There is also a documentation system for technical specifications. An important goal is to build a database that can be shared with all other governmental institutions. Standardization in procurement is also an important objective.

As a basic e-marketplace characteristic, price/quality competition is achieved by giving an opportunity to every solicitor for bidding. In other words, openness and easiness for bidding fosters competition. This system also contains computer-assisted bid assessment, that is, the e-bid reference model maintains its status as a reliable assessment system.

Figure 2. E-bid reference model for public purchasing (Source: Elektronik İhale Forumu, n.d.)

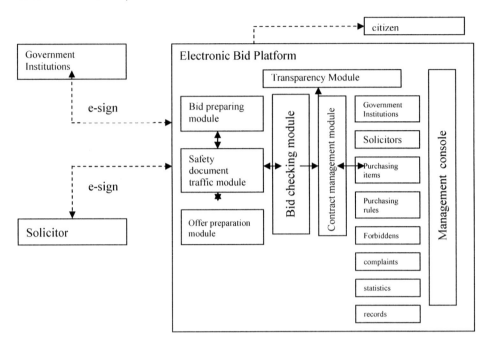

As it can be seen, the PPA platform does not feature a built-in m-procurement component. This can be attributed to the fact that even the idea of the importance of the Internet has only recently been disseminated by the public sector. Mobile commerce or m-procurement sound like futuristic ideas at this stage. However, it can be predicted that in the future, the e-procurement platform of PPA will evolve into an m-procurement-based exchange mechanism.

Future Trends

So far we have talked about business- and infrastructure-related issues and barriers to e-procurement adoption. In this section, we present some future trends and discuss how technology such as mobile can be an enabler for Turkey.

Migration to M-Procurement

The future of e-procurement is apparently m-procurement. However, mobile technologies are still at their development stage, and their full potential is yet to be exploited. Especially, hybrid products such as merging cell phones and PDAs are candidates to be the enabling devices for m-procurement.

In Figure 3, we tried to give a simple model of the migration from the classical procurement to first e-procurement and then to m-procurement. Among the infrastructures, the communication infrastructure gains more importance as this migration occurs. With the new technology, the legal system soon becomes outdated, and it also gains importance to have a robust and up-to-date legal infrastructure. Transportation and financial infrastructures are still important, but they are much more mature than communication and legal infrastructures.

Classical procurement, e-procurement, or m-procurement (mobile procurement) each require transportation, communication, financial, and legal infrastructures. Emerging markets are known to be underdeveloped in all of these dimensions. On the other hand, Turkey is closing the gap with developed countries.

Figure 3. Migration from procurement to m-procurement

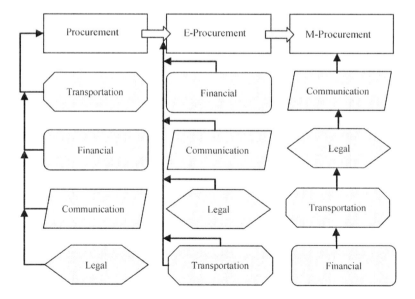

The Changing Face of the Marketing Function

Migration from classical procurement to m-procurement will change the way the marketing function operates in a firm, in that e-procurement will make the sales and procurement departments shrink as less employees will be needed. The emphasis will shift from sales to the analysis of the data obtained from digital sales-procurement activities of companies.

Thus the profile of the people in the marketing and procurement departments will be altered, and market researchers and analysts will gain value. Also, such workers will need to have expertise in using and modifying software packages. These traits are much different from those needed in the age of classical procurement.

In fact, even the marketing function is new compared to production and finance, for example. It evolved from sales and became a discipline using quantitative methods known as market research. In the sales era, the desired attribute was being presentable. However, market research needs an analytical mind.

M-procurement will be very much like the classical procurement in terms of human contact. However, since this contact is completely digitalized, it will be tracked, analyzed, stored, and data-mined. We may even see the rise of virtual selling or purchasing agents. Thus, the seemingly visible human contact will be performed by software. If even sales activities are performed by software, then what kind of jobs will be left to human beings other than computer programming?

Certainly, the final stage data analysis will still need human intellect, and employment will continue there. This will make the marketing function a part of the strategic management function; marketing and strategic management will come to be in apposition, in which both will be used interchangeably. Analysis will be based on the data collected from em-procurement activities. With the exception of some multinational firms, most of the firms consider the production and marketing functions as separate. However, e-procurement tools necessitate an integrated approach.

Conclusion

Emerging countries are different from developed countries, and even emerging countries have differences among them. In this chapter, we tried to give a picture of Turkey in terms of m-procurement, e-procurement and em-procurement activities.

In general, the e-procurement infrastructure in Turkey is developing but still insufficient. It should also be noted that even a weakness in only one of these areas of infrastructure will hinder the total e-procurement process. To date, the most significant problem is the security problem, and the most advanced area can be seen as the financial area. However, security problems weaken the strengths of the financial infrastructure.

Given the low Internet penetration but a wider mobile customer base, we see potential in Turkey first for m-procurement and then for integrated em-procurement. Of course, em-procurement requires an even more sophisticated infrastructure than just a wide customer base.

Obviously, m-procurement is still an evolving concept. Its major advantage is the freedom from the need of wired connection. In fact, in the future wireless technologies and the Internet technologies are likely to merge and become one single integrated technology. Thus we prefer the term em-procurement instead of m-procurement.

Em-procurement can be seen as the most advanced form of procurement given the available technologies. With em-procurement, the exact position of a purchased product can be tracked down, and even possible problems with the product can be detected and reported to sales.

Em-procurement is also good for tracking the performance of logistic personnel. Thus, they will be more accountable, and supervision will become easier. Also, in countries where mobile technologies are more widely used, employee training costs will be lower, since they are already accustomed to them.

The most important problem with em-procurement is that the technology is still too underdeveloped to handle the procurement needs of the companies. Cell size and life, memory size, bandwidth, and high communication costs prevent their use by all employees. At the present, only technologically-savvy middle or top managers have the privilege to use them.

For mobile technologies to make their full impact, they should become much cheaper and much more capable. After cheap broadband services are widely available, people will be able to handle their procurement activities with almost perfect human contact. At that point, the concept of m-procurement and em-procurement terms will become more meaningful.

References

Aberdeen Group Profile. (n.d.). *elcom: Delivering the benefits of Internet procurement automation without the burdens.* White paper. Retrieved July 29, 2005, from www.aberdeen.com

ADSL Abone sayısı 900bini Geçti (ADSL Subscriber's are more than 900 thousand). (n.d.). Retrieved August 8, 2005, from http://www.ntvmsnbc.com/news/336004.asp

Bovet, D., & Martha, J. (2000). *Value nets: Breaking the supply chain to unlock the hidden profits.* New York: John Wiley Sons Inc.

Croom, S. (2000). The impact of Web-based procurement on the management of operating resource supply. *The Journal of Supply Chain Management, 36*(1), 4-13.

Emel, G. G., Taskın, C., & Deniz, G. (2004). Tedarik Zinciri Yönetimi: Otomotiv Sektöründe Bir Araç Rotalama Uygulaması. *Öneri, 16*(21), 59-70.

Gebauer, J., & Segev, A. (1998). Assessing Internet-based procurement to support the virtual enterprise. *Electronic Journal of Organizational Virtualness, 2*(3), 30-43. In T. Pushmann & R. Alt (Eds.), Successful use of e-procurement in supply chains. Retrieved July 29, 2005, from verdi.unisg.ch/.../$file/Successful%20Use%20of%20eProcurement%20in%20Supply%20Chains.pdf

Giunipero, L. C., & Sawchuk, C. (2000). *E-purchasing plus: Changing the way corporations buy.* JGC Enterprises. Retrieved July 29, 2005, from http://www.sharemax.com

Gratton, S. -J., & Gratton, D. A. (2004). *Marketing wireless products.* Oxford, UK: Elsevier.

Hawking, P., Stein, A., Wyld, D. C., & Foster, S. (2004). E-procurement: Is the ugly duckling actually a swan down under? *Asia Pacific Journal of Marketing and Logistics, 16*(1).

Elektronik İhale Forumu. (Electronic Bid Forum). (n.d.). Retrieved January 14, 2006, from http://www.kik.gov.tr/eihalecs/eihale.ppt

EU - Turkey relations. (n.d.). Retrieved August 10, 2005, from http://europa.eu.int/comm/enlargement/turkey/eu_relations.htm

Johnson, P. F., & Klassen, R. D. (2005). E-procurement. *MIT Sloan Management Review, 46*(2), 7-10.

Kalakota, R., & Robinson, M. (2001). *E-business 2.0: Road map for success.* New Jersey: Addison-Wesley.

Kalakota, R., & Robinson, M. (2002). *M-business: The race to mobility.* New York: McGraw-Hill.

Kotabe, M., & Murray, J. Y. (2004). Global procurement of service activities by firms. *International Marketing Review, 21*(6), 615-633.

Kuglin, F. A., & Rosenbaum, B. A. (2001). *The supply chain network @ Internet speed: Preparing your company for the e-commerce revolution.* New York: Amacom.

Kumar Nirmalaya foreword by Philip Kotler. (2004). *Marketing as strategy* (p. vii). Boston: HBS Press.

Neef, D. (2001). *Procurement: Present and future.* Retrieved July 30, 2005, from http://www.informit.com/articles/article.asp?p=24124&seqNum=7

Ohmae, K. (2000). *The invisible continent: Four strategic imperatives of the new economy.* New York: HarperCollins Publishers.

Pride, W. M., & Ferrel, O. C. (1989). *Marketing concepts and strategies.* Boston: Houghton Mifflin.

Porter, M. E. (1998). *On competition.* Boston: Harvard Business School Press.

Puschmann, T., & Alt, R. (2005). *Successful use of e-procurement in supply chains.* Retrieved July 30, 2005, from http://www.alexandria.unisg.ch/EXPORT/DL/28242.pdf

Raisch, W. D. (2001). *The e-marketplace strategies for success in B2B e-commerce.* New York: McGraw Hill.

SAP.com. (2002). *E-procurement. Glossary.* Retrieved from http://searchsap.techtarget.com/gDefinition/0,294236,sid21_gci214418,00.html

Shah, J. B. (2002, April 1). Three steps to better procurement—through a mix of strategies, innovative companies are making strides to cut costs and improve inventory management. *EBN, Manhasset,* (1306), 29.

Stanton, A. D., & Stanton, W. W. (2002, February). The link between personality, innovativeness predisposition and adoption: A model of Internet purchasing. In *Proceedings of the American Marketing Association Winter Educators' Conference* (published as abstract, p. 42).

Tompkins, J. A. (2000). *No boundaries: Moving beyond supply chain management*. Raleigh, NC: Tompkins Press.

Turkish Statistical Indicators. (n.d.). Retrieved August 4, 2005, from www. die.gov.tr

UK Office of Government Commerce. (2005). *Overview to selling to government.* Retrieved June 13, 2005, from http://www.businesslink. gov.uk/bdotg/action/detail?r.l3=1074033478&r.l2=1073858827&r. l1=1073861169&r.s=sc&type=RESOURCES&itemId=1073792572

Vatandaşın Sadece %3'ü e-devlet hizmetlerinden yararlanıyor (Only the 3% of the citizen are benefited from e-government services). (n.d.). Retrieved August 8, 2005, from www.turkiye.gov.tr

Vigoroso, M. (1999). Buyers prepare for brave new world of e-commerce. *Purchasing, 126*(6), 4-12.

Wheatley, M. (2003, June 15). How to know if e-procurement is right for you. *CIO Magazine.* Retrieved August 8, 2005, from http://www.cio. com/archive/061503/eproc.html

Türkiye Cep Zengini (Turkey is a mobile paradise). (n.d.). Retrieved June 12, 2005, from http://www.hurriyetim.com.tr/haber/0,,sid~1@w~5@ tarih~2005-06-11-m@

Yanıklar, M. (2003, December 19-21). Bilişim (E-ticaret). In *The Published Papers of the Second SME Summit Meeting of Turkey* (p. 177).

Appendix

The following is the list of the definitions and abbreviations used throughout this chapter. They are listed here for quick reference and to facilitate a clearer understanding of the concepts developed.

ATI: Airline transportation infrastructure

e-procurement: The use of electronic technologies to flow freely and enable the procurement activities of an organization

em-procurement: The procurement activities conducted by the integrated use of both classical and electronic means (the Internet, extranets, etc), and mobile technologies

FDI: Foreign direct investment

ICT: Information and communication technologies

IMF: International Monetary Fund

m-procurement: The procurement activities conducted by the use of mobile technologies such as cell-phone, PDA, and so forth

MTI: Marine transportation infrastructure

PPA: Public procurement authority

RTI: Railroads transportation infrastructure

SME: Small and medium-sized enterprises

STI: Surface transportation infrastructure

TI: Transportation infrastructure

TIIM: Transportation infrastructure integration and management

TT: The Turkish Telecom Company

VoIP: Voice over Internet protocol

YTL: New Turkish Lira

Section III

Analyzing
Adoption

Chapter VI

Managing E-Relationships in a Supply Network

Susanna Xin Xu, National University of Ireland - Galway, Ireland

Joe Nandhakumar, University of Warwick, UK

Abstract

This chapter investigates the dynamics of the formation and transformation of electronic supply relationships (e-supply relationships) in the Chinese cultural, technological, and industrial network context. It focuses on a newly-formed large Chinese telecom company. The aim is to provide better insights into inter-organisational relationships (IORs) enabled by the application of newer types of Internet technology in different contexts, and to develop a new conceptual framework of e-supply relationships. In this research, the conceptualisation of the transformation process of e-supply relationships represents circuits of interactions between managerial actions and social structures, as well as the particular cultural and technological context within which the interactions take place.

Introduction

According to Sain, Owens, and Hill *(2004), e-procurement* can be considered as "the electronic integration and management of all *procurement* activities, including purchase request, authorisation, ordering, delivery, and payment between a purchaser and a supplier." E-procurement allows buyers to make their purchasing decisions while *Internet technology enables* suppliers to enjoy wider access to markets across the world (Dai & Kauffman, 2002). Therefore, the impact of emerging Internet technology on global competition is transforming the networked supply chain. It is claimed that supply chain management is becoming more important as a result of dynamic inter-organisational cooperation to maintain organisational global competitive advantages. Harland, Powell, Zheng, Caldwell, and Woerndl (2002) argue that the most critical partnerships to be developed and nurtured are those with suppliers and customers; the more a company can capitalise on its networks of suppliers and customers, the greater the chance it may gain a sustainable competitive advantage (Harland, 1996; Jarillo, 1993). However, technology is almost always seen as a "Western" concept (Shoib & Nandhakumar, 2003). Walsham (2000) argues that there is less emphasis on the process of globalisation and related development of Internet technology affecting the emerging economies in the world. Shoib and Nandhakumar (2003) state that global information systems (IS) are also new themes for research on emerging economies.

It is widely recognised that the world is becoming increasingly interconnected in terms of its economic, political and cultural life (Walsham, 2000). Companies are required to work in global markets; however, they still need to deal with the uniqueness of local conditions. The idea that organisations do business differently as a result of their different cultures gives the reasons why the interactions and business relationships between organisations have different consequences. Therefore, this study aims to explore the cultural issues in managing e-supply relationships by presenting the findings from an in-depth case study researching the dynamics of e-relationships in a newly-formed large Chinese telecom enterprise—TelcoX (pseudonym). It explains the cultural differences between China and the UK, as well as how and why these differences are important in an electronic setting.

Literature Review

Since 1978, the Chinese government has maintained an "economic reform," opening China to the outside world (She & Yu, 1993). In accordance with the requirement of the market and to facilitate its own development, China's telecom industry has undergone a series of major reforms over the past two decades in terms of its development and transformation (Harwit, 1998). These reforms have enabled the industry to break centralised monopolisation, introduce competition in value-added markets, and promote the rapid development of the entire industry. As seen, China is becoming more and more open to the outside world, and it has shown remarkable economic growth during the past few years. It is claimed that the Internet technologies present a great potential for network services in China. A new era of digital economy in China has led to a demand for telecom services (Chen, 1993; She & Yu, 1993). Thus, international business and electronic commerce (e-commerce) are the main driving forces for Internet technologies use in China.

Increasingly more and more global organisations are forming business relationships with Chinese partners. These relationships enable the organisation to grow and develop, and are also a constraint on their development and activities (Ford, Berthon, Brown, Gadde, Hakansson, Naude, Ritter, & Snehota, 2002). However, the management of business relationships in Chinese-based business varies from Western practice (Pang, Roberts, & Sutton, 1998). Chinese cultural context is not represented well in the literature. This is a limitation for Western organisations to build business relationships with Chinese enterprises. A growing body of organisational studies with different perspectives has been contributed to the explanation and analysis of inter-organisational relationships (IORs) (Grandori & Soda, 1995; Oliver, 1990). Many of the earlier studies, from an economics view, are based on transaction cost economics (Williamson, 1975). Different conceptual models are developed and suggested as different ways for the management of business relationships (Cousins, 2001; Lamming, Cousins, & Notman, 1996). However, Cousins (2001) argues that a relationship should be viewed as an intra- and inter-organisational process which is referred to as a "quasi-firm" (Blois, 1972) sitting between two organisations (Ford et al., 2002; Lamming, 1993). Therefore, it is essential to develop a conceptual framework focusing on the dynamics of business relationship formation and transformation process.

Moreover, there are only a few large-scale in-depth case studies on Internet technology-enabled business relationships management (Kim, Lee, & Pan,

2002; Yao, Palmer, & Dresner, 2002). From an IS perspective, despite the recognition of the importance of the wider organisational and human issues associated with the IORs and Internet technology implementation, many of these studies still ignore aspects beyond the technological issues. These studies attempt to identify factors leading to the success or failure of enterprise-wide system implementation (Aladwani, 2001; Dong, 2000; Holland & Light, 1999a; Nah, Lau, & Kuang, 2001; Shanks, Parr, Hu, Corbitt, Thanasankit, & Seddon, 2000) or to propose new models to confirm Internet technology as one solution for organisational formation and transformation (Al-Mashari, 2000; Holland & Light, 1999b; Kelly, Holland, & Light, 1999). This chapter therefore seeks to address some of these limitations. This study focuses on the implementation of a customer service system (CSS), which is understood as a specific Internet technology enabling organisational relationships.

Theoretical Foundation

Due to the complexity and multidisciplinary nature of e-relationship as well as the wider network context, this research draws on a multi-perspective theoretical foundation. As Boudreau and Robey (1999) argue the benefits of a multi-perspective study of enterprise systems to develop a conceptual framework, in this study we adopt a similar approach by drawing on mixed theoretical perspectives: relationship, cultural, technological, and structurational perspectives.

From a relationship perspective, the literature on Industrial Marketing and Purchasing group offers useful understandings on the nature of mutually-beneficial relationships by providing the interaction model (Håkansson, 1982) that characterised the short-term exchange episodes and long-term aspects of a relationship between buying and selling companies (see Figure 1).

The interaction model is developed to understand the interaction process in dyadic relationships and the embeddedness of these in industrial networks that focus on long-term mutually-beneficial relationships and the adaptation processes that occur within them. It explains individuals involved in intra-organisational interactions which can radically change inter-organisational interactions. Organisational structures are modified by these interaction processes. In addition, the wider context including industrial and social environments influences a relationship. However, is there a lack of understanding on

Figure 1. Interaction model (Source: Håkansson, 1982)

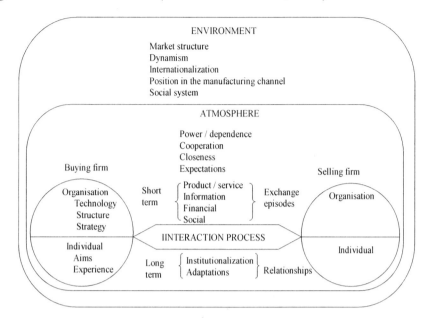

how individual interactions change the process of organisational interaction? How can the organisational structures be modified, and how can these wider contexts influence a relationship? From a cultural perspective, cultural influence on the management of business relationships is seen as a vital issue.

Recently, there has been an increasing recognition that culture is playing a crucial role in the management of business relationship. It is claimed that different national cultures make different demands on organisations and offer them different opportunities (Gabriel, 1999). Walsham (2002) focuses on the link between structural contradiction and conflict, cultural heterogeneity, and the dynamic and emergent nature of culture. A deeper examination of cross-cultural working and IS context is provided in his study. In order to provide better insights into e-supply relationships in different cultural contexts, this study therefore draws on the cultural perspective to enrich the analysis in the specific context.

From a technological perspective, there is no explanation on how technological issues influence the interaction process in the Interaction Model (Håkansson, 1982). However, technology context is another important perspective in studying Internet technology-enabled organisational relationships. There is a growing body of work which considers Internet technology as a social construction, designed and used by humans (e.g., Walsham, 1993). Orlikowski (2000) views technology in use as an emergent technological structure. These studies imply that it is very important to study the technological context in which the business relationships take place.

In order to gain a better understanding on the interactions between humans and social structures (i.e., cultural and technological properties), analyse the detailed work patterns in different cultural contexts, and the dynamics and emergent nature of culture, this study draws on the theory of structuration. Structuration theory (Giddens, 1976, 1982, 1984) provides a meta-theoretical perspective to integrate the above views. Structuration theory can be viewed as a process-oriented theory that treats structures as both a product of and a medium of human action. Giddens (1982) emphasises that we actively shape the world we live in at the same time as it shapes us. This leads to the view that humans and the social structure are mutually interacting. Jones (1999) presents a comprehensive review of structuration theory in the IS literature contexts.

Research Approach

This study employed an interpretive case study approach (Klein & Myers, 1999; Orlikowski & Baroudi, 1991; Walsham, 1993). It mainly focused on the Customer Service Department (CSD) and also pursued some practices of national and TelcoX's corporate cultures that have emerged under these particular circumstances. Data collection involved semi-structured interviews of key players, and observations of main customers and suppliers of TelcoX. Thirty-nine interviews of 60 to 90 minutes in length, in seven organisations, have been conducted with managers representing various processes including customer service management, information system management, and fulfilment and procurement management. The research commenced in the summer of 2002; most of the interviews were tape-recorded, transcribed, and then translated into English for analysis. The functions represented by those interviewed included customer service, service operation, network management, accounting, product development, and project procurement (see Table 1). They were the main actors and key members involved in the new system adoption and related business operation processes.

Informal conversations and discussions with the interviewees and other staff of the companies were held during each visit. The lead researcher regularly visited TelcoX two to three times a week. These visits varied in duration; sometimes these lasted the entire day, and at the other times the visits were limited to two to four hours. The daily work and activities in the office were observed before, during, and/or after each interview. The lead researcher observed employees' interactions and tried to "enter the world of organisational members" during their work as well as during breaks. She spent hours to observe employees' communications via telephone, e-mail systems, CSS, as well as other IS. She also tried to make conversations and informal talks when observing employees who were talking to each other. Sometimes, she joined employees' coffee and lunch breaks. Occasionally, she went to TelcoX's office during weekends when employees needed to do some overtime work.

We also use field notes (e.g., interview notes, observation notes, and conversation summaries), documents (e.g., e-mails, internal training materials, and internal operation documents) as well as related materials (e.g., posters,

Table 1. Details of data collections

(Semi-structured) Interviews		
Firms	Positions of Interviewees	Number of Interviews
TelcoX in China (including branch offices in big cities: Beijing, Shanghai, Guangzhou and Shenzhen)	Directors Senior Managers Managers GMs, Regional Office, CSSD Senior Manager, Regional Office, CSSD	10 9 6 3 1
Suppliers	Directors Senior Managers	2 3
Customers	In China	Directors	2
	In the UK	Director Senior managers	1 2
Total		39
Field Notes	**Documents**	**Other Materials**
Interview notes	E-mails	Posters
Observation notes	Internal training materials	Brochures
Conversation summaries	Internal operation documents	News from Web sites

brochures, and news from Web sites) to verify the collected data, gain more details, and "behind the scenes" information in TelcoX's wider network context.

Case Description

The Interaction Environment

According to the interaction model (Håkansson, 1982), one of the basic elements of this model is the environment within which interaction takes place. Market structure, dynamism, internationalisation, position in the manufacturing channel, and the social system are aspects in this wider context of an interaction environment. In this study, the interaction environment includes international, national, social, cultural, technological, industrial, and organisational structures.

Internationally, increasing customer demand, complexity of services, e-business which is enabled by the application of newer type of ITs, outsourcing, and globalisation are key drivers for changing webs of relationships dynamically in the supply networks (Harland, Lamming, & Cousins, 1999). The rapid growth of China's telecom, after its major reforms and restructuring since the late 1990's, is also driven partly by the emergence of competition in the global telecom market. As a result, industrial innovations and implementations of new strategies in Chinese enterprises for gaining competitive advantages are required.

The telecom enterprises have been developing new ideas on market competition through the innovations in customer service and cooperation between suppliers, customers, and competitors. An increasing number of enterprises are paying more attention to exploring new business opportunities while meeting their existing customers' needs; simultaneously, they are developing win-win business relationships with their business partners in order to effectively utilise the resources and investments, to develop national competitive advantages in this industry, and to implement strategies for competing globally.

The turbulent environments are becoming more common. Terreberry (1968) concludes that the evolution of the organisational environments is characterised by a change in the important constituents of the environment. Along with the high market competition and the rapid changes of environment, the telecom enterprises begin to realise the importance of leverage in different functions through cooperation between and across business units and departments within an organisation. Some large Chinese telecom enterprises adopted new IS such as CRM, ERP that enabled quick responses to customers, and further strategy formulation. These traditional Chinese state-owned enterprises (SOEs) are transferring to the new type of enterprises that are enabled by the application of emerging ITs. Over time, new business models influence Chinese business behaviour, which has an effect on building relationships.

China's Telecom Industry in the Global Competitive Environment

Since a supply push created by emerging ITs entering the marketplace, the introduction of local services competition and the explosion of newer types of ITs has led to heightened interests from investors. China's telecom has become a highly dynamic industry during the two decades of reform and structural changes. As a result, the telecom industry has shown an economic growth rate in the mid-to-late 1990s that few other industries could match.

The current situation about the fast-changing China telecom market offers exciting business opportunities, including China's electronic IT industry, the Internet, and e-commerce in China. Despite this significant progress, there are a number of difficulties that China's emerging large firms have encountered, such as: China's telecom firms have the difficulty of a much less transparent and more bureaucratic background of the particular domestic environment in which they operated than their international, majority state-owned competitors (Nolan, 2001). The related policies and control standards must be further systematised in order to meet international requirements.

In 2001, China's World Trade Organisation (WTO) accession changed the scenario; the managing systems of telecom are still being perfected. WTO membership provides great opportunities for foreign operators to take part in the operation of basic and value-added telecom services in China. At the same time, China's domestic telecom supervising and managing systems are confronted by more challenges along with opening to the outside world gradually.

Even more importantly, the global business environment dramatically shapes the nature of Chinese enterprises' corporate culture. The way of establishing supply relationships with Chinese firms both domestically and internationally are radically different from Western practices (Pang et al., 1998). The roots residing in traditional Chinese values, particularly Confucian (Alon & Lu, 2004; Leung, 2004), influence the way of doing business in China as well as pose even greater challenges for China's aspiring global engagement. The young Chinese companies like TelcoX stand very much at the confluence of Western and traditional Chinese culture values. Their size, mode of operation, international exposure, and adoption of modern Western practices impel them away from their traditional cultural values. It is a newer organisational form that is becoming more prevalent across China as the forces of globalisation gather momentum.

Organisational Context: TelcoX

TelcoX is one of the largest telecom carriers in China which provides a full spectrum of services and solutions to meet the broadband telecom needs of both businesses and individuals. In mid 1999, TelcoX was founded by four bodies that are affiliated with the Chinese government. With regional offices in main cities such as Beijing, Hong Kong, Shanghai, and Shenzhen, TelcoX was poised to benefit from the rapid growth of China's telecom and Internet sectors.

TelcoX merged with another large Chinese state-owned telecom company (Company A) in 2002. A subsidiary of TelcoX, providing comprehensive services to international carriers and enterprises outside China, was established in late 2003. As one of the major subsidiaries of TelcoX, this entity executed TelcoX's national strategy of "global expansion" and formed joint ventures and partnerships with foreign companies. Its responsibilities mainly lay in the operation and management of the international network asset of TelcoX and the operation of all domestic and overseas international services targeted at international operators and corporate customers. It was the first and sole domestic telecom enterprise that was dedicated to the development of all international businesses, which was also a key step in institutional reforms in China's telecom industry. Currently, business relationships with dozens of first-class operators throughout the world have been established by TelcoX. People educated in Western countries such as the United States of America, with the experience of working in multinational companies, formed the senior management team.

There were no non-Chinese staff working in this organisation, but senior managers came from various backgrounds. A few of them had the experience of working in the West or in foreign enterprises. For those people, TelcoX emphasised "ownership" and adopted Western-like professional working styles. However, those who had been working in Chinese SOEs for many years were used to following the typical Chinese working style, that is, members exist in a network of relationships and normally conduct work activities together, although individual work tasks are differentiated (Pang et al., 1998). They put an emphasis on collectivism that projects a preference for group decision-making and relationships. This working style reflects the willingness of subordinates to depend on the decisions and instructions of their superiors (Hofstede, 1991).

The Adaptation of the Customer Service System

The Customer Service Department (CSD) was providing all of TelcoX's product users with pre- and post-sale customer services. Adhering to the service idea of "at the speed of light," and "leading in service," TelcoX was following "customer first" as its guiding principle to provide customers with first-class and individualised services. In early 2001 the CSD director initiated the idea of a "distributed call centre" with the support of TelcoX's vice president. The proposed system, then called CSS system, was developed for tracking customer calls and providing better services to all TelcoX's product users. The new CSS system supported more than 30 call centres and sub-centres in China. There were about 200 customer service representatives (CSRs) and nearly 200 public switched telephone networks (PSTNs) to cover cities all over China. Through this system, not only could various local customer service demands be handled, but it also had a unified workload and standardised data management functions.

During the new call centre development, CSD people collected many detailed cases of Western companies and kept developing those cases. The newly-developed call centre was operated with a practical workflow, strict service quality standards, and a comprehensive management system. There were about 70 people in the call centre, and with the exception of a small number of second line support from CSD, most of them were the first-line CSRs that were outsourced and provided by Supplier 1 (see Figure 2). The call centre was divided into four teams: Customer calls went to the first team of CSRs who were rarely away from their desks and solved customer calls with brief responses on the spot. Their jobs typically involved customer inquiries, complaints handling, and call transfers to relevant functions. The second team was for general support. They helped to handle those customer inquiries and complaints transferred by the CSRs that needed coordination and solutions from related internal departments, and then delivered solutions to customers via phone and/or e-mail systems. The third team's main responsibilities were for handling quality control of customer calls as well as customer satisfaction surveys. The fourth team was for the CSRs' training and technical support.

Supply Relationships Establishments

With the increasing demands for services from customers, TelcoX came to realise that the existing customer service model should be replaced by a new one based on the idea of customer relationship management (CRM). As shown in Figure 2, two American enterprises, Supplier 2 and Supplier 3, were selected as the new call centre system providers.

Besides system support, the CSRs who communicated with customers directly played a very important role in the call centre. It was believed that only qualified people with certain knowledge and quicker reactions as well as insights could meet these requirements differing from those in the former call centres. These CSRs were trained with the idea of CRM and the knowledge of advanced systems. Therefore, Supplier 1, an American joint venture (JV) company, was chosen for the call centre outsourcing service. With the CSS support, TelcoX could provide better services to their customers. Those enterprises with nationwide businesses in China such as banking, finance, stock market, and insurance sectors, and some international telecom carriers (e.g., Customer 1, see Figure 2) expanding their businesses in China treated TelcoX as an important business partner, rather than simply a service provider.

The use of CSS and the needs of TelcoX's customers also determined the internal work processes. The Service Delivery Department, through the cooperation with CSD, fulfilled a business requirement from the International Business Unit, which took care of large accounts and telecom carriers. The Network Management and Maintenance Department was responsible for information networks support and any technical problems. People who had clear job allocations and responsibilities built up communications in a process

Figure 2. Emergence of supply relationships of TelcoX

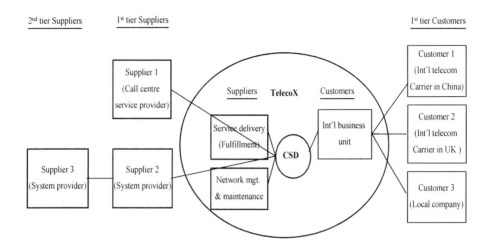

of cooperation, which was created for both internal and external customer services in TelcoX, as Figure 2 illustrates.

Analysis and Discussion

The above case description provides an overview of the emergence of e-supply relationships in TelcoX. In our analysis, we interpret the behaviours reported in the case study using the theoretical lens described above. The data analysis involved a critical examination of large amounts of qualitative data while simultaneously allowing the concepts to emerge from the empirical data.

Relationship Perspective: Dynamics of Interactions

From a relationship perspective, the interaction model (Hakansson, 1982) emphasises that the environment (wider context) must be considered when analysing the interaction between a buying and a selling firm (IMP, 1997). In the study of TelcoX, employees reflexively monitored their environment and acted accordingly. As seen, China's telecom market increasingly consists of different types of organisations, for example, Chinese state-owned enterprises (SOEs), JVs, and multinational companies. They became important actors in this environment that was comprised of national resources, investments, increased economies of scale, and developments of Internet technologies. As reviewed earlier, in order to achieve a high level performance, TelcoX's leaders decided to implement IS, such as CSS, as their first step of strategy executions.

To execute the CRM strategy, CSD people explored their surroundings and engaged in directed and undirected searches at the early stage of a new call centre establishment. The managers and team leaders overcame their frustration by exploring their understandings of their technical ability, their service patterns, and the characteristics of their resources. At the same time, they fully considered the company's further developments in terms of system plan and product selection. This was critical for meeting increasing customers' demands. Finally, they established a call centre with a national integration distributional customer service system in TelcoX. For example, to design a new call centre, CSD people were involved in customer surveys and knowledge search about how to set up a call centre. The CSD director expressed:

We cannot copy the Western countries' designs directly. We have our own special national conditions. China is broad and there are many different dialects and customs. The development of economy is imbalanced from place to place...

Some Western companies' successful experiences were good examples for them to increase their understanding. However, copies of other cases did not have any help in TelcoX's own call centre setup. To implement the new system, job reallocation to a new call centre was needed. The CSD director explained:

For the call centre, business units didn't know this system very much at first, they thought customer inquiries should come to sales people directly (not business units). But, we know it's impossible to work for 7 days, 24 hours by individuals; we must set up a system. Through a system, we can meet such requirements.

At the same time, managers were concerned about the impact CSS might have in reallocating jobs and work processes in TelcoX. To manage the impact, CSD people did a "concrete" analysis of the current situation. They collected detailed cases from other companies and kept discussing these cases. Several months later, they worked closer with business units than before. The manager said:

At first they (business units) doubt what the call centre will be? How can we set it up with nothing? ...From 'sit and watch', then to 'understand' till 'support', we are recognised and highly expected now.

In the past, sometimes, CSD lost customer inquiries or problems during their handling due to non-systematic follow-ups, which was called the "casual way" within TelcoX. In contrast, CSS with the functions of customer call handling, including customer inquiries, checking, fault reporting and customer complaints, and data recording, dispatching, and reporting, which was called "manageable co-handling," helped CSD make progress with monitoring and coordinating. It was faster than before; cycle time came down from days to hours. It was seen as a more controlled way to handle customer issues and a more managed way for data reporting. Consequently, customers found it more convenient to reach TelcoX than before. Their business ability improved as a result of the changes in internal process that were based on customer survey. Finally, they came to know what they should do and why as well as what they would like to do instead of what they have to do. The CSD manager recalled:

It was a nice memory. We worked very hard and blindly at first. Just like kids who try to write words nicely, but they put extra energy and great efforts into silly words. Like the beginners who play Shaolin Gongfu [a Chinese Kongfu, a form of boxing]... very hard, extra energy, great efforts...

This experience led them to know that a "Chinese-characterised" call centre suitable in China's conditions was required. Later, acceptance of others' experiences and a better understanding of their environment helped a new call centre design as well as development. The better understanding of their environment also helped employees to manipulate their environment and enabled them to acquire experience and then to take action for altering their environment. Clearly, in this study, the development of relationships between TelcoX and its business partners were mainly triggered by organisational problem-solving and new business opportunities exploring before, during, and after the implementation and use of CSS. The interactions between the human and their environment promoted these relationships within and across TelcoX. In this study, it can be seen that the improvement of TelcoX's performance was partly because of the relationships with its business partners. These selected suppliers and cooperative customers were very experienced Western companies having professional working styles and advanced management IS. In addition, their corporate cultures were one of the main factors in influencing the way of doing business in TelcoX. Over time, TelcoX, a newly-formed Chinese company, was shaped by this environment.

From a relationship perspective, the dynamics of organisational interactions as well as the interactions between organisational members and their environment, affected human intentions in developing their business relationships in different ways. Firstly, a closer relationship between organisational members (e.g., leaders and followers, suppliers and customers) created more opportunities to produce emerging context in which the short-term exchange episodes in a relationship and the long-term aspects of that relationship were embedded. In a wider context, this embeddedness of relationships increased the knowledge and experience for members to reproduce or change their existing context gradually. Secondly, in a dynamic environment, the degree of dynamism within a relationship and, in the wider context, influenced organisational members to take action in developing relationships. At the same time, these actions contributed to the dynamics of interactions. For instance, TelcoX's people developed their understanding of the socio-cultural realities shaping their daily work and through which they would be increasingly able to transform those realities. Such interactions challenged their existing structures. Over time, TelcoX people changed their environment including social, cultural, industrial, and technological structures, both consciously and unconsciously. This process of dynamism also can be illustrated from the emergence of culture. From a cultural perspective, the next section will further explore this issue.

Cultural Perspective: Dynamics of Culture

TelcoX had a mix of traditional Chinese and Western cultures that made it different from the more typical Chinese SOEs. This unique cultural context seemed to have a positive influence on the evolution of e-relationships. TelcoX was founded by four bodies that are affiliated with the Chinese government, and its regional structure provided a degree of decentralisation for operating units that is not common in more typical Chinese businesses, as described by Redding (1984) and Whitley (1992). With the use of CSS and other IS within TelcoX, the process management and cross-functional business units began to show a degree of differentiation that was rare in traditional Chinese SOEs (Westwood & Kirkbride, 1998). In the traditional SOEs, Chinese management philosophy centres on people (Bond & Hwang, 1986; Bond, 1991). Much of the Chinese cultural values seem to have come from the teaching of Confucius (Alon & Lu, 2004; Leung, 2004).

Use of the CSS and other IS helped TelcoX to provide quality services for meeting new requirements of customers, to lead cultural diversity, and to form e-relationships. These relationships were different from traditional ones. Traditionally, Chinese people establish their relationships via *"guanxi"* (a Chinese term) that has become a familiar term among those involved with Chinese society. *Guanxi* refers to a special kind of relationship, characterised by implicit rules, both of obligation and reciprocity (Luo, 1997; Yeung & Tung, 1996). It is briefly translated as human relationships or personal connections on which an individual can draw to secure resources or advantages when doing business as well as in their social life (Davies, Leung, Luk, & Wong, 1995).

With one fifth of the world's population and complex society, Chinese people had developed *guanxi* to obtain everyday necessities, housing, and goods that were in shortage in the past and were also major factors motivating the efforts to form *guanxi* in China (Brunner & Wang, 1988; Buttery & Leung, 1998; Pye, 1986). More importantly, *guanxi* fulfilled the Confucian ideal of reciprocity (favour-exchanging) and helped to communicate and provide for assistance when problems arise (Pye, 1986). According to Pye (1986), with its philosophical and moral support from a Confucian ethic, the right *guanxi* helps to maintain harmony in the Chinese system of doing things. As Luo (1997) argues, *guanxi* are delicate fibres woven into every Chinese individual's social life, and therefore, into many aspects of the Chinese society. Ahmed and Li (1996) explain *guanxi* as fundamental in directing social and personal behaviour in China, referring to it as the relationship between people or organisations which implicitly indicates assurance, understanding, and mutual obligation.

In China, therefore, the use of *guanxi* is the quickest and surest route to accomplishment. "Who one knows matters, rather than what one knows" (Pang et al., 1998, p. 276). A traditional Chinese *guanxi* is built on interpersonal connections and particularistic criteria, which attach more importance to personal relationships. It refers to relationships between people and can be applied to family members, kinship, friendships, educational ties, bureaucratic linkages, and so forth relations. A direct particularistic criterion is the assumption that the two individuals share some common experiences or heritage, such as two classmates who were at the same university. Those relations may lead to business relationships as *guanxi* plays an important role in helping parties to gain a commercial foothold.

Guanxi is dynamic and transferable (Luo, 1997, 2000; Pearce & Robinson, 2000). For instance, in this study, if Supplier 3 had *guanxi* with Supplier 2, and Supplier 2 had *guanxi* with TelcoX, then Supplier 3 could be introduced to TelcoX by Supplier 2. Thus, *guanxi* could be established by bridging the gaps of personal connections, which can bring potential partners for an organisation as well. The application of *guanxi* at the organisational level has become increasingly pervasive and intensive in China in the early 1980's (Luo, 2000). It requires great effort to maintain a life-long relationship once a *guanxi* has been achieved. However, a *guanxi* at an organisational level would be lost when an individual, who brought this *guanxi* connection, leaves. This largely explains the difference between *guanxi* and Westernised business relationships.

Interviews on Western working style in this study reflected that no personal feeling or interest was involved in the Westernised business relationship. Western management culture seems to have a strong impact on the development of relationships; the establishment of business relationships is simply based on business needs in the West. As the interviewees from Western countries said:

...It is purely working relationships...Personally, I think there is no such kind of personal relationship involved in business among English people. It is a friendship. I also try to manage selecting suppliers and balancing the business and personal relations during work very carefully...I make sure all

suppliers are selected based on criteria (the Contract Negotiator of Customer 2, a UK company)

We generally maintain very formal relationships with suppliers. We send them our formal contracts that are very clear, which are good for the suppliers. And then, when they complete their work to our satisfaction, we pay their invoices so they get their remuneration. We try to pay them on time; we don't delay for a long time because that causes a bad relationship, especially for the small companies... we don't want any work delay either... (The Logistics/Service Manager of Customer 2, a UK company)

The interviewees from Western countries also expressed their concerns on the practices of personal relationships. If they accepted the invitations of social activities, they must make sure to keep their principles in balancing the personal and business relationships. Otherwise, it would cause unfair business handling, although sometimes they might not want to be involved in any social activities more than going out for a drink or a meal. Moreover, reports to their bosses about what they were going to do were needed. Since a *guanxi* is built up normally through social activities, such as inviting people to dinner or gift-giving which equals to corruption in the view of some Westerners, the establishment of *guanxi* is often portrayed as an old-fashioned way of doing business. I would argue that this overemphasis on the gift-giving element of *guanxi* is inaccurate and offensive to Chinese traditions. Although the legal system in China has not been well-developed historically, Chinese people usually use their *guanxi* to resolve disputes and conflicts instead of using China's laws, rules, and regulations.

While business relationships have developed in recent years, the new practices emerged through new experiences gained in business developments in some new Chinese enterprises such as TelcoX. While business relationships developed in recent years, the new practices emerged through new experiences gained in some new Chinese enterprises such as TelcoX, even though there were still some of TelcoX's people who believed that this approach was a much more effective and efficient way to establish relationships. Therefore, guanxi, an important factor in relationships in the Chinese culture, attached importance to both personal and business relationships in China. It could not work if it was abolished completely. It was also not suitable to apply the foreign experiences in China without considering the cultural context.

Emerging Concept of the Guanxi-Platform

The main actors who were interviewed, who were involved in the processes of implementation and use of CSS, indicated that the cultivation of "*guanxi*" at an individual or organisational level both within and between organisations was very important. As seen frequently, Western enterprises and JVs expanded their businesses in China, and some foreigners could speak Chinese fluently, but they could not understand Chinese culture very well and sometimes made wrong decisions and judgments. The director of Supplier 3 told an interesting story of his American boss:

When my boss was in Singapore, he went to a Chinese school, hoping to learn something about China. But actually, the teacher did not know what had happened in China in recent years. My boss was told that to establish relations with Chinese you must invite them to a dinner. Therefore, my boss always asked me whether I had invited my customers to a dinner. I felt very funny and told him that this was very old traditional practice from many years ago. That was so-called 'guanxi'. Now, it is different. We prefer providing customers with the best solutions, resources, and services to wasting time at the dinner table. It is essential for us to establish and develop the relations with customers by full support. Success achieved by customers will strengthen our relations with them. Customers' satisfaction will help maintain the customer relationship.

This story reflects the idea of "sensation investment" in building a relationship. From the long-term strategic view, Chinese enterprises build up solid foundations with potential customers in order to gain business opportunities which are likely to emerge in the future. Therefore, to achieve this goal it is necessary to have various social activities and functions, through which people can make each other's acquaintance, promote mutual understanding, and strengthen friendly connections.

We found that the way to establish relationships was different from the traditional way of *guanxi*. In this research, we refer to the new way of practice as "*guanxi-platform.*" *Guanxi-platform* is "*a scientific platform embodying value, equality, and respect.*" It was invisible on both individual and organisational levels. Differing from the traditional practice of *guanxi*, the new practices are transparent of *guanxi-platform* above board. These new practices have ensured that the cooperation and competition among parties had "healthy" relationships with others, for example, equal opportunities and fair competition. These healthy relationships enabled parties to grow and develop, while at the same time constraining development and their activities. Although there were differences in the practices, there were also similarities. Instead of personal interests or favours that were the main concerns in building up *guanxi*, the directors from customer companies expressed their ideas in establishing *guanxi-platform*:

...In today's business environment, good products are essential for building up relationships (guanxi-platform)... (Director of Customer 1)

Companies operate in a continuously perfect system which is a prerequisite of the establishment of relationships (guanxi-platform). (Director of Customer 2)

However, the value of personal feelings in the traditional concept of *guanxi* was not completely denied in the new understanding of *guanxi-platform*. *Guanxi-platform* could meet the individual's requirements on personal relationships development. People held principles, and flexibilities were allowed only when it did not go against the principles, although all these relationships of *guanxi-platform* were restricted by the laws and regulations. That is to say, personal feelings cannot be ignored in both traditional *guanxi* and new *guanxi-platform*.

Therefore, various cultures and working styles existed within TelcoX (although they were originally Chinese) and in its wider context, cultural diversity was likely to persist. It contributed to TelcoX's corporate culture that integrated subcultures into the mainstream in a harmonious way and also reproduced the new organisational structure as well as network structure. In this particular cultural context, new practices emerged that represented the dynamic nature of culture. The emerging concept, *guanxi-platform*, is built on both personal connections and business needs. To establish a *guanxi-platform*, it was necessary for TelcoX and its business partners to have various social and business activities, through which new knowledge and experience could be gained. Besides these normal channels, systematic management was a new practice of a *guanxi-platform* in TelcoX, as well as organisations across China.

Stripped of its emotional content, there are similarities between *guanxi*, *guanxi-platform,* and Westernised business relationships. The mutual interests or business needs of both parties to the relationships are the common elements. Thus, when dealing with English business people, Chinese people need to be aware that English people do not come over and try not to be influenced by giving and receiving gifts. English people are very careful and try to avoid involving deep personal relationships in business relationships. Also, they feel comfortable with the certainty that enforceable commitments place on them and their partners.

From a cultural perspective, findings from this study indicate that relationships at both individual and organisational levels were crucial for developing and maintaining e-supply relationships. As the existing cultural context (e.g., a mix of traditional Chinese cultural values and Western management culture) influenced organisational members to form their relationships, these relationships enabled the organisation to develop, and also placed a constraint on that development. As a result, the existing cultural context is changing. Over time, the emerging cultural context (e.g., a fusion of Chinese and Western culture) is produced through mixed practices (e.g., *guanxi, guanxi-platform*, and Westernised business relationships). It can be seen that the formation and transformation of both personal and business relationships were enacted by the dynamics of the cultural context.

Technological Perspective: Dynamics of Internet-Technology-in-Use

With regard to Internet-technology-in-use, organisational members' actions reinforced and redefined certain structures by using Internet technologies. It assumed that the existing technological structure was being shaped both within TelcoX and its wider context. In this case, the implementation of CSS and the development of the call centre were the results of coordinated departmental work. The technologically-constructed nature of CSS representing certain interpretative schemes of TelcoX's departments was perceived as "manageable co-handling" by the CSD team. TelcoX's leaders provided an impetus for change through the use of Internet technologies. Changes in the CSD's job flow, TelcoX's work process, and the resulting consequences were triggered by CSS implementation. Use of CSS and other IS in TelcoX provided new structures which were shaped by this change process. The emerging structure was the result of previous actions, which enabled and constrained managers' actions for forming and transformation of e-supply relationships.

In the process of collaboration between departments and business units, a number of discussions were involved in problem-solving. This iterative process of discussion drew attention to the elements of change in the mutual shaping of the technological structure. The constraints of working within the existing technological structure reflected actors' understandings and interpretations of the use of Internet technologies. Changes in the existing structure were experienced in different ways by various individuals, groups, and organisations during the use of Internet technologies. It had shown different perceptions of Internet-technology-in-use over this process of collaboration. For TelcoX and its suppliers, it can be seen that promotion and the use of Internet technology could radically change TelcoX's work process, provide quality customer services, as well as improve business effectiveness. It was also seen as an organisational strategic choice through introducing technological structural changes to improve their work environments. In this study, this was recognised as a work process or new channels of communications in which existing technological constraints were linked to the emerging structure.

Over time, a new technological structure had emerged in TelcoX that represented the dominant view of the employees. Within the constraints some of the conflicting views had not been presented, because those views were not possible to further develop the consequence of previous actions that were often reconstructed to the existing structure. The emerging structure downplayed conflicts while simultaneously applauding success and emphasising collaboration. This ongoing dynamic process both enabled and constrained collaboration between and across TelcoX in its wider context. By engaging in this process, individuals and/or organisations redefined organisational structures and opened up new possibilities and options in the use of Internet technologies.

In this study, the formation and transformation of e-supply relationships were followed by a series of technological changes at TelcoX as well as its business partners. TelcoX seemed to be able to respond quickly to these changes. The results of this study show that managerial actions in developing and maintaining e-supply relationships were strongly linked to these changes. These e-supply relationships were enacted in the dynamic technological context by managerial actions that significantly *changed the existing technological structure.*

Structurational Perspective:
Structuring E-Supply Relationships

As managerial actions on the use of Internet technologies reinforced the technological structure in TelcoX, from the point of view of the users, the adaptation of CSS and other IS in TelcoX was seen as partly driven by the advances of these Internet technologies. Orlikowski et al. (1995) argue that the explicit contextualisation of Internet technologies and the patterns of use of these technologies facilitate organisations to use these technologies in changing their organisational forms over time. This section, from a structurational perspective, continues to address the dynamics of Internet-technology-in-use during e-supply relationship formation and transformation in TelcoX.

Giddens (1979, 1984) proposes the notion of structure (or structural properties of social systems) as the set of enacted rules and resources that mediate social action through three modalities: facilities, norms, and interpretive schemes. In this sense, TelcoX's employees drew on their knowledge of their previous actions and the situation at hand, the available facilities (e.g., organisational resource, Internet technology), and the norms that informed their ongoing practices, and then applied such knowledge, facilities, and norms to structure their current actions. In doing so, they recursively reconstituted the rules and resources that *structured* their actions.

In the early stage of the TelcoX establishment, CSD people were working on stand-alone PCs with simple applications to handle and record their customer calls. But those non-systematic follow-ups that were called the "casual way" within TelcoX did not help them to provide quality services. Senior managers decided to implement the new system of CSS. That was what they had experienced in call centre development. By using call centre and CSS, effective collaboration and communication, both internally and externally, were enabled. Since human interactions with Internet technologies are typically recurrent, so that even as users constitute a technology-in-use through their present use of a technology, their actions are, at the same time, shaped by the previous technologies-in-use that they have enacted in the past (Orlikowski, 2000). Employees' knowledge and skills in the use of CSS had been exposed over the years, which influenced the construction of CSS in TelcoX's branch offices all over China. This reflected the view of Orlikowski (2000, p. 410): "ongoing enactment of a technology-in-use reinforces it, so that it becomes regularised and reutilised, an expedient and habitual response to repeated use of a technology within the daily exigencies of organisational life."

TelcoX's people also drew on their knowledge of and experiences with their institutional contexts, that is, cultural and technological, in which they were exchanging and interacting. In this way, employees' use of Internet technologies became structured by these experiences, knowledge, meanings, norms, and relationships. In practice, such structuring enacted TelcoX's emerging set of rules and resources, which then served to *structure* future use as employees continued to interact with the Internet technologies in their recurrent practices. Thus, over time, employees constituted and reconstituted a *structure* of Internet-technology-in-use in which e-supply relationships were formed and transformed.

A Synthesised Framework on E-Supply Relationships in the Network Context

The analysis of the data from a relationship, a cultural, a technological, and a structurational perspective indicates that the implementation of CSS and other IS in TelcoX helped to form organisational business relationships. Two interacting elements that were shaping the transformation of e-supply relationships in the network context of TelcoX were identified: managerial actions and social structures.

Managerial action was perceived as planned and unplanned actions taken by managers involved in their leadership behaviours and organisational interactions. The managerial actions and changes in communication patterns were particularly looked at with respect to, and in response by, the implementation and use of CSS, and corporate and wider cultural contexts of TelcoX. Social structures included both technologies in use (e.g., use of CSS and other emerging IS that enabled and constrained interactions) and social, cultural, and industrial contexts that were reinforced and transformed by such interactions. Changes in the CSD's work process and the consequences were triggered by the new CSS system design and implementation. Use of CSS by employees and adoption of other IS in TelcoX provided a new set of features which both enable and constrain managers' planned and unplanned actions for forming e-relationships.

By drawing on Giddens (1984) and Orlikowski (2000), Figure 3 depicts this process of e-relationship formation that can be seen as circuits of interactions between human actions and social structures. As illustrated in Figure 3, the existing social structures (e.g., culture, technology, and relationships)

Figure 3. Interaction between human actions and social structures

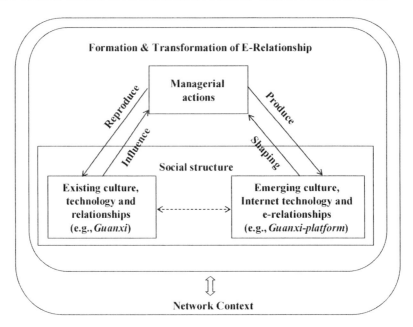

influenced managerial actions in building relationships both within and across organisations; in turn, managerial actions reproduced existing social structures, or produced new social structures (e.g., new cultural context, Internet technology, and e-relationships). As these e-relationships were enacted as emerging social structures by managerial actions, at the same time, these actions were shaped by these constituents.

Figure 4 presents the links between the cultural and the technological perspectives by adopting structuration theory as a meta-theory. The linkage of the understandings from a relationship, a cultural, a technological, and a structurational perspective strengthens the theoretical foundation in this study. Firstly, the combination of the four bodies of knowledge helped to establish a broader view on organisational relationships development. These key themes represent an important contribution in influencing e-supply relationship formation and transformation. Secondly, the emerging concept of *"guanxi-platform"* emphasises the importance of the Chinese cultural norms in the dynamics of e-supply relationships. Thirdly, a number of ideas and views from previous studies have been confirmed in this study. The findings suggest that it is important to young Chinese companies such as TelcoX to improve organisational responsiveness to the environment. Fourthly, since

Figure 4. Links between four theoretical perspectives

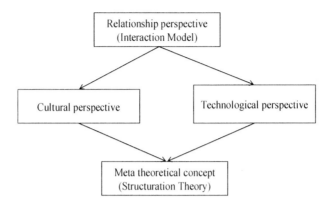

this study has been undertaken to examine the cultural issues associated with e-supply relationships formation and transformation in Chinese context, it contributes to the literature by offering an exploratory study and strengths cultural studies. In particular, this study pays attention to the socially-constructed reality, to the symbolic significance of some aspects of organisation, as well as to systems of meaning and interpretive schemes.

The findings imply that the extent and effectiveness of the use of Internet technologies is the result of several issues, which can have both direct and indirect influences on e-supply relationship management. It suggests that organisations should consider its wider context when doing business in the competitive global market. The effective communications between suppliers and customers, both within and across organisations, are critical for the organisational development and the improvement of the performance of the entire supply chain, which reinforces the wider context structuring and restructuring. At the same time, the produced and reproduced contexts shape and are shaped by the human actions and interactions with the social structures.

Conclusion

China, a large emerging economy, is becoming one of the most attractive economic markets in the world. As seen, its future is closely tied to the developments of its key industries, such as telecom and information technology (IT), which are also considered the forces to sustain future economic growth. By joining the World Trade Organisation (WTO), Internet-related businesses allow more flexibility of foreign investments in China. These also create and foster China's advantages in global competition. The emergence and employment of e-commerce emphasise the necessity of developing and maintaining international business relationships in China as well.

This study focuses on the dynamics of e-supply relationships in a Chinese telecom enterprise by using an interpretive case study approach. The findings indicate that new Chinese telecom enterprises seem to have a higher tolerance for cultural differences and a willingness to accept alternative viewpoints, but when different national and industrial factors are taken into account, wide variations exist in developing and maintaining business relationships. In particular, the key variation with respect to e-supply relationships is rooted in the Chinese cultural norms of *"guanxi"* that have important impacts on the success of the telecom enterprises in the ever-changing Chinese environment.

Through an illustrative example, this chapter presents collaborated and co-ordinated practices in TelcoX's daily work that allow the dynamism of the e-supply relationships formation and transformation to be discovered. In this study, the effects of the dynamics of interactions, the dynamics of culture, as well as the dynamics of Internet-technology-in-use are investigated. Having drawn on structuration theory (Giddens, 1976, 1982, 1984) as a meta-theory, this data analysis of a conceptual synthesis is presented in Figure 3. The empirical understanding generated in this context has implications for both theories on relationship studies and managing organisational inter-dependency of IT-based business relations.

In this research, the conceptualisation of the emergence of e-supply relationships in TelcoX represents circuits of interactions between managerial actions and social structures, and the particular cultural and technological context within which the interactions take place. The reciprocal interaction offers insights into the role of national and corporate cultures both inside and between organisations in shaping e-supply relationships in this specific context. It explains the cultural differences between China and the UK in establishing relationships. Findings of this study emphasise that these cultural differences are very important issues for studies in an electronic setting.

The empirical understanding generated in this context has implications for managing organisational inter-dependency of Internet technology-enabled business relations. For managers, these insights not only open up cultural aspects of IORs but also suggest that the emergence of different cultural norms may accompany the enactment of e-IORs. These insights would be particularly valuable for Western organisations which are forming alliances with Chinese enterprises (Xu & Nandhakumar, 2003a; Xu & Nandhakumar, 2003b; Xu, Harland, & Nandhakumar, 2004).

References

Ahmed, P. K., & Li, X. K. (1996, October). Chinese culture and its implications for Sino-Western joint venture management. *Journal of Strategic Change, 5*, 275-286.

Aladwani, A. M. (2001). Change management strategies for successful ERP implementation. *Business Process Management Journal, 7*(3), 266-275.

Al-Mashari, M. (2000). *Constructs of process change management in ERP context: A focus on SAP R/3*. Paper presented at the America Conference on Information Systems, Long Beach, CA.

Alon, I., & Lu, L. (2004). The state of marketing and business education in China. *Marketing Education Review, 14*(1), 1-11.

Blois, K. (1972). Vertical quasi-integration. *Journal of Industrial Economics, 20*(3), 253-272.

Bond, M., & Hwang, K. (1986). The social psychology of Chinese people. In M. H. Bond (Ed.), *The psychology of the Chinese people* (pp. 213-266). London: Oxford University Press.

Bond, M. H. (1991). *Beyond the Chinese face: Insights from psychology*. HK: Oxford University Press.

Boudreau, M. C., & Robey, D. (1999). *Organisational transition to enterprise resource planning systems: Theoretical choices for process research*. Paper presented at the Twentieth International Conference on Information Systems, Charlotte, NC.

Brunner, J. A., & Wang, Y. (1988). Chinese negotiation and the concept of face. *Journal of International Consumer Marketing, 1*(1), 27-43.

Buttery, E. A., & Leung, T. K. P. (1998). The difference between Chinese and Western negotiations. *European Journal of Marketing, 32*(3/4), 374-389.

Chen, Y. Q. (1993, July). Driving forces behind China's explosive telecommunication growth. IEEE *Communications Magazine, 31*(7), 20-22.

Cousins, P. D. (2001). A conceptual model for managing long-term inter-organisational relationships. *European Journal of Purchasing and Supply Management, 8*(2), 71-82.

Dai, Q. Z., & Kauffman, R. J. (2002). Business models for Internet-based B2B electronic markets. *International Journal of Electronic Commerce, 6*(4), 41-72.

Davies, H., Leung, T. K. P., Luk, S. T. K., & Wong, Y. H. (1995). The benefits of "guanxi": The value of relationships in developing the Chinese market. *Industrial Marketing Management, 24*(3), 207-214.

Dong, L. (2000). A model for enterprise systems implementation: Top management influences on implementation effectiveness. In *Proceedings of the Americas Conference on Information Systems*, Long Beach, CA (pp. 1045-1049).

Ford, D., Berthon, P., Brown, S., Gadde, L., E., Hakansson, H., Naude, P., Ritter, T., & Snehota, I. (2002). *The business marketing course: Managing in complex networks*. Baffins Lane, Chichester: John Wiley & Sons Ltd.

Gabriel, Y. (1999). *Organisations in depth: The psychoanalysis of organisations*. London: Sage.

Giddens, A. (1976). *New rules of sociological method: A positive critique of interpretative sociologies*. London: Hutchinson.

Giddens, A. (1979). *Central problems in social theory: Action, structure and contradiction in social analysis*. UK: The Macmillan Press Ltd.

Giddens, A. (1982). *Profiles and critiques in social theory*. London: Macmilan.

Giddens, A. (1984). *The constitution of society: Outline of the theory of structure*. Berkeley, CA: University of California Press.

Grandori, A., & Soda, G. (1995). Inter-firm networks: Antecedents, mechanisms and forms. *Organisation Studies, 16*(2), 183-214.

Håkansson, H. (1982). *International marketing and purchasing of industrial goods*. John Wiley & Sons, Ltd.

Harland, C., Powell, P., Zheng, J., Caldwell, N., & Woerndl, M. (2002). *Exploitation of b2b technologies: Developing SMEs and large firms' supply chain relationships—literature review report*. Bath: CRiSPS, School of Management, University of Bath.

Harland, C. M. (1996, March). Supply chain management: Relationships, chains, and networks. *British Journal of Management, 7*(Special Issue), S63-S81.

Harland, C. M., Lamming, R. C., & Cousins, P. D. (1999). Developing the concept of supply strategy. *International Journal of Operations and Production Management, 19*(7), 650-673.

Harwit, E. (1998). China's telecommunications industry: Development patterns and policies. *Pacific Affairs, 71*(2), 175-194.

Hofstede, G. (1991). *Cultures and organisations: Software of the mind*. London: McGraw-Hill.

Holland, C. P., & Light, B. (1999a, May/June). A critical success factors model for ERP implementation. *IEEE Software*, 30-36.

Holland, C. P., & Light, B. (1999b, May/June). A critical success factors model for ERP implementation. *IEEE Software*, 30-36.

IMP. (1997). An interaction approach. In D. Ford (Ed.), *Understanding business markets: Interaction, relationships, and networks* (2nd ed., pp. 3-22). London: The Dryden Press.

Jarillo, J. C. (1993). *Strategic networks: Creating the borderless organisation*. Oxford, UK: Butterworth Heinemann.

Jones, M. R. (1999). Structuration theory. In B. Galliers & W. L. Currie (Eds.), *Rethinking management information systems: An interdisciplinary perspective*. Oxford, UK: Oxford University Press.

Kelly, S., Holland, C. P., & Light, B. (1999). *Enterprise resource planning: A business approach to systems development*. Paper presented at the Americas Conference on Information Systems, Milwaukee, WI.

Kim, H. W., Lee, G. H., & Pan, S. L. (2002). *Exploring the critical success factors for customer relationship management and electronic customer relationship management systems*. Paper presented at the 23rd International Conference on Information Systems.

Klein, H. K., & Myers, M. D. (1999). A set of principles for conducting and evaluating interpretive field studies in information systems. *MIS Quarterly: Management Information Systems, 23*(1), 67-94.

Lamming, R. C. (1993). *Beyond partnership—strategies for innovation and lean supply*. London: Prentice Hall.

Lamming, R. C., Cousins, P. D., & Notman, D. M. (1996). Beyond vendor assessment: Relationship assessment programmes. *European Journal of Purchasing and Supply Management, 2*(4), 173-181.

Leung, T. K. P. (2004). A Chinese-United States joint venture business ethics model and its implications for multi-national firms. *International Journal of Management, 21*(1), 58-66.

Luo, Y. D. (1997). Guanxi: Principles, philosophies, and implications. *Human Systems Management, 16*(1), 43-52.

Luo, Y. D. (2000). *Guanxi and business*. Singapore: World Scientific Publishing Co. Pte. Ltd.

Nah, F. F.-H., Lau, J. L.-S., & Kuang, J. (2001). Critical factors for successful implementation of enterprise systems. *Business Process Management Journal, 7*(3), 285-296.

Nolan, P. (2001). *China and the global economy*. Palgrave.

Oliver, C. (1990). Determinants of inter-organisational relationships: Integration and future directions. *Academy of Management Review, 15*(2), 241-265.

Orlikowski, W. J. (2000). Using technology and constituting structures: A practice lens for studying technology in organisations. *Organisation Science, 11*(4), 404-428.

Orlikowski, W. J., & Baroudi, J. J. (1991). Studying information technology in organisations: Research approaches and assumptions. *Information Systems Research, 2*(1), 1-28.

Orlikowski, W. J., Yate, J., Okamura, K., & Fujimolo, M. (1995). Shaping electronic communication: The metastructuring of technology in the context of use. *Organisation Science, 6*(4), 423-444.

Pang, C. K., Roberts, D., & Sutton, J. (1998). Doing business in China—the art of war? *International Journal of Contemporary Hospitality Management, 10*(7), 272-282.

Pearce II, J. A., & Robinson Jr., B. R. (2000, January/February). Cultivating guanxi as a foreign investor strategy. *Business Horizons*, 31-38.

Pye, L. (1986, July/August). The China trade: Making the deal. *Harvard Business Review*, 74-80.

Redding, S. G. (1984, May). Varieties of the iron rice bowl. *The Hong Kong Manager*, 11-15.

Sain, B., Owens, J. D., & Hill, J. D. (2004). Advances in e-procurement: A focus on the product/buying situation. *Management Services, 48*(6), 10-15.

Shanks, G., Parr, A., Hu, B., Corbitt, B., Thanasankit, T., & Seddon, P. B. (2000). Differences in critical success factors in ERP systems implementation in Australia and China: A cultural analysis. In *Proceedings of the 8ᵗʰ European Conference on Information Systems* (pp. 1-8). Vienna: Vienna University of Economics and Business Administration.

She, Q. J., & Yu, R. L. (1993, July). Telecommunications services in China. *IEEE Communications Magazine, 31*(7), 30-33.

Shoib, G., & Nandhakumar, J. (2003). Cross-cultural IS adoption in multinational corporations. *Information Technology for Development, 10*(4), 249-260.

Terreberry, S. (1968). The evolution of organisational environments. *Administrative Science Quarterly, 12*(4), 590-613.

Walsham, G. (1993). *Interpreting information systems in organisations.* Chichester, UK: Wiley.

Walsham, G. (2000). IT, globalisation, and cultural diversity. In C. Avgerou & G. Walsham (Eds.), *Information technology in context: Studies from the perspective of developing countries* (pp. 291-303). Aldershot: Ashgate Publishing Ltd.

Walsham, G. (2002). Cross-cultural software production and use: A structurational analysis. *MIS Quarterly: Management Information System, 26*(4), 359-380.

Westwood, R. I., & Kirkbride, P. S. (1998). International strategies of corporate culture change: Emulation, consumption, and hybridity. *Journal of Organisational Change Management, 11*(6), 554-577.

Whitley, R. (1992). *Business systems in East Asia: Firms, markets, and societies.* London: Sage.

Williamson, O. E. (1975). *Markets and hierarchies: Analysis and antitrust implications.* New York: Free Press.

Xu, S. X., Harland, C. M., & Nandhakumar, J. (2004). *The applications of ancient Chinese military strategy in a newly-formed Chinese enter-*

prise: The dynamics of e-supply relationships. Paper presented at the 20th International Marketing and Purchasing Conference, Copenhagen, Denmark.

Xu, S. X., & Nandhakumar, J. (2003a). *E-inter-organisational networks in a newly-formed large Chinese enterprise.* Paper presented at the 8th UK Academy for Information Systems Annual Conference, Warwick, UK.

Xu, S. X., & Nandhakumar, J. (2003b). *Transformation of e-inter-organisational relationships: A study of a newly-formed Chinese enterprise.* Paper presented at the 26th Information Systems Research Seminar in Scandinavia, Haikko Manor, Finland.

Yao, Y. L., Palmer, J. W., & Dresner, M. (2002). *Impacts of electronic commerce on supply chain management.* Paper presented at the 23rd International Conference on Information Systems, Menorca.

Yeung, I. Y. M., & Tung, R. L. (1996, Autumn). Achieving business success in Confucian societies: The importance of guanxi (connections). *Organisational Dynamicsm 25*(2), 54-65.

Chapter VII

ICT Adoption in Firms by Using Endogenous Metrics

Michela Serrecchia, Institute for Informatics and Telematics, Italian National Research Council (IIT-CNR), Italy

Irma Serrecchia, Institute for Informatics and Telematics, Italian National Research Council (IIT-CNR), Italy

Maurizio Martinelli, Institute for Informatics and Telematics, Italian National Research Council (IIT-CNR), Italy

Abstract

This chapter analyzes the digital divide in Italy and the factors contributing to this situation at both the regional and provincial levels. To do this, we used the registration of Internet domains under the ".it" Country Code Top Level Domain as a proxy. In particular, we analyzed domain names registered by firms. The analysis produced interesting results: The distribution of domains registered by firms in Italian provinces is more concentrated than the distribution related to income and the number of firms, suggesting a diffusive effect. Furthermore, in order to analyze the factors that may contribute to the presence of a digital divide at the regional level, a regression analysis was performed using demographic, social, economic, and infrastructure indicators. The results show that Internet technology, far from being an "equalizer," follows and possibly intensifies existing differences in economic opportunity in industrialized countries like Italy.

Introduction

Internet growth has fired the imagination of users, policymakers, entrepreneurs, corporate managers, military strategists, social commentators, scholars, and journalists (Guillèn & Suarèz, 2004). Some researchers see the Internet as a new technological medium that will lead to a "smaller, more open world" (Tapscott & Caston, 1993, p. 313). According to others, the Internet symbolizes "the triumph over time and space," the rise of the "netizen," and the crowning of the "customer as sovereign" (Guillén & Suárez, 2004, p. 683).

According to Coffman and Odlyzko (2002), the Internet is a means of communication that is rapidly expanding. Studies carried out by the Network User Association (NUA, Ltd) estimated the worldwide online population in 1999 and in 2002, and show that in Europe the number of individuals online came to 190.91 million in 2002, compared to 47.15 million in 1999.

Companies as well as individuals turn to the Internet to exploit its communication potential. Today, information infrastructures are reaching out to the individual consumer, and telematics networks reduce the cost of communications. This statement echoes the economics literature (Hoffman, Novak, & Perlata, 1996), which confirms that the Web is becoming a dynamic and personal means of communication.

Other authors (Bassi, 2002) point out that the spread of the Internet and the functions of electronic commerce will permit individual clients to choose from a wide array of products to reduce costs by selecting and buying goods directly from the source, and allowing companies to sell while bypassing traditional channels. Scandinavia, at 8.6%, leads the region with the highest percentage of online sales, mostly computers and related products, travel, video and music, and books.

This situation could prove to be quite worrisome for traditional businesses, as emerges from a survey carried out by the Syndicate Agents Union and representatives of the Italian Chamber of Commerce in November, 2000.

However, companies must adopt entirely new forms of commercial activity for online sales to be successful. The advantages provided by the Internet for businesses are not only related to the sale of products and services (direct advantages), but can also be indirect in nature (Hansons, 2000). For example, some of the most important of these are reduced costs, image consolidation, greater customer loyalty, and a wider diffusion of products offered by the company. They are referred to as "indirect" since they do not lead directly to sales and do not generate immediate profits; however, eventually they will probably be the greatest benefits offered to businesses by the Internet.

The gradual confirmation of the Internet as a means of communication also permits companies to access data and a variety of other information; for example, it is possible to rapidly access information about the market in which one operates by visiting Web sites specializing in economic information or areas that provide updates on laws, price changes, the appearance of new operators in the field, fairs, competitive bidding, and other news of interest to operators. One can also identify and analyze the competition by means of information published on company Web sites, and so forth.

Our study analyzes the spread of the Internet among Italian firms utilizing the number of domain names registered under the country code Top Level Domain (ccTLD) ".it" as metrics. We considered domain names (names that are associated with IP addresses on the Net) since we believe it is extremely important for a firm to have a domain name, and an Italian firm can exploit the above-mentioned direct and/or indirect advantages using this name. Moreover, it is helpful for a firm to register a domain name not only in order to maintain its own Web site, but also to benefit from advantages related to online means of communications (for example, e-mails, FTP, and so on). As a matter of fact, online means of communications, unlike traditional ones (i.e., call-center services, telemarketing), are more effective, for example, by allowing firms to reach several customers at the same time, and more flexible, as some allow customers to solve problems on their own (i.e., with FAQs). In this way, 24-hour-a-day access to resources is offered. On the contrary, traditional customer care methods require intensive work and a considerable engagement of resources to ensure prompt and accessible assistance.

Analysis of the Internet presence in various social activities and economic and political areas reveals a critical issue: the existence of a "digital divide" between those who possess the material and cultural conditions to exploit the new technologies, and those who do not or who lack the crucial ability to adapt to the rapid continual change that characterizes the Internet today (Kirkman, Cornelius, P. K., Sachs, J. D., & Schwab, 2002; Norris, 2001; OECD, 2001; Rogers, 2001; Warschauer, 2002). Therefore, the announcement that the Internet's potential as "a liberty, productivity, and communication instrument, goes hand in hand with the digital divide exposure" caused by uneven Internet diffusion (Castells, 2001, p. 247) is unsurprising. The 1999 World Human Development Report, written by the United Nations Organization, considers the number of Internet users to be one of the most widely used indicators for pointing up the divide between rich and poor countries. Statistics compiled by the International Telecommunication Union indicate that by the end of 2002, Internet users in continents such as Africa, and Central and South America represent only 1% of the population while this percentage rises to 50-60% in countries such as Iceland, United States, Scandinavia, Singapore, or South Korea (ITU, 2003).

Even if researchers, organizations, and governments acknowledge the existence of the digital divide, there is disagreement as to its causes. Many researchers have acknowledged that the differences regarding Internet use between countries are fundamentally related to economic variables such as Internet access cost and per capita income.

In addition, the existence of the digital divide also depends on the nature of the data used, which differs from study to study (Guillèn & Suarèz, 2004). For example, some researchers analyzed data only for industrialized countries (Hargittai, 1999; Oxley & Yeung, 2001), while others analyzed data including both developed and underdeveloped countries (Beilock & Dimitrova, 2003; Guillèn & Suarèz, 2001; Kiiski, Sampsa, & Pohjola, 2002; Maitland & Bauer, 2001; Norris, 2001; Pohjola, 2004), discovering that in addition to socioeconomic variables and the existence of infrastructures, Internet access is also related to particular characteristics of the country of reference. For example, these authors maintain that a country is more apt to use the Internet when there is greater freedom of expression, and ideas and information circulate freely. Other researchers analyzed data only for the more industrialized countries (Bauer, Berne, & Maitland, 2002), finding that the digital divide is not only the result of income differences and access costs, but also of certain features of the telecommunications sector. In fact, according to these and other authors (Guillèn & Suarèz, 2004; Kirkman et al., 2002; Levy & Spiller, 1994; Wallsten, 2001; Wilson, 1998), a highly competitive sector that offers telecommunication services increases Internet use.

Selection of Variables

In this chapter we will analyze factors that contribute to the existence of the digital divide in Italy, taking into consideration not only economic variables, but also educational, cultural, demographic, and technological variables.

Economic Variables

Many studies claim that economic variables are an important predictor of the spread of the Internet. Chinn and Fairlie (2004) maintain that the digital divide between developed and underdeveloped countries are, to a great extent, the result of per capita income. According to a survey conducted by the NTIA, in the United States, low-income households ($<\$15,000$/year) are less inclined to use the new technologies, due to a lack of computer availability and Internet access cost; nevertheless, Internet use increased from 9.2% in October, 1997, to 25.0% in September, 2001, among people in this category. Moreover, a number of empirical studies regarding the global digital divide discovered that the average life standard calculated in terms of average income per employee is an important factor in the existence of the digital divide in a country (Guillèn & Suarèz, 2001; Hargittai, 1999; Maitland & Bauer, 2001; Norris, 2001). Analyzing data at an individual level in 24 countries, Chen, Boase, and Wellman (2002) found a strong correlation between economic variables and Internet use. Additionally, according to O'Neill (2001) and Johnson, Anantharaman, Amirtha Rajan, and Surgunam (2005), wealthier consumers are more apt to shop online.

Educational Variables

According to Hansons (2000), education consolidates the skills necessary for Internet use, characterizing professions that encourage Internet use and pastimes that motivate its use. According to the AMD Global Consumer Advisory Board (2002), in Germany the educational level is one of the foremost elements that affects Internet use: By the year 2000, 86% of people with a university degree were online compared to 8% of those with a lower educational level. In China, education seems to be more of a distinguishing factor than income. In Korea, the gap between users with a university education and less-educated users is 40%. Other studies on the digital divide have drawn the same conclusions. Chinn and Fairlie (2004) and Norris (2001) find that a country's educational levels, together with the average life standard, are important factors affecting Internet use. Moreover, De Arcangelis, Jona-Lasinio, and Manzocchi (2002) show that in addition to economic variables, a high number of employees devoted to research and development is a decisive factor influencing Internet use within a country.

Cultural Variables

According to the economics literature (Florida, 2002), there is a strong correlation between technological indicators and indicators pointing to cultural activities. In fact, according to Florida, the U.S. cities that experienced the highest rate of growth in the 1990s combined intense technological activity, an exciting social environment, and tolerance for deviance. These factors are attractive for the so-called creative class, that is, the growing sector of the economy involved in creative tasks, such as research, design, consultancy, and advertising.

Demographic Variables

According to some studies, the most urbanized areas are also most inclined to use the Internet (Dasgupta, Lall, & Wheeler, 2001; Zook, 1998). Other studies analyzing data on an individual level show that age and gender are key factors in the existence of the digital divide in a country. Kovacich (1998) and Johnson et al. (2005) showed that people between the ages of 25 and 34 are more apt to use the Internet. According to the ADM Global Consumer Advisory Board (2002), in the United States young people between 12 and 35 are the most active computer users (nearly 80%), while only one-third of people over 65 are online. In 2002, 89% of young people in the UK between the ages of 16 and 24 years had Internet access; only 14% of users were over 65 years of age. In the same year, in Germany only 5% of users over 65 were online, while in China only 3.7% of people over 50 surf the Internet, and about two-thirds of the users were younger than 35. In terms of gender, the literature suggests that more men than women use the Internet (Johnson et al., 2005; Kovacich, 1998), but the situation is changing rapidly. In the United States males and females have approximately equal rates of computer access, according to 2002 data. In the United Kingdom, males outnumber females, but the gap is narrowing. In Germany, 53% of users are male compared with 36% of female users. In Japan, more than two-thirds of Japanese males are online, but 56% of females are online as well. In China, women are closing the gap, considering that 41% of users are female (AMD, 2002).

Technological Variables

Studies regarding the diffusion of means of communication established that their use is facilitated by the availability of infrastructures. For example, telephone use is facilitated by a greater availability of telephone lines (Fischer, 1992). Several empirical studies regarding the spread of the Internet as a means of communication, utilizing data at an aggregate (Chinn & Fairlie, 2004; Guillèn & Suarèz, 2001; Kiiski et al., 2002) and an individual level (Chen, Boase, & Wellman, 2002; UCLA, 2000, 2003; U.S. Department of Commerce, 1999), show that infrastructure availability and low access cost are important factors that can lead to wide differences in Internet use.

In brief, in this chapter we test the following hypotheses:

H1: The Internet is more widespread in Italian regions with a marked productive efficiency measured in terms of added value per employee, per capita income, and total income (the greater the presence of these indicators in a province, the greater the probability will be that a domain name will be registered and the greater the penetration rate).

H2: The Internet is more widespread in Italian regions with a greater incidence of innovation expressed in terms of the number of registered patents.

H3: The Internet is more widespread in Italian regions with a higher percentage of large firms. This percentage is calculated in terms of local unities number.

H4: The Internet is more widespread in Italian regions with a marked cultural activity.

H5: The Internet is more widespread in Italian regions with a greater level of educational attainment.

H6: The Internet is more widespread in Italian regions with a low unemployment rate and in densely-populated provinces.

H7: The Internet is more widespread in Italian regions with greater investment in ICT.

Methodology

There are several ways to measure Internet diffusion. The most convenient are the so-called endogenous means which can be "obtained in an automatic or semiautomatic way from the Internet itself" (Diez-Picazo, 1999, p. 83). They have the undeniable advantage of accuracy, since they are based on automatic data collection and retrieval; in addition, they allow good geographical characterization of the phenomenon since they are based on data that allow differentiation of users on national, regional, and provincial levels. According to the literature, the most frequently used endogenous means for analyzing Internet diffusion are Internet hosts based on host-count procedures (see studies published by Internet Software Consortium or by RIPE-NCC) and second-level domain names (Bauer, Berne, & Maitland, 2002; Naldi, 1997; Zook, 1998). Despite the advantages offered by endogenous measures, there are also a few disadvantages, since in some cases they tend to underestimate and in others overestimate the phenomenon studied (Zook, 1998, 2000, 2001). Overestimation can occur when the number of hosts is used, often associated with IP addresses; if we consider the number of domains registered, more than one domain may be associated with the same registrant. Underestimation can occur because not all Internet users register a domain name under their own ccTLD, and in many countries the regulations allow foreign citizens to register under their own ccTLD (for example, Italy allows organizations and citizens of the European Union countries to register under the ".it" ccTLD).

In the case of hosts, underestimation may be due to the growing presence of firewalls and private networks (Intranet) and the use of dynamic IP addresses, increasingly accompanied by new tools for accessing the Net (i.e., mobile phones). In spite of these disadvantages, the number of hosts and Internet domains remains the best means for analyzing Internet diffusion.

To measure Internet diffusion in Italy among firms, we used the endogenous measure of second-level domain names registered under the ".it" ccTLD, managed by the Institute of Informatics and Telematics of CNR, Pisa, using data extracted from the databases of registrations, using automatic and semi-automatic procedures. We created a new database for analyzing Internet diffusion by initially consulting the WHOIS database (the latter contains information regarding domain names registered under the ".it" ccTLD, applicants who have signed a contract with IIT-CNR and technical and administrative contacts) using an automatic procedure; for example, in order to determine the category of the applicant, the automatic procedure verified whether an ORG field (organization name) and a DESCR field (description of the organization registering the domain name) were present and if so, depending on the values of these fields, classified it as a firm. If the ORG or DESCR fields were wrong, the LAR (Letter of Assumption of Responsibility, in which the applicant assumes full civil and penal responsibility for the use of the domain name requested) database (a semi-automatic procedure) was consulted. Finally, where LAR information was not sufficiently accurate, the Italian Chamber of Commerce database was consulted.

Approximately 1,000,000 domain names were analyzed and grouped into several categories (individuals, firms, universities, associations, public groups, and other registrants). As mentioned above, in this chapter particular attention was paid to the registration of domain names by firms. To be able to register a domain name under the "it." ccTLD, firms must send a LAR to the Italian Registry. The five currently available LARs differ according to the type of applicant (individual, association/foundation, public administration, professionals, and companies).

From this research performed up to December 31, 2004, it was established that the number of domains registered by firms came to 411,339 of which 407,030 were registered by Italian firms and 4,309 by foreign firms. Furthermore, 1,944 domains registered by Italian firms were not classified, since it was impossible to discover the province of origin.

Analysis and Results

Concentration Analysis

To measure the digital divide among Italian regions and provinces, we used the number of domain names registered by firms under the ccTLD ".it," the penetration rate calculated every 100 firms, an index calculated by Zook (Domain Name Specialization Ratio) and the Gini index (Gini, 1960).

The Zook index (Zook, 1998, 2000, 2001) is calculated as follows:

Domain name Specialization Ratio $= \dfrac{\text{Number of .it domains in a region / Number of firms in that region}}{\text{Number of .it domains in a country/ Number of firms in a country}}$

An index value greater than 1 indicates a greater specialization than the national average, and an index value less than 1 indicates a lack of specialization.

Table 1 shows the number of domains registered as on December 31, 2004, the penetration rate every 100 firms, and the specialization ratio of domain names registered both at a regional level (Italy is divided into 20 administrative unities called regions) and a macro area level (North, Centre, South). In Table 1, regions have been arranged in descending order according to the number of registered domain names.

The penetration rate formula is as follows:

$$\text{Penetration rate} = \frac{\text{Number of .it domains in a region} * 100}{\text{Number of firms in that region}}$$

Table 2 shows the descriptive statistics of the regional distribution of domain names.

The Kurtosis and the Skewness index in Table 2 describe the form and symmetry of distribution. In our case, the form of distribution is asymmetric to

Table 1. Top ten concentrations of domain names under ccTLD ".it" at a regional level during the period 1990-2004

Regions	Number of Registered Domains as of 12/31/2004	PR every 100 Firms	Domain Name Specialization Ratio
1. Lombardy	97,201	12.93	1.30
2. Latium	40,510	11.29	1.14
3. Veneto	38,679	10.28	1.04
4. Emilia Romagna	36,828	10.22	1.03
5. Tuscany	35,633	11.38	1.15
6. Piedmont	32,701	9.91	1.00
7. Campania	22,876	7.67	0.77
8. Sicily	15,981	6.48	0.65
9. Apulia	13,690	6.09	0.61
10. (the) Marches	11,602	9.39	0.95
Northern Italy	237,802	11.23	1.13
Central Italy	93,799	10.91	1.10
Southern Italy	73,485	6.64	0.67
Italy	405,086	9.92	1.00

Table 2. Descriptive statistics: Number of domains registered at a regional level

	No.	Min	Max	Mean	Std.	Dev.	Skewness
ICT diffusion	20	845.00	97,201	20,254.3	22,550.12	.860	6.543

the right (half the observations are to the right of the mode). The Skewness index is positive. It is calculated as the difference between the mean and the mode, divided by the standard deviation.

As suggested in the literature and as shown in Table 1, although some regions have a high specialization rate compared to the national average (Lombardy, Trentino Alto Adige, Tuscany, Latium) the variance between the analyzed regions can be extreme (Zook, 1998). For example, as shown in Table 1, some of the more populated Italian regions, such as Lombardy, register a penetration rate twice as high as the penetration rate registered by other less-populated regions such as Apulia and Sicily. It is interesting to note that when we observe the ranking of the registered domains, the first 3 regions (Lombardy, Latium and Veneto) contain more than 40% of the total amount of registered domains compared to the remaining 17 regions.

However, Internet geography cannot be simply described in terms of the total number of registered domains. Table 3 shows regions arranged in descending order according to the domain name specialization rate. Trentino Alto Adige, one of the more sparsely populated regions which has a number of registered domain names inferior to the national average (11,069 against a national average of 20,254.3) (see Table 2), proves to be the first in terms of specialization of domain names under the ccTLD .it; in fact, the specialization ratio of domain names is 1.45 (see Table 3), which is superior to regions that register a greater number of domains such as Piedmont, Latium, and Lombardy (see Tables 1 and 3).

At any rate, the considerable differences among Italian regions in terms of Internet diffusion are more easily seen at the provincial level (Italy is divided into 103 provinces).

Small provinces have a higher domain name specialization than larger provinces.

Table 3. Top ten concentrations of domain names specialization ratio and penetration rates under the ccTLD ".it" at a regional level during the period 1990-2004

Regions	Number of Registered Domains as of 12/31/2004	PR every 100 Firms	Domain Name Specialization Ratio
1. Trentino Alto Adige	11,069	14.35	1.45
2. Lombardy	97,201	12.93	1.30
3. Tuscany	35,633	11.38	1.15
4. Latium	40,510	11.29	1.14
5. Friuli Venezia Giulia	9,581	11.06	1.11
6. Veneto	38,679	10.28	1.04
7. Emila Romagna	36,828	10.22	1.03
8. Piedmont	32,701	9.91	1.00
9. Umbria	6,054	9.41	0.95
10. (the) Marches	11,602	9.39	0.95
Northern Italy	237,802	11.23	1.13
Central	93,799	10.91	1.10
Southern	73,485	6.64	0.67
Italy	405,086	9.92	1.00

Table 4 shows the first 20 Italian provinces arranged according to the number of registered domain names, while Table 5 shows the first 20 provinces arranged according to the specialization rate number of domain names.

As shown in Table 4, larger provinces, in terms of resident population, are foremost in domain name registration; Milan, Turin, Rome, and Naples, the first 4 provinces, together represent nearly 30% of registered domains compared to the other 99 provinces.

Although it is interesting to learn the concentrations of domain names in Italian provinces, it is important to compare the provinces according to their domain name specialization. Small provinces in lower positions in terms of the number of domain names (Table 5), such as Pisa and Bolzano, prove to be the most specialized provinces in terms of domain names, compared to the other provinces (the specialization rate of domain names is 1.75 and 1.65, respectively), while large provinces which come first in the list in terms of registered domains, such as Milan, Rome, Turin, and Naples, fall behind. Naples, in particular, does not even appear in the first 20 provinces listed, and

Table 4. Top 20 provinces by concentration of domain names under ccTLD ".it" during the period 1990-2004

Provinces	Number of Registered Domains as of 12/31/2004	PR every 100 Firms	Domain Name Specialization Ratio
1. Milan	54,319	16.25	1.64
2. Rome	34,201	12.67	1.28
3. Turin	19,185	11.36	1.14
4. Naples	13,425	8.73	0.88
5. Florence	11,185	12.56	1.27
6. Brescia	10,821	11.60	1.17
7. Bologna	10,055	11.96	1.21
8. Padua	8,269	10.74	1.08
9. Bergamo	8,187	10.47	1.06
10. Vicenza	7,548	11.35	1.14
11. Verona	7,436	10.76	1.08
12. Treviso	7,051	10.47	1.06
13. Varese	6,813	10.93	1.10
14. Genoa	6,567	9.86	0.99
15. Bolzano	6,535	16.37	1.65
16. Modena	6,528	11.25	1.13
17. Bari	6,334	6.61	0.67
18. Venice	5,859	9.44	0.95
19. Pisa	5.432	17.33	1.75
20. Udine	4,855	12.02	1.21
Italy	405,086	9.92	1.00

the specialization ratio is 0.88, inferior to the national average. Also Turin, which comes third in terms of registered domains, drops down to eleventh position in terms of domain name specialization; to some extent the same can be said of large provinces such as Milan and Rome, which both drop down two positions (see Tables 4 and 5).

As previously mentioned, an additional measure adopted in order to verify the existence of a digital divide in Italy is the Gini concentration index (Gini, 1960). The Gini index assumes values equal to 1 and 0. Value 0 indicates equi-distribution, and 1 signifies the maximum concentration. The aim of the "statistical theory of concentration" is to provide tools and techniques

Table 5. Top 20 provinces, concentration of domain names specialization ratio under the ccTLD ".it" during the period 1990-2004

Provinces	Number of Registered Domains as of 12/31/2004	PR every 100 Firms	Domain Name Specialization Ratio
1. Pisa	5,432	17.33	1.75
2. Bolzano	6,535	16.37	1.65
3. Milan	54,319	16.25	1.64
4. Rome	34,201	12.67	1.28
5. Florence	11,185	12.56	1.27
6. Siena	2,691	12.45	1.25
7. Trento	4,534	12.19	1.23
8. Udine	4,855	12.02	1.21
9. Bologna	10,055	11.96	1.21
10. Brescia	10,821	11.60	1.17
11. Turin	19,185	11.36	1.14
12. Vicenza	7,548	11.35	1.14
13. Modena	6,528	11.25	1.13
14. Lecco	2,624	11.12	1.12
15. Ancona	3,821	11.11	1.12
16. Varese	6,813	10.93	1.10
17. Verona	7,436	10.76	1.08
18. Como	4,572	10.75	1.08
19. Padua	8,269	10.74	1.08
20. Reggio-Emilia	4,332	10.55	1.06
Italy	405,086	9.92	1.00

for measuring the concentration in concrete situations or for comparing the degrees of concentration among heterogeneous situations.

The Gini index, calculated according to the number of registered domains (that number should not be confused with the above-mentioned penetration rate) and the Lorenz curve (Lorenz, 1905) confirm the above-mentioned results. Only firms with head offices in certain provinces of Italy register a high number of domains, while firms with head offices in other provinces (especially in the south of Italy) show barely significant percentages. The first ten provinces of the total 103 register nearly half of the domains compared to the national total (43.74%).

Table 6. Gini concentration ratio

Gini Index	
Number of registered domains	0.543
Number of firms	0.468
Total income provinces	0.466

Table 7. Top 20 provinces in terms of registered domains, number of firms, and total income

Ranking Provinces	Number of Registered Domains	Ranking Provinces	Number of Firms *	Ranking Provinces	Total Income expressed in Thousands of Euros**
1. Milan	54,319	1. Milan	334,188	1. Milan	73,790
2. Rome	34,201	2. Rome	269,986	2. Rome	65,726
3. Turin	19,185	3. Turin	168,948	3. Turin	35,410
4. Naples	13,425	4. Naples	153,699	4. Naples	32,088
5. Florence	11,185	5. Bari	95,894	5. Bari	18,602
6. Brescia	10,821	6. Brescia	93,259	6. Bologna	17,099
7. Bologna	10,055	7. Florence	89,078	7. Brescia	16,786
8. Padua	8,269	8. Bologna	84,040	8. Florence	16,540
9. Bergamo	8,187	9. Bergamo	78,164	9. Genova	15,619
10. Vicenza	7,548	10. Padua	77,022	10. Verona	15,151
11. Verona	7,436	11. Verona	69,130	11. Venezia	15,007
12. Treviso	7,051	12. Treviso	67,317	12. Palermo	14,412
13. Varese	6,813	13. Genova	66,617	13. Padua	13,601
14. Genova	6,567	14. Vicenza	66,524	14. Bergamo	13,515
15. Bolzano	6,535	15. Salerno	64,603	15. Salerno	12,510
16. Modena	6,528	16. Varese	62,335	16. Varese	12,059
17. Bari	6,334	17. Venezia	62,077	17. Catania	11,625
18. Venezia	5,859	18. Modena	58,025	18. Vicenza	11,061
19. Pisa	5,432	19. Palermo	56,421	19. Treviso	10,869
20. Udine	4,855	20. Catania	55,799	20. Modena	9,957

*Note: *Source: Italian National Institute of Statistics (ISTAT); ** Source: Tagliacarne Institute*

The study also compares the number of domains registered by firms with head offices in provinces with the income earned by the single province and the number of firms in each province in order to verify whether the distribution of registered domains is similar to the number of existing firms and income distribution. That is, we wished to verify whether the richest and most industrialized Italian regions are also the most inclined to use the Internet.

Table 6 shows that the Gini index, calculated on the number of registered domains, is higher than the index calculated according to income and number of firms; this signifies that in Italy the wealthiest and most industrialized provinces do not always come first in the registration of domain names.

Table 7 shows the trend described above and reports the first 20 provinces arranged according to the number of registered domains, to the total income and number of firms. For example, the provinces of Florence, Bologna, and Padua register more domain names than the province of Bari, which registers a higher number of firms.

The aforementioned can be demonstrated if we observe the Lorenz curve (Figure 1), which is a graphical representation of the Gini index.

The sequential reading of information contained in the various points of Figure 1 gives us a complete overview of the phenomenon of the concentration of domain names registered in the section which was studied. For example, the point (p1=0.05, q1=0.002) reminds us that the sector's smallest region, constituting 5% of the frequency of regions with firms that register domain names, contributes to the ICT diffusion with only 0.2%.

Figure 1. Lorenz curve for domains, income, and number of firms

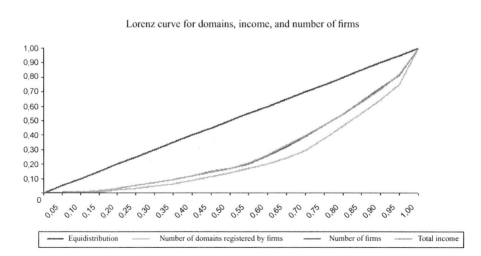

In a similar way, the point (p2=0.10, q2=0.004) informs us that the two smallest regions in the domain name registration, together representing 10% of the total number of domain names registered by firms in Italy, contribute to the diffusion of the ICT only to the extent of 0.4% and so forth.

Moreover, as shown in Figure 1, the curve representing the registration of domain names is farther from the curve of the number of firms, from that of income, and from the equi-distribution curve (we refer to equi-distribution when, for example, a firm established within a province registers the same number of domain names as every other firm established in any other Italian province).

An initial conclusion, based on the observation of the above-mentioned results, is that the Internet cannot be regarded as a spreading phenomenon capable of closing the gap among Italian regions and provinces: Domain name distribution proves to be more concentrated than income level and the number of firms, signifying that the Internet is far from being an equalizer, and instead intensifies the differences between Italian areas. The above-mentioned trend is even more prominent if we observe the domain name specialization ratios and penetration rates rather than the number of registered domain names: Some provinces that come first in terms of number of firms and registered income are not included in the first 20 provinces in terms of domain name specialization and penetration rate. For example, Naples (Campania's capital) and Bari (Apulia's capital) are both in the fifth position in terms of income and registered firms (see Table 7), while in terms of penetration rate and domain name specialization, they are not even present in the first 20 provinces (see Table 5).

In addition, it is interesting to observe that only Northern and Central Italian provinces are more specialized in the Internet diffusion; in fact, as shown in Table 5, the first 20 provinces are nearly all in the North of Italy, except for Rome, Siena, Pisa, and Florence, which are Central Italian provinces (Rome is a province of Latium; Siena, Florence, and Pisa are in Tuscany).

Factors Contributing to the Digital Divide

To identify key factors in the existence of the digital divide at a regional level (the survey was conducted at a regional rather than a provincial level since many variables were available only at a regional level), and in order to verify whether the above-mentioned hypotheses are true, we identified five models:

- **Model 1:** A stepwise regression, taking as a dependent variable the penetration rate calculated every 100 firms and, as independent variables, economic indicators

- **Model 2:** A stepwise regression, taking as independent variables those indicators expressing the cultural activity of a given region

- **Model 3:** A stepwise regression, taking as independent variables those indicators expressing the educational level of a given region

- **Model 4:** A stepwise regression, taking into consideration demographic indicators

- **Model 5:** A stepwise regression, taking into consideration as independent variables those indicators connected to ICT

Table 8. Dependent variable and independent variables used within the survey

Dependent variable
penetration rate = Ratio between domains registered in each region and the number of firms in that region multiplied by 100 (source: our elaboration)
Independent variables for Model 1. – Economic indicators: Added value for employee in a given region (Source: Tagliacarne Institute); Total income in a given region (Source: Unioncamere); Per capita income in a given region (Source: Unioncamere); Proportion between patents registered in each region by USPTO and the number of firms in that region, multiplying that proportion by 100 (Source: USPTO-Elaboration); and Percentage of local unities with a number ≥ to 250 employees (Source: ISTAT-Elaboration)
Independent variables for Model 2. – Cultural indicator: Spending on theatre and music (Source: Tagliacarne Institute)
Independent variables for Model 3. – Educational level in every region: Number of graduates every 1,000 inhabitants (Source: MIUR elaboration); Number of employees devoted to research and development (Source: ISTAT); Graduates in technical scientific subjects (Source: MIUR); and Providers/maintainers number (Source: our elaboration)
Independent variables for Model 4. – Regional demographic indicators: Resident population in every region (Source: ISTAT); and Unemployment rate in every region (Source: ISTAT)
Independent variables for Model 5. – Regional technological indicator: Ratio of IT expenditure in each region and the number of firms in that region (Source: Assinform/NetConsulting elaboration)

In the stepwise regression, independent variables are inserted into the equation if the F probability is ≤ 0.050, while they are removed from the equation if the F probability is ≥ 0.100.

The dependent and independent variables used by the models listed above are described in Table 8.

Nevertheless, all models show the multi-colinearity problem: The variables studied in each model could be correlated to the independent variables examined in the other models, generating an evaluation distortion. For example, the independent variable *number of registered patents* of Model 1 could be correlated in a positive or negative way to the independent variable *number of employees devoted to research and development* of Model 3.

Testing Hypotheses H1-H3 (Model 1)

The purpose of Model 1 is to verify whether the disadvantaged areas in terms of economic Internet diffusion among Italian regions is the *added value per employee* ($R^2 = 0.64$) (see Table 9). The rest of the variables analyzed in the model prove to have little significance as they do not reflect the above-mentioned insertion principles. Although the above-mentioned variables are not very significant in expression of variance at a regional level, economic indicators such as total income, per capita income, number of registered patents for every 100 firms, and percentage of large firms are positively correlated to the penetration rate (Pearson's correlation between penetration rate and the economic variables indicated above, proves to be equal to 0.480, 0.737, 0.702, 0.539 respectively) (see Table 10).

Table 12 indicates the ranking of the economic variables considered in this analysis and the penetration rate rank registered by firms with their head offices located in a given region.

Table 9. Coefficients (a) F= 32.62 SIG. = 0.000 R^2 = 0.644

Model		Non-Standardized Coefficients		Standardized Coefficients	t	Sig.
		B	Standard Error	Beta		
1	(Constant)	-13.383	3.909		-3.423	.003
	Added value per employee	.000	.000	.803	5.711	.000

Note: a dependent variable: Penetration rate

Table 10. Pearson's correlation matrix

	Penetration	Added Value per Employee	Percentage Large Firms	Total Income	Per Capita Income	Registered Patents per 100 Firms
Penetration	1.000					
Added value per employee	0.803**	1.000				
Percentage big firms	0.539*	0.637**	1.000			
Total income	0.480*	0.510*	0.921**	1.000		
Per capita income	0.737**	0.828**	0.314	0.166	1.000	
Registered patents every 100 firms	0.702*	0.717**	0.701**	0.611**	0.478*	1.000

*Note: ** the correlation is significant at the 0.01 level; * the correlation is significant at the 0.05 level*

Table 11. Descriptive statistics

	Penetration	Added Value per Employee	Percentage Large Firms	Total Income	Per Capita Income	Registered Patents per 100 Firms
Mean	8.85	45,972.66	.05	41,844.35	14,733.20	.20
Standard Deviation	2.61	4,331.36	.07	36,606.73	2,918.12	.17

As shown in Table 12, regions with a high added value per employee are the most inclined to use the Internet (as shown in Table 10, Pearson's correlation between added value per employee and penetration rate is 0.803). For example, Lombardy is the second region in terms of registered penetration rate, while it comes first in terms of added value per employee. The same can be said of Emilia Romagna, which is in sixth position in terms of added value per employee, and is seventh in terms of registered penetration rate. Instead, the total income does not seem to have a significant influence on Internet diffusion in Italy; as will be better illustrated later, Internet diffusion concerns only certain regions according to the total registered income and number of firms. In fact, as shown in Table 12, Trentino Alto Adige, which is in the first position in terms of registered penetration rate, loses position in terms of total income and percentage of big firms since it does not even

Table 12. Top ten regions by registered penetration rate and rank in terms of economic indicators

Regions	Penetration Rate Ranks	Added Value per Employee Ranks	Percentage Large Firms Ranks	Total Income Ranks	Per Capita Income Ranks	Registered Patents every 100 Firms Ranks
Trentino AA	1	5	14	15	2	10
Lombardy	2	1	1	1	5	2
Tuscany	3	10	6	7	6	8
Latium	4	2	4	2	7	5
Friuli Venezia Giulia	5	8	7	14	10	1
Veneto	6	9	5	3	8	6
Emilia Romagna	7	6	2	4	4	4
Piedmont	8	4	3	5	9	3
Umbria	9	11	15	17	11	11
(the) Marches	10	12	11	12	12	7

appear among the first ten regions. The same can be said about Umbria, which is in the 9th position in terms of registered penetration rate, while it is in the 15th and 17th positions in terms of percentage of large firms and total income. Also, good indicators expressing a significant correlation with the penetration rate are per capita income and the number of patents calculated per 100 firms (see Table 10). As a matter of fact, Trentino Alto Adige, in the first position in terms of registered penetration rate, is in the second position in terms of per capita income. Lombardy is in the second position in terms of registered patents every 100 firms and is also second in terms of registered penetration rate.

Testing Hypothesis H4 (Model 2)

Model 2 seems to confirm somewhat the combination of technological indicators and cultural indicators (Florida, 2002). The results are shown in Table 13.

Although the model is rather plain, it expresses only 34% of ICT diffusion variance among Italian regions ($R^2 = 0.34$); the independent variables have a statistically-significant positive effect in the ICT diffusion.

The H5 hypothesis is confirmed: The Internet is more diffuse in Italian regions where there is considerable spending on theatre and music (the correlation between the "spending on theatre and music" variable and the penetration rate is positive and significantly different from zero, Beta is equal to 0.587) (see Table 13).

Table 15 shows the aforementioned tendency even more markedly. Although the cultural indicator (spending on theatre and music) is not strictly correlated to the penetration rate, the correlation is positive (see Table 13). In fact, some regions that are in the lowest position in terms of registered penetration rate also occupy the lowest positions in terms of investment in cultural activities; for example, the Marches occupy 10th place in terms of penetration rate and 11th place in terms of spending on cultural activities.

Additionally, it is interesting to observe that, as might be expected, the cultural indicator is strongly related to the number of registered domain names (see Table 15). Many regions such as Piedmont, Lombardy, Veneto, Emilia Romagna, and Latium occupy the same positions both in terms of registered domain names and investment in spending on cultural activities investment. In fact, the Pearson relation between the number of registered domain names and cultural indicator is equal to 0.97 against a relation between cultural indicator and penetration equal to 0.58. Besides this, although it is useful to

Table 13. Coefficients (a) – $R^2 = 0.34$ F = 9.442

Model		Non-Standardized Coefficients		Standardized Coefficients	t	Sig.
		B	Standard Error	Beta		
2	(Constant)	7.464	.663		11.266	.000
	Spending on theatre and music	3.557E-05	.000	.587	3.073	.007

Note: a dependent variable: Penetration rate

Table 14. Descriptive statistics

	Mean	Standard Deviation	N
Penetration rate	8.85	2.61	20
Spending on theatre and music	38941.75	43027.62	20

Table 15. Top ten regions in terms of registered penetration rate and their ranks in terms of spending on theatre and music

Regions	Penetration Rate Rank	Registered Domains Rank	Cultural Indicator Rank
Trentino AA	1	11	13
Lombardy	2	1	1
Tuscany	3	5	5
Latium	4	2	2
Friuli Venezia Giulia	5	13	10
Veneto	6	3	3
Emilia Romagna	7	4	4
Piedmont	8	6	6
Umbria	9	16	14
(the) Marches	10	10	11

take as a dependent variable the number of registered domains, in this chapter we analyze only the penetration rate because we believe that this value better represents Internet diffusion among firms in the Italian regions.

Testing Hypothesis H5 (Model 3)

Table 16 shows that the degree of education plays an important role in ICT diffusion among firms. The model expresses 93.4% of the Internet variance diffusion among Italian regions ($R^2 = 0.938$): Regions with a number of employees devoted to research and development and with a higher number of Providers/Maintainers (Providers/Maintainers are companies that register a domain name for somebody else, offer connection to the Internet services, manage electronic mail, and so on; in practice, they are companies specialized in ICT services) are more inclined to utilize the new technology.

The following tables show the correlation matrix between the variables identified in the model, the descriptive statistics, and finally, the rank of observed variables.

Table 17 shows that the penetration rate registered by firms in the various Italian regions is strongly related to the number of Providers/Maintainers; regions with firms specializing in offering ICT-related services are more apt

Table 16. Coefficients (a) - R²=0.938 F=56.58 Sig.=0.000

Model		Non-Standardized Coefficients		Standardized Coefficients	t	Sig.
		B	Standard Error	Beta		
3	(Constant)	8.422	1.015		8.294	.000
	Providers/Maintainers per 1,000 firms	29.844	3.663	.702	8.148	.000
	Graduates in technical/ scientific subjects	-.086	.015	-.430	-5.849	.000
	Number of graduates per 1,000 inhabitants	-.033	.011	-.232	-2.884	.011
	Number of employees devoted to research and development	.442	.175	.195	2.518	.024

Note: a dependent variable: Penetration rate

Table 17. Pearson's correlation matrix

	Penetration	Providers/ Maintainers per 1,000 Firms	Graduates in Technical/ Scientific Subjects	Number of Graduates per 1,000 Inhabitants	Number of Employees Devoted to Research and Development
Penetration	1.000				
Providers/Maintainers per 1,000 firms	0.767**	1.000			
Graduates in technical scientific subjects	-0.254	0.312	1.000		
Number of graduates per 1,000 inhabitants	-0.713**	-0.448*	0.183	1.000	
Number of employees devoted to research and development	0.642**	0.488*	-0.001	-0.451*	1.000

*Note: ** the correlation is significant at the 0.01 level; * the correlation is significant at the 0.05 level*

to utilize the new technology (the correlation is equal to 0.704, positive and significantly different from zero); however, even the number of employees working in research and development is a decisive factor in Internet diffusion among firms (the correlation is equal to 0.642).

Besides this, a result worth mentioning is that the number of graduates, unlike the other variables expressing the educational attainment level at a regional level, cannot be considered as a factor affecting Internet diffusion among firms; Pearson's correlation between the number of graduates per 1,000 inhabitants and the penetration rate calculated per 100 firms proves to be negative and significantly different from zero (the correlation is equal to -0.713 at a significance level of 0.01).

The following table shows the trend described above. The factors expressing diffusion among firms at a regional level are the number of Providers/Maintainers in proportion to the number of firms and the number of employees working in research and development. As shown in Table 19, if we consider the rank based on the number of Providers/Maintainers, Trentino Alto Adige and Lombardy are in the first and second positions respectively in terms of registered penetration rate and the number of Providers/Maintainers.

Even the number of employees devoted to research and development assumes a decisive role: Some regions such as Umbria, which is in the 9th position in terms of penetration rate, is in the 8th position in terms of employees devoted to research and development. On the contrary, the variable "number of graduates per 1,000 inhabitants" shows a trend opposed to the penetration rate. Regions with a low level of educational attainment, calculated in terms of graduates, register a high penetration rate; as shown in Table 19, the

Table 18. Descriptive statistics

	Penetration	Providers/ Maintainers per 1,000 Firms	Graduates in Technical Scientific Subjects	Number of Graduates per 1,000 Inhabitants	Number of Employees Devoted to Research and Development
Mean	8.85	.13	29.27	62.30	2.34
Standard Deviation	2.61	.061	13.08	18.40	1.15

number of graduates in proportion to the population is higher in Southern regions: Abruzzo, Molise, Apulia, Campania, Basilicata, Calabria, Sicily, and Sardinia. Southern Italian regions that are less inclined to use the new technology register a higher number of graduates than Northern and Central regions except for Latium (Central region), which is in the fifth position.

The Northern and Central regions, which were in the top positions when taking into consideration all the economic, cultural, and technological indicators utilized in this chapter, are in the lowest positions in terms of graduates. This trend is explained by the fact that in less industrialized areas where job opportunities are scarce, 19-year-olds tend to continue their studies and graduate with the hope of finding a job more easily (and usually find jobs in the North or in the Center of Italy anyway), while in the more industrialized Northern and Central regions where there are more job opportunities, young people tend to discontinue their studies and start working soon after obtaining their secondary-school diploma. This can be seen in Table 19, which shows the rank according to the number of graduates per 1,000 inhabitants, and in Table 23, which shows the rank according to the registered unemployment rate. Northern Italian regions register fewer graduates per 1,000 inhabitants, but consequently they have a low unemployment rate; for example, Trentino

Table 19. Top ten regions in terms of registered penetration rates and their ranks in terms of indicators expressing cultural level of Italian regions

Regions	Penetration Rate Rank	Providers/ Maintainers per 1,000 Firms Rank	Graduates in Technical Scientific Subjects Rank	Number of Graduates per 1,000 Inhabitants Rank	Number of Employees Devoted to Research and Development Rank
Trentino AA	1	1	18	20	11
Lombardy	2	2	10	16	5
Tuscany	3	4	9	18	7
Latium	4	6	16	5	1
Veneto	6	7	12	13	12
Friuli Venezia Giulia	5	5	15	10	4
Emilia Romagna	7	11	7	19	3
Piedmont	8	9	5	15	2
Umbria	9	3	3	11	8
(the) Marches	10	10	17	12	14

Alto Adige, the region with the lowest unemployment rate in Italy, is the region with the fewest graduates per 1,000 inhabitants. In fact, the correlation between the number of graduates and the unemployment rate is equal to 0.728 with a significance level of 0.01.

Testing Hypothesis H6 (Model 4)

Model 4 shows that a linear relation exists between the demographic indicator and the registered penetration rate, partially confirming hypothesis 6: The adjustment can be considered satisfactory, as Model 4 explains approximately 68% of the total variability (**$R^2 = 0.680$**).

Regions with a high unemployment rate are less inclined to utilize the new technology; the correlation between the penetration rate and the unemployment rate is negative and significantly different from zero, being equal to -0735 (see Table 20). In fact, as shown in Table 23, Trentino Alto Adige, which comes first in terms of registered penetration rate, is the region with the lowest unemployment rate in Italy.

Moreover, although some populated regions are first in terms of registered penetration rate such as Lombardy and Veneto, the other populated regions such as Campania, Apulia, and Sicily do not even appear in the first ten positions in terms of penetration rate (see Table 23). In fact, the correlation between the penetration rate and the residing population is only equal to 0.337.

These results agree with the previous statement that the most populated regions are not always the first to take advantage of new technology.

Table 20. Coefficients (a) - $R^2 = 0.680$ F = 18.079 Sig. 0.000

Model		Non-Standardized Coefficients		Standardized Coefficients	t	Sig.
		B	Standard Error	Beta		
4	(Constant)	10.239	.719		14.231	.000
	Unemployment rate	-.263	.048	-.754	-5.488	.000
	Resident population	4.154E-07	.000	.375	2.731	.014

Note: a dependent variable: Penetration rate

Testing Hypothesis H7 (Model 5)

As expected, Hypothesis 7 is also confirmed: The infrastructure supply is a good indicator for measuring the existence of the digital divide; the technological indicator also has a statistically-significant positive effect on ICT diffusion (on the whole, Model 5 is significant given the significance of the statistics F, 0.01) (see Table 24). In addition, there is a direct relation between penetration rate and the indicator expressing infrastructures in ICT, (the beta is equal to 0.673, positive and significantly different from zero at 0.01 level); this means that some regions with a high investment in IT also register a high penetration rate.

In addition, even the above-mentioned model expresses a variance of only 45% of ICT diffusion among Italian regions.

An initial conclusion is that although as suggested in the literature (Chinn & Fairlie, 2004; Guillén & Suaréz, 2001; Kiiski et al., 2002), infrastructures play an important role in determining the digital divide in Italy; economic indicators and indicators related to educational level are also important for explaining the disparity in Internet use among Italian provinces.

Table 21. Pearson's correlation matrix

	Penetration	Unemployment Rate	Resident Population
Penetration	1.000		
Unemployment rate	-0.735**	1.000	
Resident population	0.337	0.050	1.000

*Note: ** the correlation is significant at the 0.01 level; * the correlation is significant at the 0.05 level*

Table 22. Descriptive statistics

	Penetration	Unemployment Rate	Resident Population
Mean	8.85	9.87	2,894,412.25
Standard Deviation	2.61	7.49	2,355,890.75

Table 23. Top 10 regions in terms of registered penetration rate and their ranks in terms of demographic indicators

Regions	Penetration Rate Rank	Unemployment Rate Rank	Residing Population Rank
Trentino AA	1	20	16
Lombardy	2	18	1
Tuscany	3	12	9
Latium	4	8	3
Friuli Venezia Giulia	5	16	15
Veneto	6	19	5
Emilia Romagna	7	17	7
Piedmont	8	13	6
Umbria	9	11	17
(the) Marches	10	14	13

Tables 25 and 26 reports descriptive statistics about the variables studied in Model 5 and the ranking of regions with reference to the penetration rate and the indicator for ICT infrastructures.

As we see in the table above and in agreement with the literature, ICT diffusion among Italian firms at the regional level is influenced by investment in IT. Actually, some regions that come first in terms of registered penetration

Table 24. Coefficients (a) - R^2=0.45 F=14.878 Sig. = 0.01

Model		Non-Standardized Coefficients		Standardized Coefficients	t	Sig.
		B	Standard Error	Beta		
5	(Constant)	4.705	1.162		4.047	.001
	Ratio of IT expenditure in each region and number of firms in that region	1.077	.279	.673	3.857	.001

Note: a dependent variable: Penetration rate

Table 25. Descriptive statistics

	Mean	Standard Deviation	N
Penetration	8.8490	2.60929	20
Ratio of IT expenditure in each region and number of firm in that region	3.8480	1.62975	20

Table 26. Top ten regions in terms of penetration rate and their ranks in terms of investment in IT

Regions	Penetration Rate Ranks	Technological Indicator Ranks
Trentino AA	1	6
Lombardy	2	2
Tuscany	3	8
Latium	4	1
Friuli Venezia Giulia	5	4
Veneto	6	7
Emilia Romagna	7	5
Piedmont	8	3
Umbria	9	15
(the) Marches	10	13

rate are the first positions also in terms of spending on ICT investment, and the regions in the last positions in terms of spending in investments in ICT are also in the last positions in terms of registered penetration rate. For example, Lombardy comes 2nd both in terms of registered penetration rate and in IT investment; Veneto comes in 7th in terms of ICT investments while in terms of registered penetration rate it is in the 6th position; and Liguria is in the 11th position both in terms of registered penetration rate and ICT investment.

Discussion and Conclusion

Our chapter analyzes the contributing factors in the existence of the digital divide in Italy. The econometric analysis shows that the indicators relating to education, in particular the number of firms specializing in selling ICT services, substantially contribute to the existence of the digital divide among firms that have their head offices in a given region and, as the economics literature suggests (De Arcangelis et al., 2002), the number of employees devoted to research and development also becomes a crucial element.

Another key factor in the existence of the digital divide in Italy, according to results obtained by other studies (Kiiski et al., 2002; Pohjola, 2004) is determined by economic indicators. Especially in Italy, the added value per employee is a variable that significantly expresses Internet diffusion among variance of Italian firms.

The technological indicator, calculated according to investments in IT among Italian regions, is an important factor in the existence of the digital divide in Italy: however, it does not significantly express the variance of Internet diffusion at a regional level. Some researchers disagree with this result. For example, Chen, Boase, and Wellman (2002) and UCLA (2000, 2003) find that, in addition to income, access costs are strong predictors of Internet use.

Finally, according to our results, we wish to highlight that in Italy, in disagreement with other researchers (Chinn & Fairlie, 2004; U.S. Department of Commerce, 1999), although the variable showing educational attainment at a regional level (i.e., the number of university graduates per 1,000 individuals) also has a statistically-significant effect on ICT diffusion, the correlation between this variable and the penetration rate registered by firms in a given region prove to be highly negative. This means that regions with a high number of graduates in proportion to the resident population are less inclined to utilize the new technology.

However, the results obtained in this chapter illustrate the factors contributing to the existence of the digital divide at a regional level, according to the number of domains registered by firms. It is obvious that economic indicators and other types of indicators related to education, compared to the number of graduates in Italy, such as the number of employees devoted to research and development or the providers/maintainers number, are the foremost elements contributing to the existence of the digital divide among firms.

On this point in a future study, it would be desirable to analyze Internet diffusion in Italy among individuals and compare the results with the analysis carried out in this chapter.

In conclusion, the digital divide in Italy depends on the degree of educational attainment, on regions that are productively efficient (efficiency calculated in terms of added value per employee), and with a low unemployment rate.

In addition, in this chapter we not only identified the factors contributing to the existence of the digital divide but also, by analyzing data, observed the presence of a serious issue: Italian regions with a low economic development and regions with a high unemployment rate appear to be underdeveloped even from a technological point of view. The difference between those who use the Internet and those who do not is another factor that contributes to the widening of a gap that makes geographical areas uneven (Northern and Central regions of Italy not only are wealthier and more highly industrialized, with a high productive efficiency and in the forefront compared to Southern regions, but are also the regions with higher penetration rates). In the first instance, the Internet could be a pervasive phenomenon justified by the decentralized, non-hierarchical, immaterial nature of Internet technology (Negroponte, 1995), which in principle does not have strong barriers to entry as in manufacturing (for example, if a new manufacturing company decides to enter a highly competitive sector of the market, some barriers might be big companies with strong contractual powers or high investment costs required to enter the market). This means that everyone in Italy could take advantage of the potential of the Internet due to its low cost of access. In addition, use of the Internet by an individual does not reduce its possibility of being used as a resource by someone else (immaterial nature); on the contrary, it offers benefits not only to that individual but to all users (network externality, Metcalfe Law) (Hansons, 2000). Data show that this effect does not take place at all at a provincial level. Domains are even more concentrated than the number of firms and income. Ranking of provinces by penetration rate shows that Internet distribution follows wide differences in income level: Even when some provinces have a large number of firms and high income, they do not always come first in terms of registered penetration rate.

Before drawing conclusions, these data should be compared to those on the use of domains by individuals, and this comparison is currently in progress. Our preliminary conclusion is that Internet technology, rather than serving as an equalizer, intensifies existing differences in economic opportunities.

References

AMD Global Consumer Advisory Board. (2002). First-ever comparative analysis of Internet access and use. Retrieved from http://www.amdg-cab.org/

Bassi, M. C. (2002). *La Catalogazione delle Risorse Informative in Internet.* Milano: Editrice Bibliografica.

Bauer, J. M., Berne, M., & Maitland, C. F. (2002). Internet access in the European Union and in the United States. *Telematics and Informatics, 19*(2), 117-137.

Beilock, R., & Dimitrova, D. V. (2003). An exploratory model of inter-country Internet diffusion. *Telecommunications Policy, 27*(3), 237-252.

Castells, M. (2001). *The Internet galaxy.* New York: Oxford University Press.

Chen, W., Boase, J., & Wellman, B. (2002). The global villagers: Comparing Internet users and uses around the world. In B. Wellman & C. Haythornthwaite (Eds.), *The Internet in everyday life* (pp. 74-113). Malden, MA: Blackwell.

Chinn, M. D., & Fairlie, R. W. (2004). *The determinants of the global digital divide: A cross-country analysis of computer and Internet penetration* (Working Papers 881). Economic Growth Center, Yale University.

Coffman, K. G., & Odlyzko, A. M. (2002). *Growth of the Internet.* AT&T Labs—Research.

Dasgupta, S., Lall, S. V., & Wheeler, D. (2001). *Policy reform, economic growth, and the digital divide: An econometric analysis.* World Bank—Development Economics Research Group (DECRG).

De Arcangelis, G., Jona-Lasinio, C., & Manzocchi, S. (2002). Sectoral determinants and dynamics of ICT investment in Italy. *Rivista di Politica Economica. Fascicolo V-VI (Maggio-Giugno)* 119-161.

Diez-Picazo, G. F. (1999). *An analysis of international Internet diffusion.* Masters of science in technology and policy thesis, Massachusetts Institute of Technology.

Fischer, C. S. (1992). *America calling: A social history of the telephone to 1940.* Berkeley, CA: University of California Press.

Florida, R. (2002). *The rise of the creative class and how it's transforming work. Leisure, community, and everyday life.* New York: Basic Books.

Gilder, G. (2000). *Telecosm: How infinite bandwidth will revolutionize our world.* New York: Free Press.

Gini, C. (1960). *Statistics.* Roma: Edizioni Metron.

Guillén, M. F., & Suárez, S. L. (2001). Developing the Internet: Entrepreneurship and public policy in Ireland, Singapore, Argentina, and Spain. *Telecommunications Policy, 25*(5), 349-371.

Guillén, M. F., & Suárez, S. L. (2004). Explaining the global digital divide: Economic, political, and sociological drivers of cross-national Internet use. *Social Forces, 84*(2), 681-708.

Hansons, W. (2000). *Internet marketing.* Milano: Ed. Tecniche Nuove.

Hargittai, E. (1999). Weaving the Western Web: Explaining differences in Internet connectivity among OECD countries. *Telecommunication Policy, 23*(10-11), 701-718.

Hoffman, D., Novak, T., & Perlata M. (1999). Building consumer trust online. *Communications of the ACM, 42*(4), 80-85.

ISTAT, Italy's National Statistical Institute. (2005). *Economical indicators database.* Retrieved from http://www.istat.it.

ITU (International Telecommunication Union). (2003). *World telecomunications indicators: Database.* Retrieved from http://www.itu.int/ti/pub-blications/world/world.htm

Johnson, E., Anantharaman, R. N., Amirtha Rajan, S. D., & Surgunam, S. (2005). Privacy and security concerns among Canadian Internet users: A national study. *E-Business Review, 5*, 87-90.

Kiiski, Sampsa, & Pohjola, M. (2002). Cross-country diffusion of the Internet. *Information Economics and Policy, 14*(2), 297-310.

Kirkman, G. S., Cornelius, P. K., Sachs, J. D., & Schwab, K. (2002). *The global information technology report, 2001-2002: Readiness for the networked world.* Oxford University Press.

Kovacich, G. (1998). Electronic-Internet business and security. *Computer & Security, 17*(2), 129-135.

Levy, B., & Spiller, P. T. (1994). The institutional foundations of regulatory commitment: A comparison analysis of telecommunications regulation. *Journal of Law, Economics, and Organizations, 10*(2), 201-246.

Lorenz, M. O. (1905). Methods of measuring the concentration of wealth. *Publications of the American Statistical Association, 9*(90), 209-219.

Maitland, C. F., & Bauer, J. M. (2001). National level culture and global diffusion: The case of the Internet. In C. Ess (Ed.), *Culture, technology, communication: Towards an intercultural global village* (pp. 87-128). Albany, NY: SUNY Press.

Naldi, M. (1997). Size estimation and growth forecast of the Internet. *Preprints del Centro Vito Volterra* n. 303, Roma: Università degli studi di Roma Tor Vergata.

Negroponte, N. (1995). *Being digital*. New York: Knopf.

NTIA, Economics and Statistics Administration (2002). A nation online: How Americans are expanding their use of the Internet. Retrieved from http://www.ntia.doc.gov/ntiahome/dn/nationonline_020502.htm

Norris, P. (2001). *Digital divide: Civic engagement, information poverty, and the Internet worldwide*. New York: Cambridge University Press.

NUA (Network Users Association) (2002). How many online? Retrieved from http://www.nua.com/surveys/how_many_online/index.html

O'Neil, D. (2001). Analysis of Internet users' level of online privacy concerns. *Social Science Computer Review, 19*(1), 17-31.

OECD (2004). Understanding the digital divide. Retrieved from htpp://www.oecd.org

Oxley, J. E., & Yeung, B. (2001). E-commerce readiness: Institutions and international competitiveness. *Journal of International Business Studies, 32*(4), 705-723.

Pohjola, M. (2004). *The adoption and diffusion of ITC across countries: Patterns and determinants. The new economy handbook*. Academy Press, forthcoming

RIPE-NCC (RIPE Network Coordination Centre). Internet diffusion analysis based on host count procedures. Retrieved from http://www.ripe.net

Rogers, E. (2001). The digital divide. *Convergence, 7*(4), 96-111.

Tapscott, D., & Caston, A. (1993). *Paradigm shift: The new promise of information technology*. New York: McGraw-Hill.

UCLA, Center for Communication Policy. (2000). *Surveying the digital future*. Los Angeles, CA. Retrieved from www.ccp.ucla.edu

UCLA, Center for Communication Policy. (2003). *Surveying the digital future: Year three.* Los Angeles, CA. Retrieved from www.ccp.ucla.edu

U.S. Department of Commerce. (1999). *Falling through the net: Defining the digital divide.* Washington, DC.

Wallsten, S. J. (2001). An econometric analysis of telecom competition, privatization, and regulation in Africa and Latin America. *Journal of Industrial Economics, 49*(1), 1-19.

Warschauer, M. (2002). Reconceptualizing the digital divide. *First Monday, 7*(7). Retrieved December 13, 2006 from http://www.firstmonday.org/issues/issue7_7/warschauer/index.html

Wilson, E. J., III (1998). Inventing the global information future. *Futures, 30*(1) 23-42.

Zook, M. A. (1998). *The Web of consumption: The spatial organization of the Internet industry in the United States.* Paper presented at the Association of Collegiate Schools of Planning Conference, Pasadena, CA, November 5-8.

Zook, M. A. (2000). Internet metrics: Using host and domain counts to map the Internet, *Telecommunications Policy, 24,* 6-7.

Zook, M. A. (2001). Old hierarchies or new network of centrality?—The global geography of the Internet content market. *American Behavioral Scientists, 44,* 1679-1696.

Chapter VIII

Analyzing E-Procurement Adoption Efforts:
Case Study of an Indian Steel Manufacturer[1]

Amit Agrahari, Infosys Technologies Ltd, India

Abstract

This case study looks into the evolution of various e-procurement systems at an Indian steel manufacturer, Tata Steel. This chapter argues that rather sticking to one system, organizations need to manage a portfolio of e-procurement systems to realize the full potential of the Internet. Further, these systems evolve over a period of time, thus necessitating dynamic instead of static analysis. Prior research has analyzed e-procurement and its predecessor, EDI-based IOIS, as a static game with adoption and subsidy being the key issues. However, with e-procurement increasingly being a competitive necessity, the issue is not "if to adopt e-procurement", but "how to adopt e-procurement". This chapter analyzes e-procurement adoption efforts in a dynamic game setting. First, the e-procurement adoption effort is analyzed in a "without subsidy" scenario and then in a "with subsidy" scenario. Results show that e-procurement adoption efforts are likely to be more if the buyer and suppliers are not myopic, and the rate of decay in strategic benefits from the dyadic relation is low. Further, the buyer can induce more effort from the supplier by offering him subsidies. The buyer will offer a subsidy only if he can take away more than half of the total e-procurement benefits. The level of subsidy depends on the effectiveness of the supplier's e-procurement adoption effort. Results for the game theoretic model are corroborated with the case study.

Introduction

Procurement has never been an easy task, especially if one has to handle more than 2,000 suppliers spread across a subcontinent. That was exactly the problem which Tata Steel was facing in the late 1990's. The procurement process involved lengthy paperwork, with a cycle time for purchase request to purchase order release of more than 60 days. Suppliers were demanding a more transparent selection process and better payment schedules. These inefficiencies also affected procurement planning and resulted in high inventory costs.

During 1991-1992, Tata Steel installed an IBM 2370 mainframe. An early effort to use IT in procurement was started in late 1990's, and a procurement system was developed over a DB/2 database. However, only a few key suppliers were provided the facility to see their orders and goods receipt notes (GRN). Further, this system was not equipped to support any transaction. It was not developed any further since a move to ERP was expected, and developing mainframe-based systems would have resulted in wasted efforts. In December 2001, Tata Steel adopted SAP as an ERP system, and a system for e-procurement was developed on the top of SAP. What followed is an example of how e-procurement can bring efficiencies in business processes and benefits for both buyers and suppliers. In 2003, Tata Steel was identified as the best IT user in the manufacturing sector in India by NASSCOM (an association of IT companies in India).

Industry Background

The Indian iron and steel industry is nearly a century old. Established in 1907, Tata Steel is the first integrated steel plant in Asia. Soon after India became an independent nation, the steel industry was categorized as reserved for government-owned public sector units (PSU). These reserved industries were heavily regulated through licenses and quotas. Until 1991, private organizations like Tata Steel did not have much competition, and their production capacity and distribution channels were regulated by government. Economic reforms were initiated in 1991, and the steel industry was deregulated, thus making it open for competition. Licensing requirements for capacity creation were abolished, and the industry was removed from the list of industries reserved for PSU. With a view to making the steel industry more efficient and competitive, foreign equity investments up to 100% were allowed, and price and distribution controls were removed. Restrictions on external trade, both in import and export, have been removed. Import duty rates have also been reduced drastically, making the Indian steel industry open to global competition.

The Organization

Today India is the tenth largest producer of steel in the world, with Tata Steel contributing over 13% to India's total steel production. Tata Steel is the second lowest-cost producer in the world. The company is India's single largest exporter of high-quality, value-added steel products. The company offers a diverse range of products and services. These include HR/CR coils and sheets, tubes, construction bars, forging quality steel, rods, structurals, strips and bearings, steel plant and material handling equipment, ferro alloys and other minerals, software for process controls, and cargo handling services. Tata Steel's turnover in the fiscal year 2003-2004 was nearly INR 980 billion (US$19.6 billion). The company's profit in the same year was

Table 1. Total procurement at Tata Steel for financial year 2003-2004

Category	Raw Materials	Process Consumables	Global Sourcing	Logistics and EPA	Services	Others	Profit Centers and out locations	Total
Buy Value FY 2004 ($ Million)	100	230	70	70	60	110	110	750

Note: All figures in US$ (50 INR = 1 US$ (Approximately))

INR 101.2 billion (US$2.2 billion), which is its highest-ever profit, and it produced a record-breaking 3.98 million tons of saleable steel.

E-Procurement Initiation

The move to e-procurement was initiated soon after SAP was implemented at Tata Steel. This move was the catalyst in transforming the procurement division into a knowledge-based buying organization (Figure 1). From December 1 to 5, 2001, Tata Steel observed a blackout period to implement ERP with a big-bang approach. IBM mainframes were replaced by client server architecture, and SAP was the ERP system implemented on ORACLE database. The old procurement system gave way to a Web-enabled system. The maintainence, repair and operations (MRO) team had two options in front of them, either to wait for SAP to stabilize and then develop the e-procurement system, or start developing the e-procurement system right away. It was estimated that if Tata Steel waited for ERP to stabilize, the e-procurement system could not be developed before December, 2002. Smelling the urgency and opportunity cost involved, they decided to take up e-procurement development right away.

Because of architectural similarities, expertise generated while developing the procurement system for the mainframe came very handily, and Tata Steel could develop an e-procurement system by April, 2002. Pilot implementation involved suppliers from the rapid-order segment (a low-value, high-transaction segment). Most of the suppliers in this segment are local suppliers and in vicinity to Tata Steel. They were not too technology-savvy, and most of them did not have any formal technical training for using computers and the Internet. The pilot project also enabled SAP and the e-procurement system to evolve simultaneously. By July, 2002, both SAP and e-procurement systems were stabilized, and all suppliers in the rapid-order segment were migrated to the e-procurement system.

During the dot com boom, Indian industry observed the emergence of several vertical and horizontal procurement portals. Tata Steel also had a spate of offers to join domestic and international e-commerce platforms for the steel industry. Rather than joining any ill-conceived dot com, Tata Steel set up internal e-commerce task forces to study various e-commerce models that had sprung up during the dot com boom. It came to a conclusion that while e-commerce is definitely the way forward, it would make more business sense for two or three of the largest players in a similar industry/region to come together and consolidate their e-commerce plans on a common platform. Thus, MetalJunction.com was born, which is a separate entity with equal equity of SAIL (a government-owned PSU) and Tata Steel.

Figure 1. Journey from transactional unit to a knowledge based buying organization

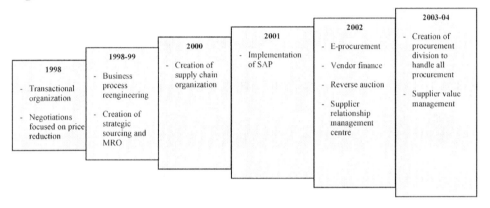

Table 2. Tata Steel's journey to e-procurement

1999-2000
➢ Auto bill payment through IBM ➢ Auto-indenting for fast and medium-moving items ➢ Electronic routing and approval ➢ Decision support system for stores
2000-2001
➢ E-procurement ➢ Lotus notes for e-mail communication ➢ Supply chain, MRO home page launched I intranet
2001-2002
➢ Implementation of SAP-MM module (i.e., stabilization completed) ➢ Implementation of e-procurement in MRO(P) ➢ Linkage of e-procurement with SAP ➢ Reverse auction ➢ Import orders to TLL thru e-route ➢ Use of intranet for receiving customer complaints
2002-2003
➢ Online "Code of Conduct" through e-procurement site ➢ Supplier satisfaction survey through e-procurement site ➢ Online bidding for price discovery

E-Procurement Adoption

Johnston and Mak (2000) observed that in traditional electronic data interchange (EDI) systems, only 20% of suppliers, by number, who account for 80% of transaction value, participate, and thus a large proportion of suppliers, usually small to medium-size enterprises (SMEs) supplying small ranges of products, remain outside the EDI. Further, e-procurement inherently carries higher adoption and implementation risks, since suppliers' adoption decision and implementation practices cannot be controlled by the initiator. To overcome these risks, Riggins, Kriebel, and Mukhopadhyay (1994) proposed various subsidy strategies. These include e-readiness audit, identifying subsidy needs, providing monitory as well as non-monitory subsidies, and so forth. The major hindrance in e-procurement adoption is the lack of technology awareness. A subsidy in the form of free training sessions is a good strategy to overcome this problem. Tata Steel conducted training sessions on internal e-procurement systems for its suppliers across the country. Since Tata Steel has to cover all its existing suppliers, the expenditure on training was quite high. The objective of these sessions included technical training and confidence building. To provide technical training, Tata Steel collaborated with a local training institute, SNTI, and installed a few computer systems where suppliers can see and feel how the e-procurement system works. They were also provided with a CD that included a tutorial on e-procurement. Suppliers who could not come to Jamshedpur or attend any meetings were offered the training modules over the net. Meetings were also scheduled in various cities with suppliers. In a bid to place an emphasis on confidence building, Tata Steel communicated to its suppliers very clearly that the system is not a threat to their business in any way. Initial resistance also included fear related to system security and information revelation. To overcome these fears, Tata Steel got a BS7799 (a security standard) certificate for its Information system including the e-procurement system. Suppliers who have already adopted an e-procurement system were called to discuss their experiences with other suppliers. Tata Steel also installed e-procurement clinics with the help of some tech-savvy suppliers. These suppliers were early adopters who helped other suppliers in their vicinity to overcome initial technical problems. Apart from these initiatives, an e-procurement help desk was also installed to redress both technical and non-technical issues and problems.

Despite these efforts to increase suppliers' e-procurement readiness, Tata Steel could not invoke a high usage rate (Figure 2). By November, 2002, over 90% of suppliers were made e-partners, that is, they were registered with Tata Steel and had access to the Internet. However, less than 35% of suppliers were using the system. In November, 2002, Tata Steel decided to make e-procurement mandatory for its suppliers.

As observed by Iacovou, Benbasat, and Dexter (1995), external pressure, especially from a trading partner, is the most prominent factor that explains a supplier's e-procurement adoption. Today, over 90% of Tata Steel's total supplier base uses the e-procurement system. There are some big vendors, NGOs, and research labs that continue to use old paper-based systems. Getting these people to use the e-procurement system is still a challenge, and Tata Steel needs to develop a strategy to have them participate.

Apart from all MRO suppliers, by February 2003, suppliers of sparse planning and outsourcing (SPOS) were also included in the e-procurement systems. This unit manufactures equipments against drawings, which are used in Tata Steel. Encouraged with the results, Tata Steel went ahead and by April, 2003, the Kolkata office also started using the e-procurement systems. Around the same time, Growth Shop, a profit centre owned by Tata Steel which manufactures equipment, also started using the e-procurement systems. Growth Shop is situated at Aadityapur, which is approximately 18 kilometers away from Tata Steel's plant. The backbone, however, was not SAP; it was BANN in Growth Shop.

Figure 2. E-procurement adoption by suppliers

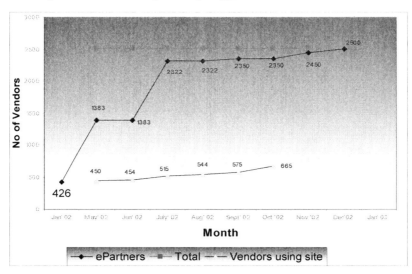

Values Generated from E-Procurement

Savings in procurement price is the most often cited benefit of the e-procurement system. However, procurement managers at Tata Steel think that the benefits are more in terms of improved efficiency and better buyer/supplier relationships. The e-procurement system has brought much needed transparency into the procurement process. Unlike the paper-based system, where audit trails were not available, e-procurement has enabled auditing of the entire process, from purchase order generation to quotations submission to final bid submitted.

Operational Benefits

Transaction costs have been lowered since lengthy paperwork and mailing of RFQs and orders are now done automatically by the computer system. E-procurement systems have reduced the cycle time for purchase request to RFQ generation to only a few hours (Figure 3). The total cycle time estimated for purchase request generation to purchase order generation is reduced to 14 days as compared to 60 days in the manual system. Savings from strategic sourcing drive is given in Figure 4. Similarly, inventory reduction in the last three years is shown in Figure 5. However, price reduction because of internal e-procurement systems alone is not available.

Price reduction because of MetalJunction.com is given in Table 3. By 2003, March-end Tata Steel had procured materials and services totaling Rs. 902.5 million (US$18.05 million) through MetalJunction.com. Procurement through MetalJunction.com has brought in more competition and has ensured that prices were either reduced or maintained.

Impact of E-Procurement Systems on Inter-Organizational Relationships

E-procurement systems have brought much needed transparency in the supplier selection process at Tata Steel. Before the e-procurement systems, suppliers frequently complained about quotations not being evaluated. Now the process provides an audit trail; any quotation submitted can be traced back, and the reason for its selection or rejection can be ascertained. This

Figure 3. Actual reduction in order lead time

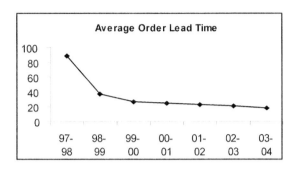

Figure 4. Projected and actual strategic sourcing savings

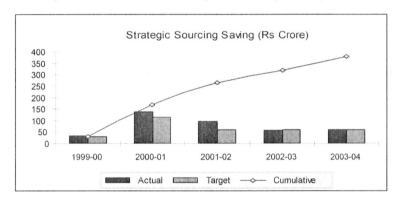

Figure 5. Inventory reduction in last three years

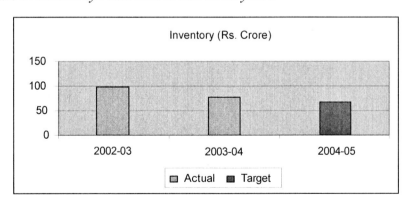

Table 3. The savings in procurement using metaljunction.com for financial year 2002-2003

Category (All figures in US$ {50 INR = 1 US$, approximately})	Value Procured	Actual Savings over Last Procured Price	% Savings
Chemicals	4,056,600	647,700	15.97%
Electrical Consumables	3,350,320	355,060	10.60%
Explosives	2,712,000	75,460	2.78%
Ferro Alloys	481,800	5,700	1.18%
General Consumables	2,939,880	254,760	8.67%
Instruments	2,124,740	497,840	23.43%
Logistics	7,732,000	449,720	5.82%
Mechanical Consumables	1,883,200	244,400	12.98%
Non-Ferrous Metal, Iron Metallics	8,467,200	0	0.00%
Petroleum by-products	1,686,920	166,380	9.86%
Pharmaceuticals	21,820	0	0.00%
Refractories	3,570,760	44,420	1.24%
Total	39,027,240	2,741,420	7.02%

can lead to enhanced trust between Tata Steel and its suppliers. Further, the e-procurement system has enabled suppliers to participate in any bidding process despite their physical location. This means that suppliers do not have to lose business just because they are not in close proximity. However, the impact of different e-procurement systems on inter-organizational relationships cannot be assumed to be the same. Suppliers using MetalJunction. com have reported pressure on their profit margins. The head of Tata Steel's procurement division thinks that suppliers prefer bidding online rather than participating in the tender process. The reason for this preference stems from greater transparency in the online procurement process, because the rules are predefined and the lowest price is known to all participants. Since the time required for negotiation is reduced to just an hour or so, it frees their time to develop new business. Further, as online procurement is rarely "maverick buying", hence despite margins coming under pressure, a supplier's order position is more secure. Similarly, in internal e-bidding, since the numbers of suppliers have remained more or less the same, the impact of this system was limited to reduced transaction cost and better transparency. Since volume integration does not take place, it was not perceived by suppliers as a move to increase Tata Steel's bargaining power and competition among suppliers.

Managing a Portfolio of E-Procurement Systems

In the late 1990's, Tata Steel started its move to e-procurement. Today it procures almost everything through the e-procurement system except capital goods and imports. Over a period of time, Tata Steel has adopted four e-procurement systems. They can be broadly classified as consortium-sponsored and internal e-procurement systems. MetalJunction.com is a consortium-sponsored system, whereas the next three are internal e-procurement systems:

1. MetalJunction.com, an e-market promoted by a consortium of SAIL and Tata Steel

2. An internal e-bidding system

3. E-negotiation system

4. Online stock information from vendor through the Internet

MetalJunction.com, an industry portal, conducts reverse auctions and market-making activities for procurement and sales. It charges different fees for different services offered. Fees range from a low of 0.1% to a high of 7.5% of goods sold/procured (in 2002-2003), and it is revised every year. Together Tata Steel and SAIL produce over 60% of India's total steel production. Therefore, the market-making services offered by MetalJunction.com enable Tata Steel to reach to a broader supplier base. Today, MetalJunction. com provides e-procurement, e-selling, and channel finance services to Tata Steel, and has saved INR 53.7 million (US$1.07 million) or approximately 5.96% of total procurement cost.

The internal e-procurement site offers Web-based multi-directional flow of transactional and business information, between participants. All cross-organizational elements of the inbound supply chain, including enquiry/RFQ details, online and off-line quotation logging, order placement, delivery compliance monitoring, order amendments, material receipt, and payment tracking are covered and transacted through this site. This site offers three kinds of e-procurement systems, namely e-bidding; e-negotiation, and online stock information.

An internal e-bidding system was developed that has integrated internal ERP systems with the e-procurement system. To avoid any conflict of interest with MetalJunction.com, only Tata Steel's existing suppliers are allowed to participate in this system. This means that new suppliers cannot bid through the internal e-bidding system.

The e-negotiation system facilitates one-to-one negotiation with multiple suppliers simultaneously. In this system, suppliers cannot see the lowest bid offered by other suppliers. In addition, value-added services such as negotiation chat rooms, transactional correspondence (mails initiated on a transaction hitting appropriate mailboxes), and e-mail notifications and acknowledgments are also offered.

An online stock information system is also initiated with VMI suppliers, which enables inventory information sharing between a buyer and a supplier. Suppliers have to upload inventory information using a Web server, and Tata Steel's e-procurement system retrieves it and provides it automatically to the internal users. Information regarding inventory at the supplier's premises, stock in transit, and inventory at Tata Steel are provided by this system. This system is in the early stages, and so far only one supplier has implemented this system. Unlike other e-procurement systems, this system requires a substantial investment by suppliers in Web servers, and operating costs are also high for the suppliers.

These systems differ in e-procurement adoption effort and the number of suppliers which are participating. E-procurement adoption effort is a function of the level of integration and the number of document sets transacted through e-route. MetalJunction.com is not integrated with Tata Steel's internal system, but the number of suppliers which are participating is significantly higher. Tata Steel's internal systems are low in number of participants, but high on e-procurement adoption effort. Though there is a general preference towards the internal e-procurement system, MetalJunction.com is still used quite often. MetalJunction.com is preferred when the volume is quite high, and the buyer feels a need for scanning the entire market. Every year, Tata Steel carries out a buy analysis to decide whether to go for cost savings or increase buying efficiency. Based on this analysis, the right channel mix is decided (Figure 9).

Figure 6. Graphical representation of Tata Steel's procurement process

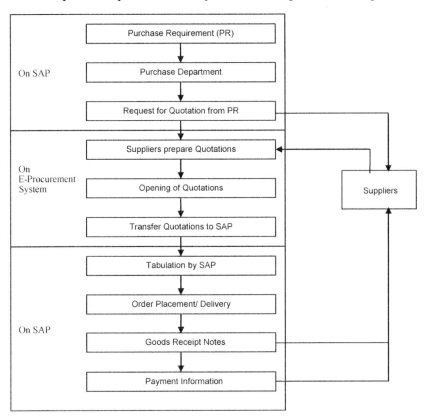

Figure 7. Graphical representation of internal e-procurement system

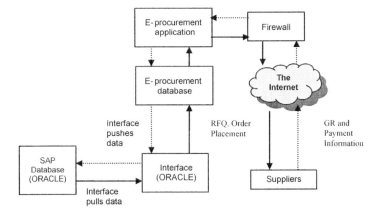

Figure 8. Graphical representation of metaljunction.com architecture

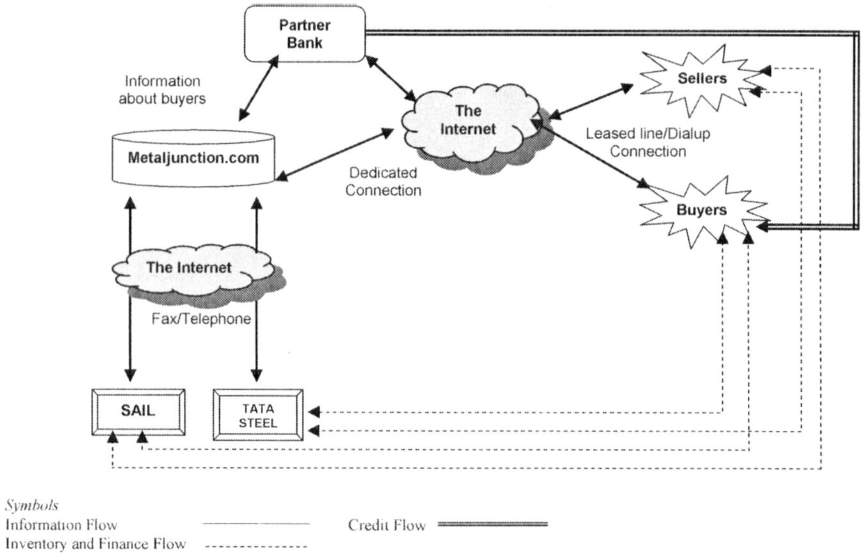

Figure 9. Portfolio of e-procurement system

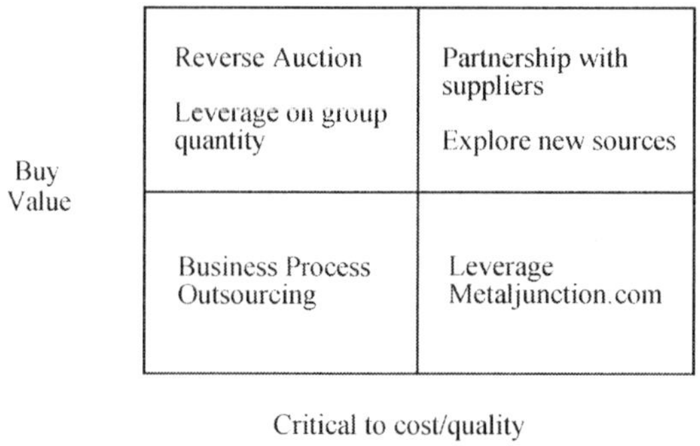

Reverse Auction Leverage on group quantity	Partnership with suppliers Explore new sources
Business Process Outsourcing	Leverage Metaljunction.com

Buy Value

Critical to cost/quality

Analyzing E-Procurement Adoption Effort: A Differential Game Theoretic Approach

In the previous section, we have illustrated the evolution of various e-procurement systems at TATA Steel. To generalize our findings, we will develop a game theoretic model and corroborate findings from our case study. E-procurement can be analyzed using various lenses such as transaction costs economics, value chain, inter-organizational interdependencies, and so forth. Unlike its predecessor, EDI-based IOISs (Inter-Organizational Information Systems), e-procurement has greater reach and can fundamentally change the way organizations generate and add value. Existing literature on e-procurement and IOIS have widely used transaction cost economics (TCE) because of the mathematical tools and techniques it offers. This section reviews existing literature on e-procurement and IOIS to analyze e-procurement in a differential game setting. Unlike EDI-based IOIS, e-procurement is dynamic in nature and evolves over a period of time. Therefore, rather sticking to any one e-procurement system, firms are developing a portfolio of e-procurement strategies to leverage the full potential of the Internet.

Analyzing E-Procurement Using Transaction Cost Economics

Transaction cost economics was first used by Malone, Benjamin, and Yates (1987) to identify two IOIS configurations corresponding to the two major governance structures. Transaction cost economics suggests market and hierarchy as two mechanisms of coordination, and any middle-range solution was considered to be inferior. Over the years, transaction cost economics has been revised to reflect the empirical reality that middle range solutions could be actually more effective (Williamson, 1991). Choudhury (1997) enhanced the Malone et al. (1987) model and proposed three kinds of IOIS design, namely electronic monopolies, electronic dyad, and multilateral IOIS. However, the impact of information systems on the organization of economic activity is a debatable question. Following are two competing hypotheses that analyze the impact of information systems on procurement.

E-Market Hypothesis: Malone et al. (1987) proposed three kinds of transaction cost efficiencies that IOIS can offer. They are electronic brokerage (low search cost), electronic communication (faster and efficient transmission of information) and electronic integration (efficient dyadic relationships that go beyond exchange of routine information). They proposed that transactions for products with high-asset specificity and/or complexity of description will be supported by electronic hierarchies, while transactions for other products will be supported by electronic market. They have also suggested that the increasing adoption of IT will lead to a greater degree of outsourcing and hence less vertically-integrated firms. Moreover, since search costs are reduced, firms will rely more on search, leading to the emergence of e-markets.

Table 4. A comparison of e-hierarchy and e-markets (Source: Dai & Kauff-man, 2003)

Dimensions	E-Hierarchy	E-Markets
Network features	Private networks—only open to pre-selected business partners	Open networks—accessible to a large set of potential business partners
Market-making	Limited market-making functions and restricted set of trading partners	More market-making functions and easier access to a larger pool of potential partners
Information sharing	Both transactional and strategic information can be shared	Mostly transactional information is shared
Implementation costs	Higher costs to have additional participants in the network	Lower costs to add additional participants to the network

E-Hierarchies Hypothesis: Clemons, Reddi, and Row (1993) argued that factors such as transaction economy of scale, learning curve effects, and so forth, favor a move towards long-term relations with a small set of suppliers. Transaction cost economics typically focuses on ownership structure. Malone et al. (1987) coupled coordination with ownership. As per transaction cost economics, explicit coordination increases transaction costs (coordination cost and transaction risks). IT can reduce both coordination costs and transaction risks. Reduction in transaction risks leads to a greater reliance on outsourcing to achieve economy of scale, scope, and specialization, which is called a move to the middle (cooperation is the middle point between market and hierarchy).

Using Game Theory to Understand E-Procurement

Game theory has been used extensively to analyze issues related to IOIS adoption and implementation. Typically, the buyer firm initiates the IOIS, and suppliers have the option either to join or not to join the IOIS. If they decide to join, the buyer firm might offer them some subsidy, and if they decide not to join, they might be dealt with severely by the buyer firm. Further, joining IOIS will result in various fixed and variable costs to suppliers. Various studies have analyzed IOIS initiation and adoption using game theory (Barua & Lee, 1997; Riggins, Kriebel, & Mukhopadyay, 1994; Seidmann & Sundararajan, 1997; Wang & Seidmann, 1995). These studies mainly focus on suppliers' adoption and the effect of network externality on IOIS growth. Nault and Tyagi (2001) and Bakos and Nault (1997) have studied ownership pattern in e-markets using value analysis. Dai and Kauffman (2003) and Peleg, Lee, and Hausman (2002) have identified e-market and long-term relationship as two e-procurement strategies. Our model is more closely related to these two studies.

Peleg et al. (2002) have used a newsvendor ratio to analyze short-term versus long-term e-procurement strategy and compare it with a mixed strategy. They have concluded that there is no dominant strategy. However, this analysis does not take suppliers' adoption into consideration, and price is the only decision variable which is considered. Dai and Kauffman (2003) have analyzed e-procurement strategies using network externality, operational, and strategic benefits. These two studies assume that e-procurement adoption is a static game. In fact, except for Seidmann and Sundararajan (1997), no other studies have analyzed e-procurement or IOIS as a dynamic game.

EDI-based IOIS has been analyzed as a static game because of system incompatibility and higher setup cost, therefore forcing firms to develop a proprietary system and offer subsidies to get maximum possible supplier

Table 5. A summary of e-procurement/IOIS research

Issues	Main Findings	References
Network externalities and subsidy	For buyers, IOIS exhibit positive network externalities, but for suppliers it exhibits negative externalities. Buyer may offer subsidies to encourage supplier participation.	Riggins, Kriebel, and Mukhopadyay (1994); Wang and Seidmann (1995); Barua and Lee (1997); Riggins and Mukhopadhyay (1999)
Operational benefits	Reduced document processing and transmission time, improved data quality because of fewer errors	Johnston and Vitale (1988); Riggins and Mukhopadhyay (1994); Mukhopadhyay, Kekre, and Kalathur (1995)
Market-making benefits	Lower search costs enable firms to evaluate more suppliers and find better deals.	Malone, Yates, and Benjamin (1987); Bakos (1991); Garicano and Kaplan (2001)
Information sharing/ Strategic benefits	Inventory levels and sales data may be shared that enables better production planning and collective forecasting. Sharing product design information and market expertise can result in product innovation and market expansion. Specific investments from suppliers can benefit the buyer in terms of responsiveness, higher quality, innovation, and technology adoption.	Bakos and Brynjolfsson (1993); Seidmann and Sundararajan (1997); Riggins and Rhee (1999); Lee and Whang (2000); Chatfield and Yetton (2000); Lee, So, and Tang (2000); Kauffman and Mohtadi (2003)

adoption. However, the Internet has brought down system development and implementation cost. Further, various systems could be integrated seamlessly, and network implementation costs are also low. Therefore, apart from deciding whether to join or not, suppliers and buyer also have to decide upon the level of effort they would like to put into e-procurement adoption. As illustrated in the case study, various e-procurement systems differ in the level of adoption effort and the value generated from the e-procurement system. Therefore, these issue areas are analyzed in a differential game setting. The differential game will further enhance our understanding about how organizations make e-procurement adoption decisions over a period of time.

Differential Game Theory

A differential game is a dynamic game, played in continuous time. It allows the modeler to introduce a set of variables to characterize the state of the dynamic system at any instant of time during the play of the game, which makes the dynamic game a state space game. A set of differential equations describe the evolution of the state variable over time. Dockner, Jorgensen, Long, and Sorger (2000) have studied the differential game theory in detail.

Denote time by t and suppose that the players agree to play the game on the time interval [0,T]. All players can take actions at each time $t \in [0,T]$ thereby influencing the evolution of the state of the game as well as their own and their opponent's objective functional. The state of a dynamic system at any particular instant of time is characterized by an n-vector of state variables $x(t) = (x_1(t),....,x_n(t)) \in X$ where $X \subseteq R^n$ is a set containing all possible states. The state vector represents payoff relevant history of the game at time t. The initial value of the state vector is fixed and equals to $x_0 \in X$. Assuming that the evolution of the state can be described by the ordinary differential equation:

$$x'(t) = f(x(t), u(t), t) \ ; \ x(0) = x_0 \tag{1}$$

where $u(t) = (u_1(t), u_2(t), ... u_m(t)) \in R^m$ is the vector of action chosen by the decision-maker. u(t) is called the control variable. The choice of a control must respect the constraint $u(t) \in U(t, x(t))$ the set of all feasible action if state is x(t). Function f is defined on the set $\Omega = \{(x,u,t) \mid x \in X, u \in U(x, t), t \in [0,T]\}$ and takes value in R^n.

The goal of the decision-maker is to choose the control path u: [0, T] → R^m in an optimal way. Assuming that the decision-maker has the objective functional:

$$J(u(.)) = \int_0^T e^{-rt} F(t, x(t), u(t))dt + e^{-\rho T} Z(x(T)) \qquad (2)$$

where:

ρ = Const ≥ 0 is the discount rate

Z $_=$ Salvage value

The decision-maker has to maximize the above objective function over all control paths u(.) which satisfies u (t) ∈ U (x(t), t) while taking into account system evolution and the initial value of the state vector. The term F (x(t), u(t), t) measures the instantaneous utility derived by choosing the control value u(t) at time t when the current state of the game is x(t). This is a basic optimal control problem.

- **Definition 1:** A control path u: [0, T] → R^m is feasible for the optimal control problem stated in (2) if the initial value problem (1) has a unique absolutely-continuous solution x (.) such that the constraints x (t) ∈ X and u (t) ∈ U(x(t), t) hold for all t and the integral in (2) is well defined. The control path u (.) is optimal if it is feasible and if the inequality J(u(.)) ≥ J(ũ (.)) holds for all feasible control paths ũ (.).

Clearly an optimal control path can have none, one, or more than one feasible and optimal path. Hamilton-Jacobi-Bellman equation is the heart of the dynamic programming approach to the optimal control problem. Denote the optimal value of the objective function in (2) as V(x, t). HJB is defined as:

ρ V (x, t) – V_t (x, t) = max {F(x, u, t) – V_x (x, t) f(x, u, t) | u (t) ∈ U(x(t), t)}

- **Theorem 1:** Let V: X × [0, T]→ R be a continuously differentiable function which satisfies the HJB equation:

$$\rho V(x, t) - V_t(x, t) = \max \{F(x, u, t) - V_x(x, t) f(x, u, t) \mid u(t) \in U(x(t), t)\}$$

(3)

and the terminal condition:

$$V(x, T) = Z(x)$$

(4)

for all $(x, t) \in X \times [0, T]$. Let $\Phi(x, t)$ denote the set of controls $u \in U(x(t), t)$ maximizing the right-hand side of (3). If u (.) is a feasible control path with corresponding state trajectory x(.) and if u (t) $\in \Phi(x(t), t)$ holds for almost all $t \in [0, T]$ then u(.) is an optimal control path. Moreover V(x, t) is the optimal value of the control problem.

Model Development

The proposed model analyzes a dyadic relation between a single buyer and an exclusive supplier. This will help in staying away from the analytical complexity that arises from the competition among suppliers. Results are not likely to change in the case of a buyer procuring through multiple non-competing suppliers.

Buyer b and suppliers s can control their rate of e-procurement adoption efforts. E-procurement adoption efforts are denoted by b(G,t) for buyer and s(G,t) for supplier. Cost function C (.) is quadratic in e-procurement efforts and is given by

$$C(s) = \frac{h}{2} s^2$$

$$C(b) = \frac{h}{2} b^2$$

where h ≥ 0 is positive parameter. Buyer and supplier both are assumed to be facing similar cost function. This assumption is quite valid as most e-procurement service providers charge either on a usage basis or a user license basis. This form of cost function is fairly common in marketing channel research (Chintagunta & Jain, 1992). Convex cost function implies increasing marginal cost of effort.

If the buyer decides to subsidize the supplier's e-procurement adoption cost, then the supplier's revised cost function can be written as

$$C(s) = \frac{h}{2}s^2 - \theta s$$

$$C(b) = \frac{h}{2}b^2 + \theta s$$

where $\theta \geq 0$ is the discounts offered by manufacturer. Benefits from e-procurement could be operational or strategic in nature. Operational benefits, such as reduced paperwork cost, lower cycle time, and so forth, are linearly depended on the adoption efforts b and s .Therefore operational benefit is $\pi_0 = \alpha_b b + \alpha_s s$, where $\alpha_b, \alpha_s \geq 0$ is the e-procurement adoption efforts' effectiveness in creating operational benefit. Adoption efforts by buyer and suppliers also generate strategic benefits. It evolves as Nerlove and Arrow (1962) equation

$$G'(t) = \lambda_b b(G,t) + \lambda_s s(G,t) - \delta G(t) \, ; \, G(0) = G_0 \qquad (5)$$

where λ_b, λ_s, $\delta \geq 0$. λ_b and λ_s represent the effectiveness of adoption efforts by buyer and supplier, respectively, in creating strategic benefits. G_0 is the strategic benefit from the dyadic relation at the beginning of the game, and δ is the rate of decay in strategic benefit. The rate of change in the strategic benefit from the dyadic relation will depend on other interventions such as innovation, specific investment, and so forth. However, the interest here is to study e-procurement adoption efforts, and hence these interventions are assumed to be constant. Total benefit from e-procurement is given as follows

$$\pi = \alpha_b b + \alpha_s s + G$$

Discount rate ρ is assumed to be positive and constant for both buyer and suppliers. The buyer takes away η part of the total benefit and the supplier gets the rest. The game is assumed to be played in an infinite time horizon.

The buyer's objective function can be written as

$$J_b = \int_0^\infty e^{-\rho t}[\eta(\alpha_b b + \alpha_s s + G) - \frac{h}{2}b^2 - \theta s]dt \qquad (6)$$

The supplier's objective function can be written as

$$J_s = \int_0^\infty e^{-\rho t}[(1-\eta)(\alpha_b b + \alpha_s s + G) - \frac{h}{2}s^2 + \theta s]dt \qquad (7)$$

The above objective functions show that the buyer and supplier's control decision, that is, e-procurement adoption effort, will be a function of time and current strategic benefit from the dyadic relation. However, at any instant of time, both players essentially face the same game; hence it is possible to make a simplification here by restricting to stationary strategies b(G) and s(G) (Jorgensen, Sigue, & Zaccour, 2000). Now we will study e-procurement adoption efforts by buyer and supplier in two scenarios, namely "without subsidies scenario" and "with subsidies scenario".

E-Procurement Adoption without Subsidies

In this scenario, the buyer does not offer any subsidies to the supplier for his e-procurement adoption efforts. Therefore $\theta = 0$. Proposition 1 states the main results in this scenario.

> **Proposition 1:** If the manufacturer offers no subsidy, the Nash equilibrium adoption effort is given by:

$$b = \frac{1}{h}[\eta\alpha_b + \lambda_b \frac{\eta}{\delta + \rho}] \qquad (8)$$

$$s = \frac{1}{h}[(1-\eta)\alpha_s + \lambda_s \frac{(1-\eta)}{\delta + \rho}] \tag{9}$$

Proof: Appendix A

Equations 8 and 9 show control for e-procurement adoption efforts. Symmetry in these equations is because of the symmetry in objective functions. The effort level for e-procurement adoption will depend on both operational and strategic benefits derived. This result is quite intuitive. Effort levels are indirectly related to the rate of decay in strategic benefits and discount functions. Therefore we will see higher e-procurement adoption efforts in dyadic relation with low strategic benefit decay rates. This result corroborates findings from Tata Steel's case study, where we have seen high e-procurement adoption efforts in products that are critical to cost/quality. Usually these products are very complex in nature and require heavy specific investments from both buyer and supplier. Similarly, if buyer and supplier both employ a lower discount rate, then they will tend to put more effort in e-procurement adoption. This result is similar to Choudhury (1997), who found lower adoption efforts when market volatility is high (market volatility is defined as the rate at which players in the industry change over time). We have assumed a similar discount function for buyer and suppliers. However, in some cases, a supplier can have a higher discount rate than the buyer, as the risk-free interest rate is usually higher for smaller organizations. In that case, we are likely to see a lower effort from the supplier. The buyer can offer some adoption subsidies to suppliers to get a higher adoption effort from them and hence increase his own benefit from e-procurement.

E-Procurement Adoption with Subsidies

Let us assume that the buyer plays channel leader and provides incentives to the supplier for his e-procurement adoption efforts. The buyer's objective is to offer subsidies to the supplier in a way that can maximize his own benefit from e-procurement adoption. Hence the buyer plays a Stackelberg leader and the supplier plays a Stackelberg follower, which means that the supplier observes the buyer's move, that is, effort and subsidy level, before choosing its own effort level.

Proposition 2: If the manufacturer offers a subsidy of θs for an adoption effort of s by the supplier, the Nash equilibrium adoption effort is given by:

$$b = \frac{1}{h}(\eta\alpha_b + \lambda_b \frac{\eta}{\delta + \rho})$$ (10)

$$s = \frac{1}{h}((1-\eta)\alpha_s + \theta + \lambda_s \frac{1-\eta}{\delta + \rho})$$ (11)

$$\theta = \frac{(2\eta - 1)}{2}[\alpha_s + \frac{\lambda_s}{\delta + \rho}]$$ (12)

Proof: Appendix B

Subsidy does not affect the buyer's effort level. This was expected since it is unlikely for him to change his effort level because of subsidies offered to the supplier. On the other hand, the supplier will now exert more effort by a factor of θ/h. Further if θ ≥ 0 then η ≥ ½, hence the buyer will offer any subsidy only if he can take away more than half of the total benefit generated from the e-procurement system. This was also observed in the case study. In the case of big vendors, NGOs, and research labs, Tata Steel did not offer any subsidy, and they remained out of the e-procurement net. Further rate of subsidy also depends on the effectiveness of the supplier's e-procurement adoption efforts in deriving operational benefits and strategic benefit. Decay in strategic benefit and discount rate is inversely related to the subsidy rate. Therefore the buyer will offer more subsidies to suppliers who are more effective and with whom he is wishes to have a long-term relationship. This result is also in line with findings from the case study.

Conclusion

Prior research in the area of inter-organizational information systems (IOIS), EDI, and e-procurement have tended to support either the "electronic market hypothesis" (Malone et al., 1987) or "move to middle hypothesis" (Clemons et al., 1993). In the present case study, we have seen evidences that support both hypotheses. Hence, we can propose that to get full benefit of the Internet, organizations should use or develop a portfolio of systems.

In this chapter, we have looked into the evolution of various e-procurement systems at Tata Steel. These systems can be divided into internal or consortium-sponsored systems. The internal e-procurement systems can be further divided into internal e-bidding system, e-negotiation, and online stock information. These systems differ in the level of e-procurement adoption effort and the number of suppliers reached. Their impact on price reduction and transaction cost reduction also differ. They differ as well in terms of the effect on operational efficiency and inter-organizational relationship. The consortium-sponsored e-market increases the bargaining power of initiators and brings down prices, but it has a very low level of integration. A high level of integration can lead to more strategic and relational benefits. Hence we can conclude that to realize full benefits of the Internet, organizations will use a portfolio of e-procurement systems. Since these systems are evolved over a period of time, thus it necessitates dynamic rather than static analysis. Thus we used the differential game theory to analyze e-procurement adoption effort.

This chapter has analyzed e-procurement in a differential game setting. To the best of our knowledge, this kind of analysis has not been done before in e-procurement literature. Unlike proprietary information systems, Internet-based information systems are much more flexible, less costly, and can be seamlessly integrated. This enables them to evolve over a period of time, and organizations can manage a portfolio of system rather than sticking to any one system. In a similar spirit, a recent article by Ba, Stallaert, Whinston, and Zhang (2005), have used evolutionary game theory to find out the effect of product characteristics on market evolution.

Differential game theory is used to analyze dyadic e-procurement adoption effort in "with subsidy" and "without subsidy" scenarios. Results can be extended to one buyer and several non-competing suppliers. However, we have not analyzed e-procurement adoption effort in the presence of network externality. This issue can be taken up in future research. Further, to keep the proposed model simple, product volume/demand is not analyzed, as a variable. Since demand are mostly stochastic in nature, hence modeling it in a differential game setting might make the model unmanageably complex.

This chapter raises questions about how suppliers can be motivated to adopt an e-procurement system, when the initiator does not posses the necessary bargaining power. Prior research (Choudhury, 1997) has suggested that a consortium-sponsored e-market can enhance the bargaining power of organizations at the same level of the value chain, and hence suppliers can be coerced to join. However, in the present case study, we have not seen evidence that can support this strategy.

References

Ba, S., Stallaert, J., Whinston, A. B., & Zhang, H. (2005). Choice of transaction channels: The effect of product characteristics on market evolution. *Journal of Management Information Systems, 21*(4), 173-197.

Bakos, J. Y. (1991). A strategic analysis of electronic marketplaces. *MIS Quarterly, 15*(3), 295-310.

Bakos, J. Y., & Brynjolfsson, E. (1993). Information technology, incentives, and the optimal number of suppliers. *Journal of Management Information Systems, 10*(2), 37-54.

Bakos, J. Y., & Nault, B. R. (1997). Ownership and investment in electronic networks. *Information Systems Research, 8*(4), 321-341.

Barua, A., & Lee, B. (1997). An economic analysis of the introduction of an electronic data interchange system. *Information Systems Research, 8*(4), 398-422.

Chatfield, A. K., & Yetton, P. (2000). Strategic payoff from EDI as a function of EDI embeddedness. *Journal of Management Information Systems, 16*(4), 195-224.

Chintagunta, P. K., & Jain, D. (1992). A dynamic model of channel member strategies for marketing expenditures. *Marketing Science, 11*(2), 168-188.

Choudhury, V. (1997). Strategic choices in the development of inter-organizational information systems. *Information Systems Research, 8*(1), 1-24.

Clemons, E. K., Reddi, S. P., & Row, M. C. (1993). The impact of information technology on the organization of economic activity: The "move to the middle" hypothesis. *Journal of Management Information Systems, 10*(2), 9-35.

Dai, Q., & Kauffman, R. J. (2003). *To be or not to B2B: Evaluating managerial choices for e-procurement channel adoption* (Working paper). Minneapolis, MN: MIS Research Center Carlson School of Management. University of Minnesota.

Dockner, E. J., Jorgensen, S., Long, N. V., & Sorger, G. (2000). *Differential games in economics and management science*. Cambridge, MA: Cambridge University Press.

Garicano, L., & Kaplan, S. N. (2001). The effects of business-to-business e-commerce on transaction costs. *The Journal of Industrial Economics, 49*(4), 463-485.

Iacovou, C. L., Benbasat, I., & Dexter, A. S. (1995). Electronic data interchange and small organizations: Adoption and impact of technology. *MIS Quarterly, 19*(4), 465- 485.

Johnston, H. R., & Vitale, M. R. (1988). Creating competitive advantage with inter-organisational information systems. *MIS Quarterly, 12*(2), 153-166.

Johnston, R. B., & Mak, H. C. (2000). An emerging vision of Internet-enabled supply chain electronic commerce. *International Journal of Electronic Commerce, 4*(4), 43-59.

Jorgensen, S., Sigue, S. P., & Zaccour, G. (2000). Dynamic cooperative advertising in a channel. *Journal of Retailing, 76*(1), 71-92.

Kauffman, R. J., & Mohtadi, H. (2003). *Open versus proprietary systems in B2B e-procurement: A risk-adjusted transactions cost perspective* (Working paper). Minneapolis, MN: MIS Research Center Carlson School of Management, University of Minnesota.

Lee. H. L., So, K. C., & Tang, C. S. (2000). The value of information sharing in a two-level supply chain. *Management Science, 46*(5), 626-643.

Lee., H. L., & Whang, S. (2000). Information sharing in a supply chain. *International Journal of Technology Management, 20*(3), 373-387.

Malone, T. W., Yates, J., & Benjamin, R. I. (1987). Electronic markets and electronic hierarchies. *Communications of ACM, 30*(6), 484-497.

Mukhopadhyay, T., Kekre, S., & Kalathur, S. (1995). Business value of information technology: A study of electronic data interchange. *MIS Quarterly, 19*(2), 137-156.

Nault, B. R., & Tyagi, R. K. (2001). Implementable mechanisms to coordinate horizontal alliances. *Management Sciences, 47*(6), 787-779.

Nerlove, M., & Arrow, K. J. (1962). Optimal advertising policy under dynamic conditions. *Economica, 29*(114), 129-142.

Peleg, B., Lee, H. L., & Hausman, W. H. (2002). Short-term e-procurement strategies versus long-term contracts. *Productions and Operations Management, 11*(4), 458-479.

Riggins, F. J., Kriebel, C. H., & Mukhopadhyay, T. (1994). The growth of interorganizational systems in the presence of network externality. *Management Science, 40*(8), 984-998.

Riggins, F. J., & Mukhopadhyay, T. (1994). Interdependent benefits from inter-organizational systems: Opportunities for business partner reengineering. *Journal of Management Information Systems, 11*(2), 37-57.

Riggins, F. J., & Mukhopadhyay, T. (1999). Overcoming adoption and implementation risks of EDI. *International Journal of Electronic Commerce, 3*(4), 103–115.

Riggins, F. J., & Rhee, H. S. (1999). Developing the learning network using extranet. *International Journal of Electronic Commerce, 4*(1), 65-83.

Seidmann, A., & Sundararajan, A. (1997). Building and sustaining inter-organizational information sharing relationships: The competitive impact of interfacing supply chain operations with marketing strategy. In K. Kumar & J. I. DeGross (Eds.), *Proceedings of the International Conference of Information System, Atlanta* (pp. 205-222).

Wang, E. G., & Seidmann, A. (1995). Electronic data interchange: Competitive externalities and strategic implementation policies. *Management Science, 41*(3), 401-418.

Williamson, O. E. (1991). Comparative economic organization: The analysis of discrete structural alternatives. *Administrative Science Quarterly, 36*(2), 269-296.

Endnote

[1]   The views expressed in this chapter are purely personal, and have no connection with the policies or views of my employer, Infosys Technologies Ltd.

Appendix A

Proof of Proposition 1

Suppose that there exists bounded and continuously differentiable function $V_i : R+ \to R$ $i \in \{b, s\}$. Using theorem 1, Hamilton-Jacobi-Bellman (HJB) equations for the buyer can be defined as:

$$\max \{\eta(\alpha_b b + \alpha_s s + G) - \frac{h}{2} b^2 + V'_b(G)(\lambda_b b + \lambda_s s - \delta G(t))\} = \rho V_b(G)$$

(A.1)

Supplier's HJB equation will be written as follows:

$$\max \{(1-\eta)(\alpha_b b + \alpha_s s + G) - \frac{h}{2} s^2 + V'_s(G)(\lambda_b b + \lambda_s s - \delta G(t))\} = \rho V_s(G)$$

(A.2)

Maximizing A.1 with respect to b yields:

$$b = \frac{1}{h}(\eta \alpha_b + \lambda_b V'_b(G))$$

(A.3)

Maximizing A.2 with respect to s yields:

$$s = \frac{1}{h}((1-\eta)\alpha_s + \lambda_s V'_s(G))$$

(A.4)

Substituting value of b and s from A.3-A.4 into A.1 gives us:

$$\eta G(t) + [\frac{\eta^2 \alpha_b^2}{2h} + \frac{\eta(1-\eta)\alpha_s^2}{h}] + [\frac{\eta \alpha_b \lambda_b}{h} + \frac{(1-\eta)\alpha_s \lambda_s}{h}]V_b'(G) + \frac{\eta \alpha_s \lambda_s}{h}V_s'(G) +$$
$$\frac{\lambda_b^2}{2h}V_b'(G)^2 + \frac{\lambda_s^2}{h}V_b'(G)V_s'(G) - \delta G(t)V_b'(G) = \rho V_b(G)$$

(A.5)

Let us define the following variables:

$$D_b = \frac{\eta^2 \alpha_b^2}{2h} + \frac{\eta(1-\eta)\alpha_s^2}{h}$$

(A.6)

$$E = \frac{\eta \alpha_b \lambda_b}{h} + \frac{(1-\eta)\alpha_s \lambda_s}{h}$$

(A.7)

$$F_b = \frac{\eta \alpha_s \lambda_s}{h}$$

(A.8)

$$H = \frac{\lambda_b^2}{h}$$

(A.9)

$$I = \frac{\lambda_s^2}{h}$$

(A.10)

Substituting these variables into A.5 gives us:

$$\eta G(t) + D_b + EV_b'(G) + F_bV_s'(G) + \frac{H}{2}V_b'(G)^2 + IV_b'(G)V_s'(G) - \delta G(t)V_b'(G) = \rho V_b(G)$$

(A.11)

Similarly substituting values of b and s from A.3 – A.4 to A.2 yields:

$$(1-\eta)G(t) + D_s + EV_s'(G) + F_sV_b'(G) + \frac{I}{2}V_s'(G)^2 + HV_b'(G)V_s'(G) - \delta G(t)V_s'(G) = \rho V_s(G)$$

(A.12)

where:

$$D_s = \frac{\eta(1-\eta)\alpha_b^2}{h} + \frac{(1-\eta)^2 \alpha_s^2}{2h}$$

(A.13)

$$F_s = \frac{(1-\eta)\alpha_b\lambda_b}{h}$$

(A.14)

Following Dockner et al. (2000), we will show that linear value function:

$$V_b(G) = X_1 G + X_2$$

(A.15)

$$V_s(G) = Y_1 G + Y_2$$

(A.16)

solves HJB in A.11 and A.12 respectively. Obviously $V_b{}'(G) = X_1$ and $V_s{}'(G) = Y_1$. Substituting these values in A.11 and A.12 we get:

$$(\eta - \delta X_1 - \rho X_1)G + D_b + EX_1 + F_bY_1 + \frac{H}{2}X_1{}^2 + IX_1Y_1 - \rho X_2 = 0$$

(A.17)

$$(1 - \eta - \delta Y_1 - \rho Y_1)G + D_s + EY_1 + F_sX_1 + HX_1Y_1 + \frac{I}{2}Y_1{}^2 - \rho Y_2 = 0$$

(A.18)

Since the above equations must hold for any non-negative G, the coefficient of value function A.13 and A.14 must be chosen as:

$$X_1 = \frac{\eta}{(\delta + \rho)}$$

(A.19)

$$X_2 = \frac{1}{\rho}[D_b + E\frac{\eta}{(\delta + \rho)} + F_b\frac{(1-\eta)}{(\delta + \rho)} + \frac{H}{2}(\frac{\eta}{\delta + \rho})^2 + I\frac{\eta(1-\eta)}{(\delta + \rho)^2}]$$

(A.20)

$$Y_1 = \frac{1-\eta}{\delta + \rho}$$

(A.21)

$$Y_2 = \frac{1}{\rho}[D_s + E\frac{(1-\eta)}{(\delta + \rho)} + F_s\frac{\eta}{(\delta + \rho)} + H\frac{\eta(1-\eta)}{(\delta + \rho)^2} + \frac{I}{2}(\frac{1-\eta}{\delta + \rho})^2]$$

(A.22)

Putting these values in A.3 and A.4 yields:

$$b = \frac{1}{h}(\eta \alpha_b + \lambda_b \frac{\eta}{\delta + \rho})$$

$$s = \frac{1}{h}((1-\eta)\alpha_s + \lambda_s \frac{(1-\eta)}{\delta + \rho})$$

which are the values of adoption efforts by the buyer and the supplier given in equation (8) and (9). Inserting these values in equation (5) yields:

$$G'(t) = \lambda_b[\frac{1}{h}(\eta \alpha_b + \lambda_b \frac{\eta}{\delta + \rho})] + \lambda_s[\frac{1}{h}((1-\eta)\alpha_s + \lambda_s \frac{(1-\eta)}{\delta + \rho})] - \delta G(t)$$

$$(A.23)$$

Obviously the steady state:

$$\tilde{G}(t) = \frac{1}{\delta}[\frac{\eta \alpha_b \lambda_b}{h} + \frac{(1-\eta)\alpha_s \lambda_s}{h} + \frac{\eta \lambda_b^2}{\delta + \rho} + \frac{(1-\eta)\lambda_s^2}{\delta + \rho}]$$

$$(A.24)$$

Solving A.21 gives us an equation for strategic advantage from e-procurement:

$$G(t) = (G_0 - \tilde{G})e^{-\delta t} + \tilde{G}$$

$$(A.25)$$

This completes proof for Proposition 1.

Appendix B

Proof of Proposition 2

Since the buyer is now offering a subsidy, hence we can rewrite HJB equations for the buyer as:

$$\max\{\eta(\alpha_b b + \alpha_s s + G) - \frac{h}{2}b^2 - \theta s + V'_b(G)(\lambda_b b + \lambda_s s - \delta G(t))\} = \rho V_b(G)$$

(B.1)

Supplier's HJB equation can be rewritten as:

$$\max\{(1-\eta)(\alpha_b b + \alpha_s s + G) - \frac{h}{2}s^2 + \theta s + V'_s(G)(\lambda_b b + \lambda_s s - \delta G(t))\} = \rho V_s(G)$$

(B.2)

Maximizing B.2 for s yields:

$$s = \frac{1}{h}((1-\eta)\alpha_s + \theta + \lambda_s V'_s(G))$$

(B.3)

Substituting value of s in the buyer's HJB in B.1:

$$\max\{\eta(\alpha_b b + \frac{\alpha_s}{h}[(1-\eta)\alpha_s + \theta + \lambda_s V'_s(G)] + G) - \frac{h}{2}b^2 - \frac{\theta}{h}[(1-\eta)\alpha_s + \theta + \lambda_s V'_s(G)]$$

$$+ V'_b(G)(\lambda_b b + \frac{\lambda_s}{h}[(1-\eta)\alpha_s + \theta + \lambda_s V'_s(G)] - \delta G(t))\} = \rho V_b(G)$$

(B.4)

Maximizing B.4 with respect to b yields:

$$b = \frac{1}{h}(\eta \alpha_b + \lambda_b V_b'(G))$$

(B.5)

Maximizing B.4 with respect to θ yields:

$$\theta = \frac{1}{2}[(2\eta-1)\alpha_s + (V_b{}'(G) - V_s{}'(G)\lambda_s)]$$

(B.6)

Substituting values of b and θ from B.5-B.6 into B.4 yields:

$$\eta G(t) + D_b + [E + \frac{\lambda_s\theta}{h}]V_b{}'(G) + [F_b - \frac{\lambda_s\theta}{h}]V_s{}'(G) + \frac{H}{2}V_b{}'(G)^2 + IV_b{}'(G)V_s{}'(G)$$

$$+[2\eta-1]\frac{\alpha_s\theta}{h} - \frac{\theta^2}{h} - \delta G(t)V_b{}'(G) = \rho V_b(G)$$

(B.7)

where the values of D_b, E, F_b, H, I are defined in A.6-A.10.

Similarly substituting values of s, b and θ from B.3, B.5 and B6 respectively to the suppliers' HJB in B.2 yields:

$$(1-\eta)G(t) + D_s + [E + \frac{\lambda_s\theta}{h}]V_s{}'(G) + F_sV_b{}'(G) + \frac{I}{2}V_s{}'(G)^2 + HV_b{}'(G)V_s{}'(G)$$

$$+\frac{(1-\eta)\alpha_s\theta}{h} + \frac{\theta^2}{2h} - \delta G(t)V_s{}'(G) = \rho V_s(G)$$

(B.8)

where the values of D_s and F_b are defined in A.13-A.14.

We can now proceed to find the solution of HJB defined in B.7 and B.8 by using similar approach that we have taken in appendix A. The coefficients of the value functions defined in A.15 and A.16 will be:

$$X_1 = \frac{\eta}{\delta + \rho}$$

(B.9)

$$X_2 = \frac{1}{\rho}\{D_b + [E + \frac{\lambda_s\theta}{h}]\frac{\eta}{\delta+\rho} + [F_b - \frac{\lambda_s\theta}{h}]\frac{(1-\eta)}{\delta+\rho} + \frac{H}{2}(\frac{\eta}{\delta+\rho})^2 + I\frac{\eta(1-\eta)}{(\delta+\rho)^2}$$

$$+[2\eta-1]\frac{\alpha_s\theta}{h} - \frac{\theta^2}{h}\}$$

(B.10)

$$Y_1 = \frac{1-\eta}{\delta+\rho}$$

(B.11)

$$Y_2 = \frac{1}{\rho}\{D_s + [E + \frac{\lambda_s\theta}{h}]\frac{1-\eta}{\delta+\rho} + F_s\frac{\eta}{\delta+\rho} + \frac{I}{2}(\frac{1-\eta}{\delta+\rho})^2 + H\frac{\eta(1-\eta)}{(\delta+\rho)^2}$$

$$+\frac{(1-\eta)\alpha_s\theta}{h} + \frac{\theta^2}{2h}\}$$

(B.12)

where:

$$\theta = \frac{(2\eta-1)}{2}[\alpha_s + \frac{\lambda_s}{\delta+\rho}]$$

Substituting these values in B.1 and B.5 we get:

$$s = \frac{1}{h}((1-\eta)\alpha_s + \theta + \lambda_s\frac{1-\eta}{\delta+\rho})$$

$$b = \frac{1}{h}(\eta\alpha_b + \lambda_b\frac{\eta}{\delta+\rho})$$

These are the values of b, s and θ given in Proposition 2. This completes proof for Proposition 2.

Section IV

Technical Perspective

Chapter IX

A Service-Oriented Agent-Based Model for Electronic Procurement

Manas Ranjan Patra, Berhampur University, India

Abstract

Globalization has evoked rethinking in organizing the business processes of many enterprises in order to keep pace with the competition and dynamic nature of the market. There has been continuing research for suitable paradigms and technologies that can facilitate efficient and yet less expensive solutions, a feature that is so important for small and medium-sized enterprises (SMEs). Towards this end, the chapter presents a service-oriented framework that is based on the notion of Internet-accessible services to represent applications and to integrate business processes. This model propounds a metadata-driven approach to dynamically publish, discover, and select services in heterogeneous settings while engaging in business transactions such as e-procurement across organizational boundaries. The concept of software agents is also employed as a means to automate the activities relating to a procurement cycle. The central theme of this chapter is to motivate the adoption of a service-oriented agent-based framework which can provide an effective and efficient solution to e-procurement.

Introduction

Recent developments in the field of information and communication technology (ICT) have revolutionized the way business can be conducted in a dynamic and globally-competitive market environment. This has led to a profound change in the traditional business models leading to the adoption of an e-business philosophy that is manifested in the form of e-procurement, supply chain management (e-SCM), customer relation management (e-CRM), e-auction, e-tendering, e-payment, and so forth. Application of ICT is no longer an afterthought, but an inevitable driver for business enterprises to facilitate cost-effective, timely, and customer-centric solutions in an electronic market place (*e-marketplace*). An e-marketplace provides a virtual space wherein parties meet to accomplish their business objectives. One of the major application areas that can enjoy the real benefit of such a virtual marketplace encompassing several organizational boundaries is *e-procurement*. A buyer firm can streamline its purchasing activities using the Internet as a procurement channel and maneuver its way out of the tedious process of supplier-selection, placing an order, and tracking all activities until the shipment is received and payment is settled. Thus, e-procurement can help enterprises in automating the workflow associated with an entire procurement cycle and various related tactical processes, thereby helping to reduce the massive paper trails to a large extent. In recent times, the service-oriented paradigm for application development has been manifested in the form of Web services that promise interoperability and pragmatic interaction behavior among business partners, thereby bringing about business agility (Chiu, Cheung, Till, Karlapalem, Li, & Kafeza, 2004; Huhns & Singh, 2005; Myerson, 2002; Peltz, 2003). This helps one to envisage an environment where businesses can expose their current and future applications as Web services that can be easily discovered and consumed by interested parties. However, the real benefit of such an application environment can be appreciated, provided most of the operations can be carried out with a minimum of human intervention. Software agents can contribute to a great extent as an accompanying technology to provide value addition by automating most of the activities in an e-market scenario (Petrie & Bussler, 2003).

Electronic Procurement

Electronic procurement (e-procurement) essentially includes all aspects of procurement-related functions that are supported by different electronic communication channels. It is being extensively practiced both in public and private sectors with varied forms, namely:

- **Electronic data interchange (EDI):** An inter-organization information system that uses structured data exchange formats
- **Enterprise resource planning (ERP):** Tries to automate procurement-related workflows through auto-emailing, auto-faxing, and other forms of messaging systems to directly communicate with the parties involved in a procurement process
- **Electronic tendering (e-tendering):** A process of receiving offers from vendors/suppliers through electronic means
- **Electronic auction (e-auction):** A way of conducting auctions by inviting bids over the Internet and publishing the results of an auction
- **Electronic MRO (e-MRO):** Facilitates online procurement of materials for maintenance, repair, and operations

There are several definitions of e-procurement that one can find in the literature; some of them include the following:

- E-procurement is a technology solution that facilitates corporate buying using the Internet. It has the power to transform the purchasing process because it pervades all of the steps identified by the supply manager (Presutti, 2002).
- E-procurement technology is defined as a technology designed to facilitate the acquisition of goods by a commercial or a government organization over the Internet (Carabello, 2001).

- E-procurement is an Internet/intranet-based purchasing application or hosted service that streamlines buying and trading with partners, maximizes trade efficiency across the entire supply chain, and provides strategic e-commerce capabilities (ITRG, 2002).

E-Procurement Activities

In this section, various phases of a typical e-procurement cycle are discussed (as depicted in Figure 1). This helps one to understand the suitability of the proposed service-oriented agent-based framework in the realization of electronic procurements. Some of the key procurement activities that can benefit from the framework include the following:

- **Purchase requisition phase:** This involves identification of the purchasing needs of an organization that may be triggered through a human decision-making process or semi- automated through a software system such as enterprise resource planning (ERP).

- **Sourcing phase:** The objective of this phase is to locate potential suppliers and business partners who can facilitate procurement of intended items or services. Activities in this phase include: request for information (RFI) on items/services such as description, price, availability; and shipment particulars; request for quotes (RFQ); and evaluation of offers based on information received through RFI/RFQ as well as historical data about suppliers, possibly from a supplier relationship management application (SRM).

- **Negotiating phase:** This phase involves negotiation, possibly with a number of potential suppliers short-listed from the previous phase. The content of negotiation could relate to price, terms, and conditions. The outcome of this phase is the selection of one or more suppliers who would finally execute the purchase order.

- **Transaction phase:** Once decision is made on the supplier(s), the rest of the activities follow a workflow starting with purchase approval, placing of order, order fulfillment, and payment.

- **Supplier relationship management:** Additionally, an organization may maintain a database of suppliers reflecting their quality of service,

Figure 1. E-procurement process cycle

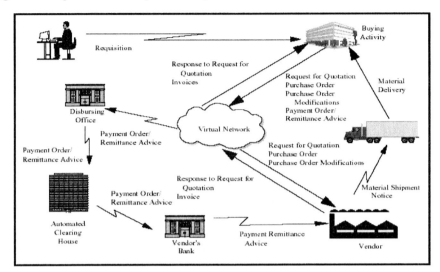

trustworthiness, and other relevant information, which can be used for decision-making in future procurements.

Paradigms and Challenges in E-Procurement

Paradigms

In this section, some common forms of procurement are discussed, starting with straightforward but passive forms to more dynamic and interactive procurement.

- **Take or leave:** This is a catalogue-based procurement process wherein a seller publishes all its items with prices in an electronic catalogue, which is browsed by customers. A customer has to buy items at the specified price, and there is no interaction with the seller. The customer either takes an item (if satisfied) or leaves it (if not satisfied). Thus, it is a very passive form of e-procurement.

- **Auction:** This form of procurement involves several rounds where interested customers announce their offers to buy itcm(s), and finally the highest bidder is awarded. There are different variations of an auction process, such as English auction, reverse auction, double auction, and Dutch auction. This is an interactive form of procurement.

- **Negotiation:** Here, a customer is allowed to negotiate with a seller on price or on any other matters such as terms and conditions, customer service, or maintenance. This provides for one-to-one interaction.

- **Multi-market package e-procurement:** The multi-market package procurement of goods and services can be defined as the procurement of a package of interdependent items and services from different heterogeneous sources, while satisfying one's own preferences and constraints. The sources of procurement could be electronic marketplaces, service providers, and retail sellers. Such procurement scenarios are complex in the sense that services are often interrelated, which could take different forms such as alternative (*one or the other*), co-requisite (*one and the other*) or prerequisite (*if one only, then the other*). Commercial applications such as Ariba Buyer (Ariba, n.d.), Enterprise Buyer (Commerce One, n.d.), are being used to automate activities in an e-procurement. But, none of them deals with the complexities involved in multi-market package e-procurement. Procurement of interrelated items/services from different sources, negotiating with them, and synthesizing the results into one common package is a real challenge. This requires innovative paradigms and implementation strategies for effective execution of complex procurement processes.

Challenges to E-Procurement

In the present competitive market economy, firms are confronted with the real challenge of streamlining the procurement process in a cost-effective way. Some such key challenges are:

- To reduce order-processing costs and cycle times
- To enable purchase requisition to be raised from individual employee's desktop
- To provide enterprise-wide access to corporate procurement capabilities

- To achieve integration of procurement software with a firm's back-office system/legacy system
- To cope with the dynamic nature of the market where new suppliers join, product details vary, and special purchase offers are made

Yet another major challenge in e-procurement is matchmaking, which involves aggregation of product as well as supplier information, and selecting the most suitable one that conforms to certain criteria. Some approaches to deal with aggregation and matchmaking are discussed in (Dai & Kauffman, 2001), which are as follows:

- **Aggregation through private and buyer-specific e-cataloging:** In this approach, suppliers prepare e-catalogues, keeping in view specific buyer categories, depending on the items that they might be interested in. Such buyer-specific catalogs are favored in transactional purchasing to reduce operating costs. This is useful when purchases are made frequently and with large quantities. Price discovery and search for product information is not the focus in such situations; rather, buyers might have established long-term relations with their suppliers and thus select their suppliers off-line. The only requirement here is proper system integration and connectivity with suppliers for streamlining the whole purchasing process with a view to minimizing operating costs. This model is being adopted by many firms, for instance, Schlumberger, Inc., which is a Texas-based oil exploration and technology services company that uses Commerce One's e-procurement solution system for purchasing via the Internet (Ovans, 2000).
- **Aggregation through public and buyer-neutral e-cataloging:** In situations when price volatility is low and purchases are time-critical, buyers find it difficult to identify relevant suppliers much in advance. In such cases, online catalogs that are publicly accessible are preferred, which greatly lowers the search costs. This is particularly useful when the demand exhibits a high variety, but less in quantity and frequency.
- **Matching via dynamic trading processes:** Dynamic trading processes are similar to electronic auctions which may additionally consider a number of other aspects, namely: the criteria for bidding as well as the final selection may be based on quality, delivery, warranty, and other dimensions besides price; and the bidding process may allow for

counter-offers to be made. Further, participants can withdraw, reject, counter, or accept offers. They are not required to accept the highest bid; both Yankee auctions as well as reverse auctions may be used, and both public and private negotiation mechanisms may be used.

- **Matching via private negotiation mechanisms:** In certain electronic markets, it might be possible for member firms to pre-select participants for evaluation. Auctions may take place within a group of prequalified suppliers. In these cases, firms benefit by being able to negotiate deals electronically with various partners, while maintaining privacy. Such private negotiation mechanisms might be useful for purchasing direct products in large quantity, such as spare parts for automobiles. These products are usually of high strategic significance to buyers, and hence, supplier reliability and qualification are of great concern, rather than achieving the lowest price. Buyers usually identify qualified suppliers based on their previous purchasing experiences, and they attempt to maintain these established buyer-supplier relationships. Private negotiation helps them to achieve this by rewarding a few preselected suppliers with their business, thereby lowering the search costs.

- **Matching via public bidding mechanisms:** It may be beneficial for buyers to adopt a public bidding mechanism for their online corporate purchases when they intend to procure products in small batches. For instance, sometimes buyers can find items of their choice when suppliers wish to dispose of excess inventories. This would not have been possible through traditional mechanisms. Thus, public bidding mechanisms create great reaches both for sellers and buyers.

Service-Oriented Paradigm

Service-orientation is a new way of thinking about software systems that require interoperability. The suitability of this paradigm to the contemporary business world has been highlighted in Hull, Benedikt, Christophides, and Su (2003) and Rust and Kannan (2003). It helps one to identify certain high-level functionalities that can be deployed as logical units. The notion of *service* has been defined in different ways in the literature. Each of these definitions contributes to the appropriateness of the service-oriented paradigm in modeling interoperable distributed heterogeneous business applications. In

Lomow and Newcomer (2005), *service* has been defined as a location on a network that contains machine-readable descriptions of messages it receives and optionally returns, after appropriate internal processing. *Service* has also been described as a functionality of an application that can be used in the development of distributed applications through an integration paradigm called service-oriented computing (Dijkman & Dumas, 2004). *Service* has been described as an encapsulated unit of functionalities (Talwar, Milojicic, Wu, Pu, Yan, & Jung, 2005). In the context of Web services, a *service* is viewed as an application or business logic that can run on a Web server by exposing its functional capabilities to clients (Greenwood & Calisti, 2004). One thing that is apparent in all these definitions is that *service* is a conceptual entity that facilitates certain actions in response to a set of stimuli from its environment. The stimuli can be in the form of messages or explicit invocation of programs that trigger some internal processing at a service provider, which may not be visible to a service consumer.

In the sequel, service-oriented computing has emerged as a possible computing paradigm to provide common interface to applications, thereby enhancing the interoperability and reusability of already available functionalities of applications running on different platforms. This would help in rapid integration of applications and automate most of the business processes of enterprises. This appears to be an ambitious proposition; but the way the notion is being supported by current technologies, it seems to provide the next generation of computing infrastructure for enterprise integration.

Importance of the Service-Oriented Model in the Emerging Economy

The present economy is geared towards globalization, profitability, transparency, and accessibility. This can only be achieved through strategic use of the available technology in all areas of business. In the emerging economy, business functions of any enterprise, irrespective of its size and scale, could involve parties cutting across geographical boundaries. For small and medium-size enterprises to participate and benefit from such global business activities, their visibility and ease of operation is of paramount importance. This can be achieved to a large extent by adopting the service-oriented model, which enables one to design and deploy modular services. Further, the model provides higher-level abstraction for organizing applications for large-scale, open, and dynamic environments, thereby improving productivity and application quality. The notion of service-oriented development can assert and guarantee transactional properties, can provide for flexible decision-support, and can relate the functioning of the service components to the enterprises that they represent for transparent business interactions.

Basic Components of the Service-Oriented Paradigm

The service-oriented paradigm centers around three service entities, namely: *service provider*, *service consumer*, and *service registry*. The entities interact with each other to facilitate a service (Figure 2).

- **Service provider:** A service provider is one that wishes to provide a service either as a means of generating revenue or to facilitate interaction with partners. In order to expose its service(s), the provider publishes the service(s) along with service descriptions. It further provides standard interfaces to access service(s).

- **Service consumer:** A service consumer is one that wishes to use a service to meet its business needs. Thus it tries to locate one and, if successful, begins to interact with the service. The only requirement here is that service consumers and service providers must have common and standardized means to access and interact with a service.

Figure 2. Components of service model

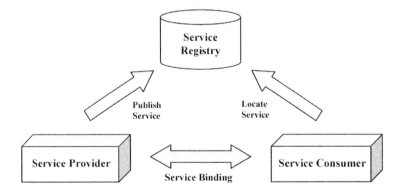

- **Service registry:** The service registry provides a location for publishing and locating services. The registry must provide a consistent taxonomy to facilitate a uniform means of describing the service being provided, description of the service provider, and information regarding how to access and interact with a particular service. Besides this, the registry needs to provide a programmatic means of publishing and locating services.

Web Services

Web services seek to implement the service-oriented paradigm. Those are viewed as self-contained modular business applications that are loosely coupled and can be accessed directly via the Internet using standard interfaces. According to the WWW Consortium (W3C, 2004) Web services are software applications identified by a universal resource indicator (URI), whose interfaces and bindings are capable of being defined, described, and discovered as XML artifacts. This standard communication allows Web services to be accessed by other Web services as well as customers, suppliers, and trading partners independent of hardware, operating system, or even programming environment. The concept of Web services reduces the time for application integration and lowers the overall cost of ownership compared to the existing business integration practices. Web services seek to provide a number of benefits both for intra- and inter-business interactions. These include:

- **Business agility:** Developers will be able to respond quickly to the demanding business needs for linking up with partners or for providing access to existing business assets in one's own organizational network.
- **Interoperability:** Functionality from heterogeneous development platforms (CORBA, J2EE, .NET) can be quickly integrated into business applications.
- **Platform-agnostic:** The Web services paradigm, being platform-agnostic, solves the basic business integration problem that requires uniform interfaces to business applications.
- **Leverage:** Investments made in the firm's Internet infrastructure can be leveraged to provide new channels for providing service to its customers.

- **Ubiquity:** Applications developed in any language can be exposed as Web services using Web services tools; in future, Web services tools will be available on all development platforms.

- **Investment protection:** Web services advocate the use of clean interfaces that allow a business asset to be wrapped within the interface; this helps one to replace and modify business processes without affecting customers who access the services offered by different businesses.

- **Component reuse:** It is possible to integrate business solutions offered as Web services by third parties in order to build new and powerful applications.

Supporting Technologies

As discussed above, Web services advocate interoperability and platform-neutral communications, as opposed to specific development languages or component models. In contrast to CORBA, COM, and EJB, which allow platform interoperability but employ their own component model and format for distributed information communication, Web services are standards-based and provide for flexible application integration. It is a conglomeration of several key technologies as presented below.

Extensible Markup Language (XML)

XML provides a standardized and platform-neutral syntax for exchanging data across heterogeneous setups. It has the simplicity of HTML but the power and extensibility of SGML. An XML document is written as a plain text containing data that is structured between user-defined tags.

Simple Object Access Protocol (SOAP)

SOAP is a lightweight protocol for exchange of information. It defines a simple model to envelop messages encoded in XML. SOAP provides a modular packaging model to express application semantics and a way to encode data within modules. Besides the basic transport, it also supports built-in extensions to provide security and transaction functionalities. These features of

SOAP make it suitable to envelop service request and response messages that are exchanged between service providers and service consumers.

Web Services Description Language (WSDL)

WSDL defines a standard description mechanism for Web services. It is an XML-based description language used for describing abstract service interfaces, service endpoints, and protocol bindings for accessing services. A WSDL document embodies a description of the functionality that a Web service offers along with the location where it is accessible. It has a flavor of CORBA and COM IDL, but it is independent of the underlying service implementation language or component model, and focuses on an abstract description. A WSDL document can be compiled to generate a client proxy, which can invoke a Web service using SOAP.

Universal Description, Discovery and Integration (UDDI)

UDDI is a specification which is used to define a registry of available Web services. It supports the concept of global electronic yellow pages enabling service providers to publish their service descriptions. Service requesters can

Figure 3. Interdependencies among the Web technologies

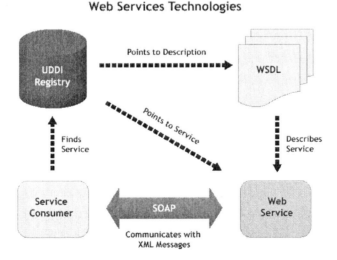

send their service requests to a service registry in the form of SOAP messages conforming to a standard UDDI schema. In a nutshell, a Web Service is a URL-addressable software resource that is designed to perform one or more function(s), and can be located by its listing in an UDDI. Further, Web services can communicate using SOAP as a standard protocol. An overall view of how the key technologies relating to Web services interact with each other is depicted in Figure 3.

Web Service-Based Systems

Web services are not just a concept, but several systems based on this concept have been implemented. The followings are some of the prominent systems being used in the business domain.

RosettaNet

RosettaNet is a global consortium that standardizes the way trading partners do business using XML messages across the Internet. Each public business process between trading partners is defined as a RosettaNet partner interface process (PIP). PIPs are specialized, system-to-system, XML-based dialogs. Each specification includes one or more business documents with a vocabulary and the choreography of the message dialog. PIP specifications also include quality of service attributes such as time-to-acknowledge messages and information on whether document transmission must be secure or if non-repudiation is required. RosettaNet standards are being extended to use service registries such as UDDI, to allow dynamic service discovery. B2B interactions in different domains such as information technology, procurement of electronic components, and supply chains are being handled by RosettaNet.

BizTalk

Microsoft's solution to the Web services initiative (.NET) is a good illustration of how the various standards work together. It defines all layers in the Web services stack, including transport with SOAP, registries with UDDI, service description with WSDL, and business modeling with XLang. Microsoft relies on components of BizTalk for transactional support. BizTalk, a component of .NET, is Microsoft's solution for enterprise application integration (EAI), which allows distributed applications to communicate with each other.

The BizTalk framework defines rules for creating loosely-coupled messages called BizTalk Messages. The framework supports SOAP, XML, and MIME standards. All BizTalk messages are composed of BizTalk documents. These documents are SOAP messages that contain specific business documents (for example, a purchase order) and the message-handling semantics for BizTalk.

The BizTalk Server is a Microsoft product used for creating collaborative business processes by automating document interchange between business entities. The BizTalk Server provides functions for validating and transporting business documents and for translating between different data formats and schemas. The BizTalk Mapper component is capable of transforming between different XML representations of data. BizTalk also provides its own mechanism for tracking transactions. Finally, the BizTalk Orchestration technology adds business process modeling capabilities to BizTalk. BizTalk Orchestration is a visual modeling tool based on the XLANG protocol that is used for modeling business processes.

ebXML

ebXML is an initiative that is being sponsored by OASIS and UN/CEFACT. Similar to the .NET/BizTalk strategy, ebXML defines many of the layers in the Web services stack, including registries, business process modeling, service description, and transport. The ebXML specification takes the best of a number of different standards, including work from BizTalk, CommerceOne, Ariba, W3C, RosettaNet, XML/EDI, and XML.ORG. The goal of ebXML is to have a global electronic market where enterprises of any size, anywhere, can:

- Find each other electronically
- Conduct business through exchange of XML-based messages using standard message structures with clear business semantics
- Use off-the-shelf business applications

The overall objective of ebXML is to facilitate the exchange of electronic business data, not only for large businesses but to extend its reach to small and medium-sized enterprises. ebXML divides Web services into two logical views: the functional service view (FSV) and the business operational view (BOV). The FSV defines service level protocols, interfaces, and functional capabilities, whereas the BOV is concerned with the semantics of business transactions and trade agreements. BOV also defines a business process and information models. The process, its service description, and protocols for process collaboration are registered in a service registry. The collaboration protocol agreement and the information model are used to determine the contents of the ebXML message payload.

An ebXML specification outlines how trading partners can register and discover other trading partners in similar markets. Documents defined in ebXML can provide information about each trading partner, what businesses they support, and their interfaces to these services. A trading partner profile (ebXML TPP) describes a company's capabilities, constraints, and the business processes it supports. A trading partner agreement (ebXML TPA) is created during a business engagement between two parties. It contains information that outlines the service and the process requirements agreed upon by the concerned parties. The conversations between trading partners are actually managed by the Trading Partner Markup Language (tpaML).

Software Agent Technology

Service is a conceptual entity, and thus requires a suitable computing paradigm for its realization. In recent times, software agents have been successfully integrated into the engineering of Web services (Greenwood & Calisti, 2004). Software entities with characteristics such as responsiveness, proactiveness, autonomy, and social abilities are often termed as software agents. Software agents possess knowledge about their environment, namely, the presence of other similar agents with their roles and the services they offer. Agents adopt reactive behavior in response to events, which are realized through message communication, and trigger execution of appropriate internal processing. Agents also exhibit proactive behavior by taking initiatives as and when situations demand and send messages to other agents. Such characteristics of agents make them suitable for use in an environment where human-like flexible behavior is desired. There is a plethora of applications of agent-based systems that have been conceptualized, proposed, and implemented. Some of the interesting ones include the following. A multi-agent-based infrastructure has been envisioned in Matos and Afsarmanesh (2004), to provide flexible specialized healthcare services to elderly people. In Li, Shen, and Ghenniwa (2004), a multi-agent-based solution is provided to integrate distributed and heterogeneous product data management systems across enterprise boundaries. Software agents have also been used for information and knowledge sharing among customers, suppliers, and business partners in manufacturing enterprise networks (Shen & Norrie, 2004). In Patra and Moore (2000), an agent-based information infrastructure has been proposed to facilitate information access for manufacturers intending to collaborate on joint manufacturing projects. With the growing trend of Internet use, agents have been advocated as the most appropriate technology for realizing the real benefit of Web services (Huhns, 2002). Besides these, agents have been considered as basic software components for building complex software systems (Jennings, 2001). Thus, an integration of software agent technology with that of service-oriented paradigm can influence the implementation of next-generation business applications to a great extent.

A Service-Oriented Agent-Based E-Procurement Model

In most of the organizations, a procurement scenario typically includes activities such as raising requisitions for purchase by different departments/individuals, evaluation and validation of the requisitions by the purchase department, sending of purchase order to seller firm, processing of purchase order by seller firm in consultation with the inventory system, contacting suitable shipping agency for shipment, and settling of payments through their bank once the items are delivered. A sketch of a complete e-procurement cycle is depicted in Figure 4, indicating the major players and the business flow. Each of the business entities is represented by a software agent to carry out required interactions with other entities in a procurement context. The elements of the proposed model are introduced in the following sections.

Figure 4. Agent mediated e-procurement

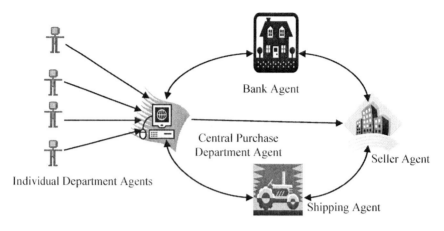

Figure 5. Sequence diagram for e-procurement

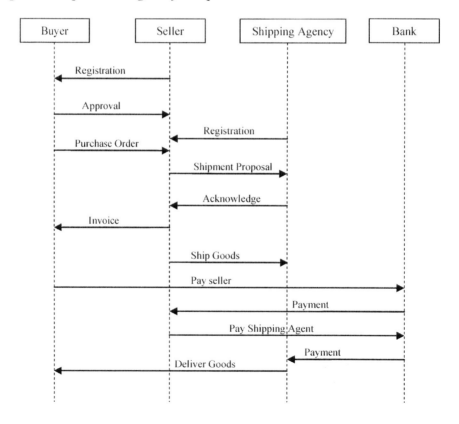

Service Point

A service point refers to a physical or logical unit where users' requests for services can be processed. Essentially, a service point provides a set of well-defined services, which can be invoked by interested users through appropriate service requests. A service point publishes certain high-level services (represented at the root-level of a service hierarchy) through its interface, which are made available to users. This notion helps one to model a loosely-coupled distributed application environment (such as e-procurement) as consisting of a set of service points. In the e-procurement example, the central purchase department, the seller, the shipping agent, and the bank are modeled as service points. The internal processing at each of these service points is hidden from the consumer of the associated service. Users can only access service through the interface provided at a service point. Some typical service-related interactions are depicted in Figure 5.

Service Composition

A service point tries to provision a requested service by invoking one or more fine-grained subservices or low-level functions. The process of enabling a

Figure 6. Class diagram for service

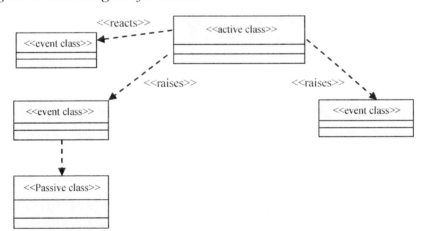

service with the help of a set of fine-grained services is referred as *service composition.* In the literature, it is also referred as *service orchestration* (Dijkman, Quartel, Pires, & Sinderen, 2003). Service composition involves activities like selecting appropriate subservices/low-level functions, determining the order in which those are to be orchestrated, and executing them.

Service Collaboration

There may be occasions where a service point receives a service request, which cannot be composed with the help of the finer-grained services and/or primitive functions available at a service point. However, it may be possible for a service point to collaborate with other service points that it is aware of (along with their service capabilities), and try to facilitate the requested service. Such a collaborative effort to realize a service is termed as *service collaboration* or *service choreography*. This can be made possible through a service catalog wherein the service points can register their service capabilities for others to view. In the context of enterprise integration, the need for open and dynamic collaboration among individual services has been highlighted in *Yokoyama, Yoshida, and Matsuda (2002)*, where the concept of service brokerage has been used to ensure safe business transactions.

Service-Flow

Akin to a workflow, a *service-flow* focuses on the *services* available at different *service points* and their interrelations. The service composition and service collaboration logic determines the form of the service-flow in a given context. Further, a suitable mechanism is needed to execute and monitor a service-flow. Similar to the multi-agent approach reported in Buhler and Vidal (2005), a software agent approach has been adopted to drive the service-flow in the proposed model.

Service-Flow Hierarchy

The notion of service can be viewed at different levels of granularity. To start with, a service request is placed at the highest level of granularity. Now the realization of the service request may require execution of one or more lower-level services. The decomposition process can continue to lower levels until atomic services are available which can be directly realizable from the implementation point of view. While modeling business processes, each of the business partners that physically exist can be viewed as a service point. The business partners (service points) collaborate because of their interdependence in different business contexts. To begin with, the business flow across business partners can be modeled as a service-flow (at level 1) that connects the service points. Each service point is associated with two types of channels, one corresponding to the incoming service requests (input service channel) and the other to the service delivery (output service channel). A service point is associated with a software agent, referred as a *service enabling agent* (SEA), which is responsible for initiating appropriate processing in response to service requests. While processing a service request, an SEA may have to trigger another level of service-flow (say, level 2) involving lower-level services within a service point. Thus, in reality one can visualize a hierarchy of service-flows being executed in order to process a service request.

Service-Flow Diagram

Here, we use the notion of service-flow diagrams to conceptually specify cooperative behavior of different service providers. The structure of a service-flow diagram depends on the service relationships among the interacting service providers in a given context. This is depicted through a class diagram as in Figure 6. The classes represent the specification of services that are invoked and delivered, and the messages that are exchanged among the service points. Three different types of classes are identified, namely: *passive class*, *active class*, and *event class*. A passive class is used to specify only data contents that do not trigger any action, for instance, a product description; an active class specifies the behavior along with events that trigger action (i.e., attributes and functions); and an event class specifies events that trigger action as well as events raised by an active class because of certain behavior manifestation.

A business activity may involve service invocations from several participants. For instance, procurement of certain item(s) would involve the services of the seller, the shipping agency, the bank, and so forth. It is necessary to coordinate the activities taking place at individual participants for consistency and traceability. The notion of service-flow coordination diagram (SCD) is introduced to model the coordination required to integrate the services that are invoked and delivered at different stages of an e-procurement process.

Figure 7. Serviceflow coordination diagram

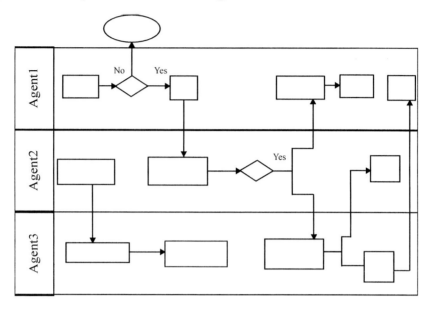

Figure 8. Class diagram for central purchase department

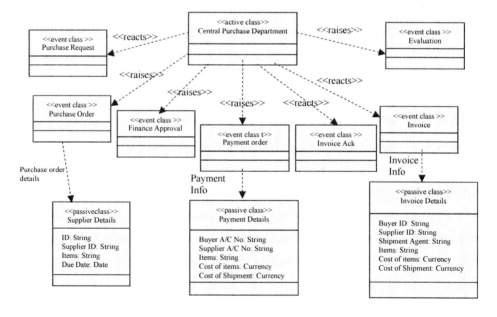

An SCD essentially consists of horizontal swim-lanes, each corresponding to a participating agent. The internal processing that enables a service at an agent is depicted along a swim-lane. Service invocations across participating agents are shown through vertical arrows across the swim-lanes. There is also provision for both sequential as well as parallel service invocations. A skeleton SCD is depicted in Figure 7.

Applying the Service-Flow Diagram

In order to make use of the notion of the service-flow diagram and related class diagram to an e-procurement scenario, one has to identify the three different types of classes, namely: *passive class*, *active class,* and *event class.* A detailed class diagram for the Buyer Agent (the purchase department) is provided in Figure 8. The *supplier details, payment details,* and *invoice details*

Figure 9. Serviceflow coordination for e-procurement

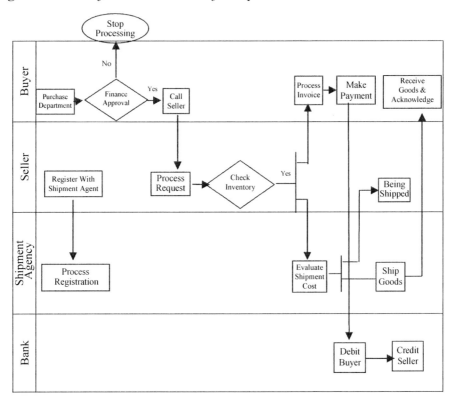

are modeled as passive classes as those specify only data contents and do not trigger any action. The purchase department, the supplier, the shipping agent, and the bank are modeled as active classes, which are characterized by a set of attributes and behavior specifications. The event class has been classified into two groups, namely: the events that trigger action in a service-flow, and the events that are raised by the active classes. For instance, purchase order, finance approval, and payment order are the events that are raised by the purchase department, whereas purchase requests, invoice, and so forth, are events that trigger action at the purchase department.

The service-flow coordination diagram for an e-procurement scenario is shown in Figure 9. Upon receiving purchase requests from different departments, the central purchase authority initiates the necessary processing. It first obtains approval from the finance department regarding the purchase of goods, and then invokes the services of seller agents who are already registered with the buyer organization. A buyer agent prepares a purchase order and sends it over to a seller. The seller in turn checks its inventory and invokes the services of a shipping agency. The seller agent, after receiving relevant information from the shipping agent, generates an invoice and sends it to the buyer agent. The buyer agent informs the seller about the payment

Figure 10. Agent architecture

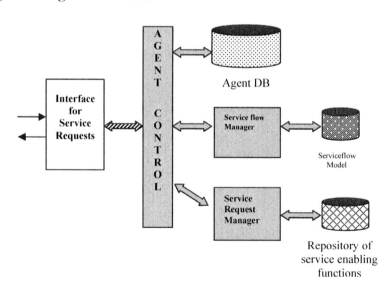

using the services of a bank. The goods are shipped to the buyer's site and acknowledged by the buyer agent.

Architecture of Service-Enabling Agent

The architecture for the agents that enable service at a service point is provided in Figure 10. The role of an agent deployed at a service point is to receive service requests (in the form of XML messages) from users as well as other service points, process them, and deliver the requested service, which is either returned to the user or passed on as input to the next service point for further processing. Keeping this in view, an agent has been structured as consisting of a set of well-defined functional components that execute instructions to exhibit appropriate agent behavior. The architecture depicts the functional components of an agent that operate in a concerted manner to process events (arrival of messages) and take appropriate action(s) by triggering internal processing and/or external actions by sending messages. The *Communication Manager* receives incoming messages at an agent's external interface and passes them on to the *Agent Control* for interpretation. It also sends messages to other agents as a result of internal processing. The *Agent Control* interprets incoming messages and instructs other modules for appropriate action. It also performs certain actions proactively when the situation demands while executing a service-flow. For example, seller agents may keep sending

Figure 11. Purchase order generation

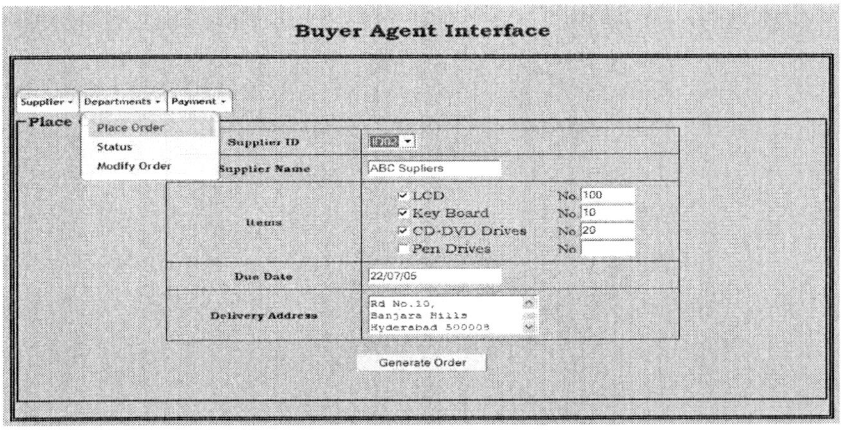

Figure 12. Seller registration

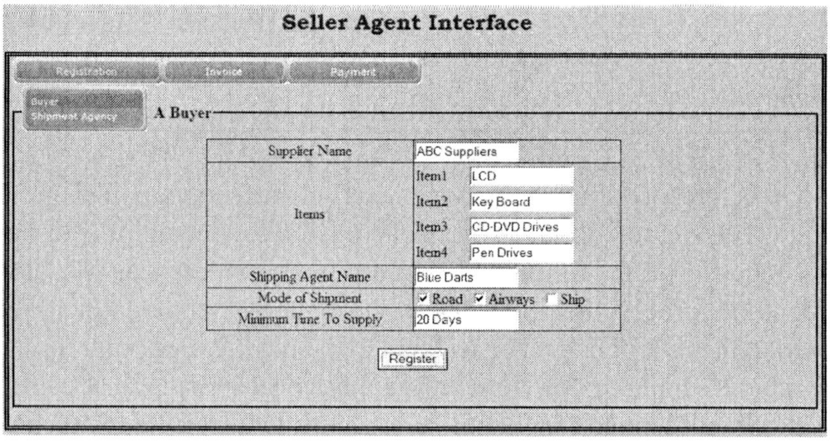

their service updates to different prospective buyers. The *Message Template Manager* takes care of preparation of messages using appropriate message templates. The most important module is the *Service-flow Manager,* which monitors execution of activities right from the moment a service request is received until an appropriate response is notified.

Implementation Framework

A prototype implementation has been attempted using XML, J2EE, and Web Services Development Tomcat 5.0 application server. The buyer and seller agent interfaces are shown in Figure 11 and 12. A buyer places an order with a registered seller through the buyer agent interface. The buyer inputs are transformed to an XML document, which is sent to the designated seller agent. The seller agent extracts the data from the XML document and checks the inventory levels to fulfill the request. Below, we provide an outline of processing taking place at a seller agent.

1.   < Registration with Buyer Agent: Proactive behavior >

    1.1   Prepare an XML file containing details of items that seller is capable of supplying

    1.2   Send the XML file to the Buyer agent

2.   \<On receiving a purchase order: Reactive Behavior>

    2.1   Extract necessary details from purchase order

    2.2   Check the inventory levels and acknowledge the buyer

    2.3   Contact the shipping agent regarding the shipment

3.   \< On receiving shipment information from shipping agency >

    3.1   Prepare Invoice with cost and delivery date.

    3.2   Send the invoice to the buyer agent.

4.   \< On receiving payment order from Buyer agent >

    4.1   Instruct shipping agency to dispatch.

    4.2   Make payment to shipping agency.

5.   \< On receiving delivery notice from Buyer agent >

    5.1   Add to sales database

Discussion and Challenges

The proposed framework promises major improvements in the management of procurement, which include:

- Better access to information and transparency in markets, specially for small and medium-sized enterprises (SMEs)
- Cost savings as a result of reduced labor cost, and better price offers because of direct buyer-supplier relations
- Process efficiency as most of the activities are semi-automated, resulting in reduced paperwork and thus, less human errors
- Better information flow between buyers and suppliers
- Streamlining of supply chain by automating most of the transactions
- Ability to implement "just-in-time" strategies to maintain optimum inventory level

The proposed model holds great promises for developing agile business applications, but faces many challenges, which need to be addressed for its successful deployment. Some of the major research issues include the following:

- There is need for suitable language support for the specification/description of services.

- One of the major challenges is to develop suitable methods for service discovery and recommendation systems through the use of efficient matchmaking algorithms. Software agents can be employed to intelligently handle matchmaking scenarios.

- There is need for efficient methods for service orchestration and choreography.

- As the technology is supposed to facilitate business transactions in an open environment, it is prone to security threats. Ensuring reliable message communication and service delivery could be a bottleneck for the success of this promising technology. Thus, a lot has to be done to provide information security both when it is stored and when it is being communicated.

Conclusion

Service-oriented computing has emerged as a possible computing paradigm to provide common interface to applications, thereby enhancing the interoperability and reusability of already available functionalities of applications running on different platforms. This would help in rapid integration of applications and automate most of the business processes. The service-oriented paradigm is being adequately supported by the Web Services technology, which is fast evolving and finding rapid adoption in enterprises. Web Services can provide a way to design seamless and flexible interaction among business applications both within and across enterprise boundaries. This is a very important feature for SMEs to collaborative while fulfilling procurements. Further, the software agent technology has brought in ways to automate most of the business interactions, which is a most sought-for feature in an open distributed market environment where business transactions need to be fulfilled under heavy time constraints. It appears that the service-oriented paradigm, augmented with the agent technology, is going to provide the next generation of computing infrastructure for enterprise integration facilitating several electronic transactions.

References

Ariba. (n.d.). Retrieved December 10, 2005, from http://www.Ariba.com

Ben-Ameur, H., Vaucher, S., Gérin-Lajoie, R., Kropf., P., & Chaib-draa, B. (2002). Towards an agent-based approach for multi-market package e-procurement. In T. G. Crainic & B. Gavish (Eds.), *Proceedings of the Fifth International Conference on Electronic Commerce Research (ICERC-5)* (pp. 1-14).

Buhler, P. A., & Vidal, J. M. (2005). Towards adaptive workflow enactment using multi-agent systems. *Information Technology and Management, 6*, 61-87.

Carabello, L. (2001). E-procurement can reduce expenses. *Healthcare Financial Management*, 82-83.

Chiu, D. K. W., Cheung, S. C., Till, S., Karlapalem, K., Li, Q., & Kafeza, E. (2004). Workflow view-driven cross-organizational interoperability in a Web service environment. *Information Technology and Management, 5*, 221-250.

Commerce One. (n.d.). Retrieved December 10, 2005, from http://www.xcbl. org/sox/downloads/soxtutorial10r1.pdf

Dai, Q., & Kauffman, R. J. (2001). Business models for Internet-based e-procurement systems and B2B electronic markets: An exploratory assessment. In *IEEE Proceedings of the 34th Hawaii International Conference on System Sciences*.

Dijkman, R. M., & Dumas, M. (2004). Service-oriented design: A multi-viewpoint approach. *International Journal of Cooperative Information Systems, 13*(4), 337-368.

Dijkman, R. M. , Quartel, D. A. C., Pires, L. F., & Sinderen, M. J. V. (2003, July). The state of the art in service-oriented computing and design (Ref. No. ArCo/WP1/T1/V1.00).

Greenwood, D., & Calisti, M. (2004). Engineering Web services-Agent integration. In *Proceedings of the IEEE International Conference on Systems, Man and Cybernetics* (pp. 1918-1925). Retrieved April 20, 2005, from www.whitestein.com/resources/papers/ieeesmc04.pdf

Huhns, M. N. (2002). Agents as Web services. *Internet Computing, 6*(4), 93-95.

Huhns, M. N., & Singh, M. P. (2005, January/February). Service-oriented computing: Key concepts and principles. *IEEE Internet Computing, 9*(1), 75-81.

Hull, R., Benedikt, M., Christophides, V., & Su, J. (2003, June). E-services: A look behind the curtain. In *Proceedings of the 22ⁿᵈ ACM Symposium on Principles of Database Systems (PODS)*, San-Diego, CA.

ITRG (Info-Tech Research Group). (2002). *A success guide for e-procurement.* London; Canada.

Jennings, N. R. (2001). An agent-based approach for building complex software systems. *Communications of the ACM, 44*(4), 35-41.

Li, Y., Shen, W., & Ghenniwa, H. (2004). Agent-facilitated integration of distributed PDM systems. *International Journal of Networking and Virtual Organizations, 2*(2), 133-152.

Lomow, G., & Newcomer, E. (2005). *Introduction to SOA with Web services.* Addison Wesley. Retrieved February 4, 2005, from www.informit.com/articles/

Matos, L. M. C., & Afsarmanesh, H. (2004). A multi-agent-based infrastructure to support virtual communities in elderly care. *International Journal of Networking and Virtual Organizations, 2*(3), 246-266.

Myerson, J. M. (2002). *Web service architectures* (Tech. Pub. pp. 1-15). Retrieved November 5, 2005, from http://www.webservicesarchitect.com /content/articles/myerson01.asp

Ovans, A. (2000, May/June). E-procurement at Schlumberger. *Harvard Business Review, 78*(3), 21-22.

Patra, M. R., & Moore, R. (2000, November). A multi-agent-based information infrastructure for manufacturing. *Proceedings of the 4th International Conference on the Design of Information Infrastructure Systems for Manufacturing (DIISM 2000)*, Melbourne, Australia (pp. 388-395).

Peltz, C. (2003, January). *Web services orchestration: A review of emerging technologies, tools, and standards* (Tech. Rep., pp. 1-20). Hewlett-Packard.

Petrie, C., & Bussler, C. (2003, July/August). Service agents and virtual enterprises: A survey. *IEEE Internet Computing, 7*(4), 2-12.

Presutti, Jr., W. D. (2002). Supply management and e-procurement: Creating value addition in the supply chain. *Industrial Marketing Management, 32*, 219-226.

Rust, R. T., & Kannan, P. K. (2003). E-service: A new paradigm for business in the electronic environment. *Communication of the ACM, 46*(6), 37-42.

Shen, W., & Norrie, D. H. (2004). An agent-based approach for information and knowledge sharing in manufacturing enterprise networks. *International Journal of Networking and Virtual Organizations, 2*(2), 173-190.

Talwar, V., Milojicic, D., Wu, Q., Pu, C., Yan, W., & Jung, G. (2005, March-April). Approaches for service deployment. *IEEE Internet Computing*, 70-80.

W3C. (2004). *W3Schools online Web tutorials.* Retrieved May 2005, from http:// www.W3.org/TR/2004/NOTE-ws-arch-20040211/

Yokoyama, K., Yoshida, E., & Matsuda, S. (2002). Requirements for open service collaboration among Web services. In *Proceedings of the Symposium on Applications and the Internet (SAINT)*, Nara, Japan (pp. 214-217).

Appendix

A sample XML code for seller registration:

```
<?xml version="1.0" encoding="UTF-8" ?>
<!DOCTYPE reg [
<!ELEMENT reg(Supplier+)>
<!ELEMENT Supplier (name,items+,address)>
<!ELEMENT name (#PCDATA)>
<!ELEMENT items (item+)>
<!ELEMENT item (#PCDATA)>
<!ATTLIST item id CDATA #REQUIRED>
<!ELEMENT address (URL,phone)>
<!ELEMENT URL (#PCDATA)>
<!ELEMENT phone(#PCDATA)>]>
<reg>
  <Supplier>
   <name>ABC Suppliers</name>
   <items>
        <item id="1">lap tops</item>
        <item id="2">LCD panel</item>
        <item id="3">key boards</item>
        <item id="4">Pen Drives</item>
        </items>
   <address>
        <URL>http:abc.com</URL>
        <phone>04012345678</phone>
   </address>
  </Supplier>
</reg>
```

Chapter X

Application of Web Services in the Context of E-Procurement:
An SME Foci

Stanley Oliver, University of Bolton, UK

Kiran Maringanti, University of Bolton, UK

Abstract

This chapter highlights the importance of e-procurement and the barriers affecting its widespread adoption in the context of small and medium enterprises. The chapter takes a technical perspective and critically analyzes the importance of information systems in the procurement domain and the integration challenges faced by SMEs in today's digitally networked economy. Next, the role of XML-based Web services in solving the integration challenges faced by SMEs is discussed. Subsequently, a procurement transformation framework enabled by Web services which provides a clear methodology of the way in which information systems should be introduced in the procurement domain is discussed. The chapter concludes by a discussion of the measures that must be undertaken by various stakeholders like the government and universities in increasing the awareness levels of SMEs to the latest e-business mechanisms.

Introduction

Micro, small and medium-sized enterprises (SMEs) play a central role in the world economy. They are a major source of entrepreneurial skills, innovation, and employment. There are an estimated 75 million SMEs worldwide, which represent about 99 percent of all companies (IBM, 1998). Zheng, Caldwell, Harland, Powell, Woerndl, and Xu (2004) find that the "Internet presents many opportunities for SMEs to harness the benefits of Information and Communications Technologies (ICT)" (p. 27-39). E-procurement, which is the utilization of the Internet in enabling and streamlining the entire procurement cycle, has been identified as a very important area of concentration for SMEs (ABI, 2003; OGC, 2005). "Electronic procurement specifically and eCommerce generally will knit supplier and buyer business processes together to deliver seamless transactions" (Cavinato & Kauffman, 2000). Large enterprises have already invested huge amounts of resources in e-procurement and are reaping the benefits of it. E-procurement is being championed by larger enterprises, mainly to save transaction costs and reduce prices. But potentially they also offer opportunities for SMEs to find new business partners and to benefit from closer integration into the value chains of large companies (ABI, 2003).

It is pertinent to study the impact of e-procurement on SMEs owing to many factors:

1. Many large organizations' supplier base consists of small and medium enterprises (SMEs), and without the full participation of these SMEs, the initiatives of large corporations will not be successful.

2. The application of emerging information technologies (IT) has often proven to be a complex job for SMEs.

3. SMEs are often at a disadvantage in terms of finance, technology, human resource development, and networking (UN-ECE, 1997); in the case of information technologies, the task seems even more daunting, owing to the highly complex evolving process and also the challenge in successfully deciphering a business case for the justification of its investment.

In this chapter, we will look at the evolution of procurement and look at the importance of e-procurement for SMEs. We will also look at the barriers to the widespread adoption of e-procurement and how the deployment of Web services will help overcome those barriers.

Background

This section offers primary insight into procurement, e-procurement, inter-organizational information systems, and supply chain management. We believe these areas are closely knitted and usually overlapping.

Procurement

Every business, irrespective of its size and sector, are involved in some form of buying and selling. Procurement is an unavoidable and important business function. A typical firm spends at least half of its revenues on external purchases of goods and services (Markham, Morales, & Slaight, 2000). Procurement is defined by Gebauer, Beam, and Segev (1998) as "including all activities involved in obtaining, transporting and moving material towards the production process." Though procurement has long been overlooked as a backwater, repetitive function, nevertheless it is indispensable, it forms the bedrock of the company, and it is a core business function. A study made by AT Kearney on European and North American manufacturers found that in 1985, 30% of the total manufacturing cost stemmed from purchased material and services. In 1995, the figure rose to 55%, and for 2005, it was estimated to rise to 85%, which makes procurement a very important function (Knusden, 2003). Since the procurement process is located at the beginning of the value chain, any ripples created here will be echoed right across the supply chain. But traditional procurement processes are muddled with inefficiencies, and leave scope for non-compliance with existing procurement policies.

Procurement, purchasing, and supply management are simply different terms used in the literature to describe the same activity. But we prefer the usage of the term "procurement." Knusden (2003) justifies the usage of the term "procurement" by asserting that "it neither rules of the operational nor the strategic aspect of acquiring external resources." Procurement is the name given to a very broad purchasing function which includes basic steps like making a requisition for goods, to much more complex aspects like sourcing and logistics. Thus, the scope of procurement is very wide, making it a very important component of supply chain management. Typically, a company's procurement function is subdivided into strategic and operational processes, since activities and priorities in these two areas are entirely different (Kaufmann, 1999; Lamming, 1995), as depicted in Figure 1.

However, traditionally procurement was often neglected as a back room function. A glance at the organization chart of many organizations reveals that purchasing departments are located in many areas of the organization. Separate purchasing departments for manufacturing and sales made it difficult to have a centralized purchasing policy. Heywood, Barton, and Heywood (2002, p. 8) note that "traditional buyers have long argued that their work does not lend itself to automation because much of the information that appears on a purchase order or contract is unstructured text, and most purchasing systems find this difficult to accommodate. A blank purchase order with terms and conditions written in the very small lettering on the back is the way they like to work. Because there was never a big push from the buyers to automate, traditional purchasing departments were usually left to their own devices and persisted with manual paper systems that satisfied only the needs of the buyers."

This is one of the reasons why procurement functions were never automated, as insufficient emphasis was placed on this important corporate function. Neef (2001) notes "traditionally, the external resources that were acquired by the company have been broken down into two major categories, that is, Direct and Indirect goods."

Figure 1. Procurement classification model (Source: Authors)

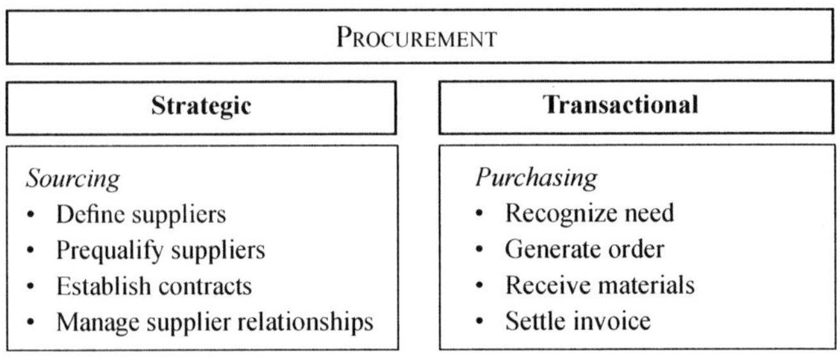

PROCUREMENT	
Strategic	**Transactional**
Sourcing • Define suppliers • Prequalify suppliers • Establish contracts • Manage supplier relationships	*Purchasing* • Recognize need • Generate order • Receive materials • Settle invoice

1. **Direct goods:** Typically, direct goods are 80% by value and 20% by volume of many organizations expenditure on procurement. Direct goods include goods which are used in the production of core products and services of the company. Direct goods are central to the running of the business, and are very crucial because any disruption in this area of purchasing can cause havoc and ultimately challenge the survival of the company. Procurement strategies for direct goods assume the highest significance for any company and have to be planned with utmost care. They improve the efficiency of the company, which in turn will help it in gaining competitive advantage in the market.

2. **Indirect goods:** Typically, indirect goods are 20% by value and 80% by volume. Indirect goods can be classified as goods which aid in the running of the business. Indirect goods are classified again as below.

    *   **Maintenance, retail, and operation (MRO):** MRO goods are very crucial to the business as these include obtaining parts for the various machinery and other high-end instruments which perform the actual production.

    *   **Office supplies:** Office supplies include all other expenditure which is helpful in performing routine jobs. These include stationery, lighting, and so forth. These are not mission-critical goods and can be bought at any period with off-contract suppliers as they can be substituted easily.

Figure 2. Traditional procurement process (Source: Heywood et al., 2002)

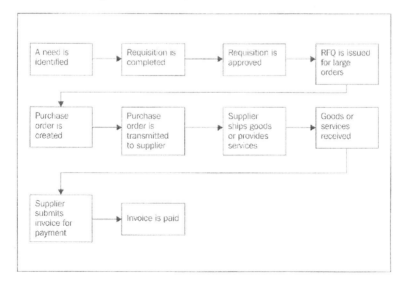

Complexity is an inherent attribute of procurement. Companies have always been trying to simplify this extremely crucial aspect of their business, in extracting optimal quality and accurate transactions at a lowest possible cost. For example, Figure 2 demonstrates the routine tasks involved on the operational side of a traditional procurement life cycle. As garnered, the process was very labor-intensive, which was a source of inefficiency in most organizations. The solution to cut down drastically on the inefficiency was through the introduction of information systems. Thus, the concept of inter-organizational information systems (IOIS) came to the fore.

Inter-Organizational Information System (IOIS)

Generally, the need for sharing procurement-related information is found to be on a higher scale between participant organizations. The emergence of IOIS attempted to solve that problem. An IOIS is defined as a computer and communication infrastructure, crossing company boundaries and enabling information sharing (Cash & Konsynski, 1985). IOIS facilitate technology-based cooperation across organizations (Bakos, 1991). Basically, IOIS enables two companies to exchange business-related documents in some pre-agreed proprietary format. As processes evolved, we saw the rise of electronic data interchange (EDI), a variant of IOIS during the period of the 1980s.

Electronic Data Interchange (EDI)

Electronic Data Interchange has been around for a long time and has been widely used for the exchange of business documents by large firms. EDI is often confined to data exchange using EDI VAN (value added network) or EDI standard protocols such as UN/EDIFACT (United Nations/EDI for Administration, Commerce and Transport) and ANSI (American National Standards Institute) ASC (Accredited Standards Committee) x12 (Shimada, 2004). Many large firms have been applying technology to the purchasing process for several decades through electronic data interchange (EDI). It was still expensive to implement, often running into millions of dollars (Presutti, 2002). However, the high costs associated with EDI can be afforded only by the large companies (Khazanchi, 1999). Competing standards, high-entry barriers and lack of suitability for real-time transactions meant that EDI was not an option for SMEs. But with the anvil of e-business, the concept of doing business electronically with a multitude of partners has become affordable for even the SME community.

E-Business

Human race has been involved in buying and selling of products and services to each other for as long as recorded history. McMillan (2002) notes that the "trading of goods and services for other goods or for money is central to the concept of human socialization." While the basic philosophy has remained the same, means of achieving the ends have changed profoundly. The success of the PC-based model of computing, coupled with the emergence of the World Wide Web, has opened up new and exciting opportunities for businesses. The Internet in general, and in particular, e-business has changed the centuries-old practices/methods dramatically at an unprecedented pace. Businesses all over the globe wanted to gain the benefits offered by this new channel of communication. While the most visible manifestation of the Internet has been in the emergence of electronic commerce as a new retail channel, it is likely that the Internet will have a profound impact on business-to-business interaction, especially in the area of supply chain integration.

The consumer-centric business-to-commerce (B2C) model dominated the embryonic stages of the Internet. But it will be their B2B successors who will leverage the full potential of this newfound electronic economy. Gartner Group, an IT research firm, predicted that the worldwide B2B market would be $ 7.2 trillion by 2003. True to predictions, B2B/e-business is already the fastest growth area in the superheated new Internet economy and carries potential almost beyond measure. In the field of e-business, e-procurement is regarded as having far greater potential for cost savings and business improvements than online retailing or enterprise resource planning systems (Aberdeen, 2000; Neef, 2001). Many studies have clearly indicated that the biggest savings from e-business initiatives will occur in the area of e-procurement (Knusden, 2003).

Supply Chain Management (SCM)

Supply chain management can be described as the chain linking each element of the manufacturing and supply process from raw materials to the end user, encompassing several organizational boundaries (New & Payne, 1995;

Scott & Westbrook, 1991). Increasingly, organizations are looking to squeeze costs out of the supply chain to gain competitive advantage over other firms. Christopher (1998) also notes that the goal of supply chain management is to link the marketplace, the distribution network, the manufacturing process, and the procurement activity in such a way that customers are serviced at higher levels but at lower total cost. Seventy percent of a firm's sales revenues are, on average, spent on supply chain-related activities from material purchases to the distribution and service of finished products to the final customer (Presutti, 2002). Supply chain management has thus evolved into a very important area of study for many researchers and companies attributable to the symbiotic relationship between supply chain and organizational performance. Supply chain management is seen as paramount to delivering high customer satisfaction with reduced lead times and costs (Bhattacharya, Coleman, & Brace, 1996).

The emergence of e-business has provided a fresh impetus for re-invigorating the supply chain. Today, there is an increased use of geographically-dispersed suppliers by firms to retain their competitive advantages. This act requires a high degree of orchestration between the geographically-dispersed partners. The role played by information technology in synchronizing these partners is profound. Cagliano, Caniato, and Spina (2003) note that "e-business is particularly important for the supply chain literature as a consequence of the increasing need to integrate activities and information flows and to optimize the processes not only at the single company level, but also at the level of inter-company processes." Chen and Meixell (2003) point towards the symbiotic relationship between supply chain management and information technology. Due to the dynamic nature of supply chain management, new breed information technologies can offer significant contributions in optimizing supply chains for better performance. This makes SCM more responsive to the dynamics of the marketplace. E-procurement is a subset of supply chain management.

E-Procurement and SMEs

E-procurement is a collective term for a range of e-business software solutions which utilize the latest information and communication technologies (especially the Internet), that can be employed to automate the internal and external processes associated with strategic sourcing and purchasing, which includes catalogue search, item requisition request, approval, purchase order, delivery, receiving, payment, identification of sourcing opportunities, supplier evaluation, negotiation, and contract. Examples of the e-business software solutions include e-procurement software, business-to-business (B2B) auctions, B2B market exchanges, purchasing consortia, e-tendering, e-auctions, e-marketplaces, and e-sourcing.

The e-business software solutions that aid the procurement process automation utilize the latest information and communication technologies, such as electronic data interchange, Internet, e-mail, software and hardware, but excludes other means of communication such as telephone, fax, and so forth. E-procurement technologies fundamentally aim to hammer out inefficiencies associated with manual-based procurement systems.

From the above discussion, we can deduce that e-procurement is mainly the effective utilization of the modern Internet standards for streamlining the entire corporate procurement activities. The emergence of e-procurement, which leverages the potential of the Internet to improve the procurement process, has gathered considerable interest amongst academia and business practitioners.

Benefits of E-Procurement to SMEs

We spoke about how e-procurement can help organizations in improving over traditional procurement processes. Especially for an SME, if they adopt electronic procurement, a small percentage of savings in procurement expenses can help them reduce operation costs and improve the profit margin considerably, as procurement is an expensive business activity. This improves their competitiveness as well, which would ultimately benefit the economy (Chan & Lee, 2003).

This section lists the benefits of e-procurement which are exclusive to SMEs, as highlighted by many authors (ABI, 2003; NEPP, 2004; Office of Government Commerce, 2002):

- Competition with any other supplier, regardless of their size; any supplier with access to the Internet is now on a par with even the largest suppliers

- Being strategically valuable, as it helps them to win other business elsewhere
- Receiving payment more quickly as there is less of a paper chase at the buyer end
- Business does not need to be limited to one geographical area
- Removal of some of the process costs associated with supplying to government
- Efficiency (doing things better through pure cost reduction in current procurement and selling business processes)
- Effectiveness (doing better things, through supply chain integration driving costs out of the supply chain, and strategic sourcing to establish new competitive supply sources)
- Evolution (doing things differently promoted through transparency and intelligence)
- B2B re-engineering (promoting business intelligence and transparency in the customer and supply chain partners and encouraging innovation through collaboration)

But on a precautionary note, it must be understood that e-procurement does not replace procurement. E-procurement is only a strategic tool that enhances the entire procurement operation. The aim that an e-procurement system attempts to achieve could be divided into two categories, that is, internal and external, as depicted in Figure 3.

The functionality that is set forth to be achieved on the internal side of e-procurement could be achieved through either:

- An ERP system
- Specialized e-procurement software

The functionality that is set forth to be achieved on the external side of e-procurement could be achieved through:

- B2B marketplaces
- E-auctions
- e-tendering

Figure 3. Essentials of a good e-procurement system

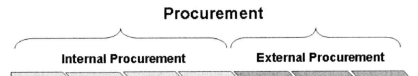

There is no particular variant of e-procurement that will dominate the entire industry. Different models are suitable for different industries, and the kind of solution to be embraced is also dictated by the size of the company. Davila, Gupta, and Palmer (2003) note that "e-procurement software and B2B auctions are better suited to the needs of large corporations, while market exchanges and purchasing consortia better serve the needs of smaller companies and non-profits." Thus, electronic marketplaces have been identified as the preferred way for SMEs to conduct electronic procurement.

New, Meakin, and Southworth (2002) note that "one of the most misleading aspects of much that has been written about the Internet and its effects on organizations is the lumping together of different types of organizations operating in different types of markets. Firms differ in many significant ways." Echoing the above thoughts, firms, especially SMEs, vary significantly in their procurement patterns, and it is often difficult to prescribe a particular model for a group of firms. Instead, SMEs have to mix and match solutions that best serve their purpose from the wide gamut of e-procurement solutions available.

B2B Marketplaces

B2B marketplaces are the umbrella term which embraces all variants of external e-procurement models. There are many names by which B2B marketplaces are addressed. In this chapter, they would be addressed as B2B marketplaces as they focus on business-to-business transactions and engage in product, service, or information exchange between buyers and sellers. "The existence of Marketplaces in human society has a long history from before the agora of Ancient Greece to the online trading places of the 21st century" (Stockdale & Standing, 2004). The concept of an Electronic Marketplace dates back to the mid-1940s, when the first documented EM system, known as Selevision, was used to remote-market Florida citrus (Henderson, 1984).

B2B marketplaces basically provide the infrastructure for the transfer of information, service, or product between the concerned partners. The ability of the marketplaces to interoperate extends the idea of liquidity and network effect by joining more buyers with more suppliers, but does not sacrifice the ability of each marketplace to be highly specific to the supply-chain node or target buyer group it serves. B2B marketplaces have emerged as the best mechanism to unlock that value, which aligns buyers and sellers in product or industry-focused Internet marketplaces for the exchange of goods and services (Aberdeen Group, 2001).

Schmid (1993) and Bakos (1991) consider B2B marketplaces as manifestations of the neo-classical market ideal, reducing transaction costs to a negligible minimum. Malone, Yates, and Benjamin (1987) conclude that markets are the preferred coordination mechanism for products with low asset specificity and low product description complexity. B2B marketplaces offer compelling features like price discovery, aggregation of buyers and sellers, automation of processes, and expanding markets to buyers and sellers (Bakos, 1998; Kaplan & Sawhney, 2000). However, there have been various viewpoints on the positioning of B2B marketplaces:

- Is a B2B/e-marketplace an inter-organizational information system? (Bakos, 1991)
- Is a B2B/e-marketplace an e-procurement solution? (Segev & Gebauer, 1999)
- Is a B2B/e-marketplace a medium? (Schmid & Lindemann, 1998)
- Is a B2B/e-marketplace a meeting point? (Kaplan & Sawhney, 2000)
- Is a B2B/e-marketplace an intermediary? (Dai & Kauffman, 2000)
- Is a B2B/e-marketplace just a listing? (Bradley & Peters, 1997)

We consider that B2B marketplaces fall under the ambit of e-procurement, which is consistent with Segev and Gebauer (1999) who note that "compared to many other electronic procurement solutions, electronic marketplaces represent a relatively neutral position between buyer and seller, providing services to both sides of a transaction. An electronic marketplace represents a virtual place where buyers and sellers meet to exchange goods and services."

The electronic markets hypothesis (EMH) by Malone, Yates, and Benjamin (1987) predicted that electronic marketplaces will be the favored mechanisms for coordinating material and information flows among organizations in the presence of electronic communication technologies. True to their hypothesis, the rise of the B2B marketplaces has been stupendous. Technically, e-marketplaces are more strategic by enabling firms to interact with other firms in a market setting than electronic data interchange (EDI) systems in a relational setting (Grewal, Comer, & Mehta, 2001).

B2B Marketplaces Classification

Generally, B2B marketplaces can be classified into public, private, and industrial/consortia marketplace.

- **Public marketplace***: A public marketplace could also be termed as a third-party or a neutral marketplace. They provide content, value-added services, and transaction capabilities.

- **Private marketplace:** Private marketplaces are exclusively the networks built by large enterprises to deal with their group of suppliers. In these kinds of marketplaces, the establisher of the network provides the infrastructure, and thus it is tightly integrated with the enterprises and its suppliers. Typical examples of such kind of marketplaces are Click2Procure (Siemens), Wal-Mart, and UPS.

Figure 4. B2B marketplaces classification

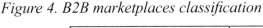

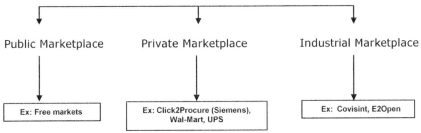

- **Industrial or consortia marketplace:** Industrial marketplaces are generally established by a group of large enterprises to leverage their buying power. In these kinds of environments, the marketplaces are integrated with the establishing enterprises. Examples of such marketplaces are Covisint, E2Open, and so forth.

Barriers to Electronic Procurement for SMEs

Numerous studies highlight the fact that the adoption of e-business among SMEs is not in tune with the expectations, and the reasons cited are numerous. Many studies have been conducted to investigate the inhibitors to the adoption of e-business among SMEs. MacGregor and Vrazalic (2005) summarize the inhibitors to the adoption of e-business among SMEs.

A study conducted by Davila et al., (2003) has pointed out that user's of e-procurement technologies report that they can acquire goods over the Internet from only 15% of the supply base. A majority of suppliers in the supply base are SMEs because of their common role as suppliers for dominating manufacturers (Hauser, 2000).

This indicates that the uptake of e-procurement is low among small and medium enterprises. However, the barriers related to the adoption of e-procurement among SMEs and the solutions to overcome those barriers is an under-researched area, and there exists very little rigorous academic and empirical research in these areas. Since there is a wealth of information available on the barriers to the adoption of e-procurement among large corporations, a summary of the barriers is presented in Table 2. These barriers were summarized by Hawking and Stein (2004) from their study of 38 major Australian firms' e-procurement adoption.

Hawking and Stein (2004) note that "the main barriers to the uptake of e-procurement are infrastructure, technology, and integration-based. This seems to indicate that the complex technological issues—both within and between organisations in the procurement process—are crucial."

A study was commissioned by IMPAQ (which specializes in developing e-procurement technologies to enable SMEs to trade with blue-chip customers) on top FTSE 350 companies to identify the extent to which e-procurement is enabling blue-chip buying organizations to enhance trading with SME suppliers. The study signifies that "61% of the blue-chip buyers felt the need to promote the adoption of e-procurement among SMEs." Corporate buyers

Table 1. Summary of the inhibitors to e-business adoption amongst SMEs (Source: MacGregor & Vrazalic, 2005)

Barriers to E-Commerce Adoption	Related Literature
• High cost of e-commerce implementation; Internet technologies are too expensive to implement	• Iacovou et al. (1995), Quayle (2002), Purao and Campbell (1998), Lawrence (1997), Riquelme (2002), and Van Akkeren and Cavaye (1999)
• E-commerce is too complex to implement	• Quayle (2002)
• Small businesses require short-term ROI and e-commerce is a long-term investment	• Lawrence (1997) and McGowan and Madey (1998)
• Organisational resistance to change because of the fear of new technology amongst employees	• Lawrence (1997) and Van Akkeren and Cavaye (1999)
• Preference for and satisfaction with traditional manual methods, such as phone, fax, and face to face	• Lawrence (1997), Venkatesan and Fink (2002), and Poon and Swatman (1999)
• Lack of technical skills and IT knowledge amongst employees; lack of computer literate/specialised staff	• Quayle (2002), Lawrence (1997), Riquelme (2002), Van Akkeren and Cavaye (1999), Iacovou (1995), and Chau and Turner (2001)
• Lack of time to implement e-commerce	• Walczuch et al. (2000), Lawrence (1997), and Van Akkeren and Cavaye (1999)
• E-commerce is not deemed to be suited to the way the organisation does business, or the way our clients do business	• Hadjimonolis (1999) and Iacovou et al. (1995)
• E-commerce is not deemed to be suited to the products/services offered by the small business	• Walczuch et al. (2000), Kendall and Kendall (2001), and Hadjimonolis (1999)
• E-commerce is perceived as a technology lacking direction	• Lawrence (1997)
• Lack of awareness about business advantages/opportunities that e-commerce can provide	• Iacovou et al. (1995) and Quayle (2002)
• Lack of available information about e-commerce	• Lawrence (1997)
• Concern about security of e-commerce	• Quayle (2002), Purao and Campbell (1998), Riquelme (2002), Van Akkeren and Cavaye (1999), Poon and Swatman (1999), and Hadjimonolis (1999)
• Lack of critical mass among customers, suppliers and business partners to implement e-commerce	• Hadjimonolis (1999)
• Heavy reliance on external consultants (who are often considered by small businesses to be inadequate) to provide necessary expertise	• Lawrence (1997), Van Akkeren and Cavaye (1999), and Chau and Turner (2001)
• Lack of e-commerce standards	• Tuunainen (1998)

perceive that the lack of understanding of e-procurement and the cost of the technology are the main barriers to adoption by SMEs (IMPAQ, 2004).

Bennett, Managing Director of IMPAQ (2004), notes that "whilst Britain's largest companies are seeing tangible benefits from e-procurement, many are not recognizing the technology's full potential due to the overriding issue of getting buy in from the SME supplier community."

Another study conducted on the adoption of e-procurement by SMEs in Canada concludes that e-procurement in Canadian SMEs has a slow accep-

Table 2. Summary of e-procurement barriers among large organizations (Source: Hawking & Stein, 2004)

E-Procurement Barriers
Inadequate Technical Infrastructure
Lack of Skilled Personnel
Inadequate Technological Infrastructure of Business Partners
Lack of Integration with Business Partners
Implementation Costs
Company Culture
Inadequate Tech Infrastructure of Partners
Regulatory and Legal Controls
Security
Cooperation of Business Partners
Inadequate E-Procurement Solutions
Upper Management Support

tance rate compared to other Internet-based solutions. Multiple factors such as lack of management support, high cost, and uncertainty about benefits of e-procurement were the major barriers cited by the respondents and, surprisingly, information and data security were not considered a significant barrier (Cuthbert, Hamzic, & Archer, 2003). This study was conducted between June and July, 2003. A total of 53 companies responded to the questionnaire in a survey distributed primarily by email.

A recently-released benchmarking survey report on SME e-procurement adoption in the Northwest of England notes that "the rate of adoption of e-procurement by SMEs in the Northwest of England is extremely low. Multiple factors such as technical integration problems and lack of top management support were cited as barriers to the adoption of e-Procurement" (Bigonline. org, 2005). This benchmarking survey was conducted on 50 manufacturing SMEs in the Northwest of England. The methodology employed was mixed methods, which involves the sequential usage of quantitative and qualitative methodologies. For the first phase of the study, a quantitative survey was conducted on 50 SMEs to understand the adoption trend of e-procurement among them. Poon and Swatman (1998) have indicated that "the survey provides the broad and unbiased overview and generic understanding of key issues related to small-business Internet use in a non-anecdotal manner.

For the second phase of study, five SMEs were selected from the respondent SMEs, and case studies were conducted on them. The multiple case-study research then served as a flexible and adaptive means to pursue the investigation of these issues in an in-depth manner." Gallivan (1997) indicates that in studying the impact of new technologies on organizations such as e-commerce, the use of mixed method studies provides opportunities to gather mixed-level data, which can be useful in linking the individual to the organizational level of analysis.

Case Study

This section presents two case studies of SMEs, highlighting the challenges to their adoption of e-procurement.

Case Study 1

Company A are designers, builders, and installers of high-quality windows, doors, and conservatories for over 25 years. It employs modern manufacturing methods which incorporate the use of computer-aided design and manufacture, which ensures the production of precision window frames. Currently, the company has an annual turnover of £3.5 million and employs 50 people.

Profile of Company A

Number of employees:	50
Industry sector:	Manufacturer
Turnover:	£ 3.5 million
Number of computers:	5
Position:	IT Manager/Buyer

Company A uses basic Microsoft Word and Excel for record-keeping and communication, and a bespoke program for designing windows. At present, the organization conducts most of the procurement-related tasks manually.

There is a facility in the bespoke program for stock-keeping, stock control, and purchasing which are not used currently. The organization issues 200-300 purchase orders per month, and currently there are five buyers involved in the procurement process. The organization sends purchase orders via fax, as only one PC has Internet access. No procurement-related information goes directly into their financial system (Sage Line 50). There is no integration between the systems of the organization to enable a better coordinated flow of procurement-related information. The company is planning to implement a network server in the future, which will facilitate other PCs in the manufacturing side with Internet access to place purchase orders electronically via e-mail or suppliers Web-based ordering systems.

Issues Affecting Adoption of E-Procurement

The purchasing and IT manager of Company A notes that the main reasons for the lack of implementation of e-procurement are:

- **Lack of knowledge and awareness about the benefits offered by e-procurement:** He notes that:

  unless I understand what's involved, how it works you are in a disadvantage position. (Anon, A., personal communication, June 2005)

- **Lack of top management support and the willing to do is missing:** On the issue of non-implementation of the modules in the Be-spoke package, he notes:

  I have been pushing to take that module option but from the M.D's view it is an expense which he will manage without. But from my point of view it is money well spent, because basically as a business I process windows and when orders go out automatically reallocate stock and re-order as and when required, which to me is excellent but he won't go that route yet. (Anon, A., personal communication, June 2005)

Case Study 2

Company B provides anechoic and screened room solutions for all EMC and RF Protection environments. It also manufactures cabinets for the telecommunications industry and various other subcontractor works. Their two main clients are British Telecom and Marconi Systems, for which Company B makes cabinets and private telephone exchanges. This case company also makes cabinets for a high speed ADSL Internet service provider. The company employs 55 and has an annual turnover of £4 million.

Profile of Company B

Number of employees:	55
Industry sector:	Engineering
Turnover:	£ 4 million
Number of computers:	> 20
Average IT spending:	£ 5,000 – £ 15,000
Position:	IT/Production Engineer/Buyer

Current Status of the Organization

With an annual procurement expenditure of around £2 million and issued purchase orders nearing 200 per month, procurement occupies a pivotal role in this company. At present, the organization has an in-house developed internal procurement system. Currently, the stock levels are driven straight out of the database. The company runs SAGE Line 100 software which generates the requirements and, depending on how the supplier wants to receive the orders, they are sent out via fax, e-mail, or post. Currently, the organization has a supply base of around 900 suppliers who cover a multiplicity of products and services. These suppliers cover most of the procurement needs of the organization. The company realizes that it is a burden to maintain such a vast array of suppliers and has started a disembarkation program. The supply base has been trimmed down to around 600. IT manager, Mr. X, justifies having such a vast supply base and notes that "since our procurement is so diverse, it is warranted that we have such a range of suppliers." The company's supply base consists of a diverse mix starting with a micro-company in Aston to a large global distributor like TDK.

Issues Affecting Adoption of E-Procurement

This diversity causes the potential problem of having to deal with different suppliers in different ways. A micro-SME would not be able to receive orders electronically, while a medium to large company might possess the capability to trade electronically. The IT manager feels that currently smaller suppliers are not yet ready to deal with them electronically and that integration of systems with heterogeneous suppliers is still a pain point.

He further adds that:

Technically it is a big challenge for the other parties to implement or consume information in real-time. For me, a proper e-procurement system would be for us feeding data direct from our database to supplier's database, so that is real time. Basically at the moment it is halfway there. We are doing everything automatically, but they are still ending up with a piece of paper at their end or either an email in their inbox. It is a bit of dream to get everybody on board, their existing systems automatically generating orders, so orders are coming in automatically. That's the way things should be. But I think that is still long away. (Anon, B., personal communication, June 2005)

The company also notes that change management is a big issue in implementing e-procurement. It is not easy to change the mindsets of people who have been used to doing things in a particular style. People are interested, but they do not want to change and there is not much you can do about it. Without the explicit support of senior management, we feel that we are not in a position to change their mindset. The senior management, I think, if it does not really affect them, they will not be really interested. Most of the time, they do not bother about it, if they have to spend some time and money. From their point of view, as long as the material is procured and they are on time, it is "task accomplished," no matter which method is used. If they want to manufacture

Table 3. Classification of barriers

Hard Barriers	Soft Barriers
Technology Problems	Organizational Barriers Lack of Domain Knowledge

Table 4. Summary of barriers

HARD BARRIERS			Soft Barriers
Technical Integration Problems	**Technical Infrastructure Problems**	**General Problems**	**Soft Barriers**
Lack of robust technical standards that are needed to make IOIS adoption economical	Lack of adequate tools and systems	Inadequate e-procurement solutions	Company culture
Complexity in inter-organizational communication	Access to and availability of strategic e-business resources	Esoteric nomenclature usage in literature	Business processes
Infrastructure integration	High cost of technology implementation	The small number of suppliers accessible through many organizations e-procurement procurement systems	Cooperation of business-partners
Integration with existing technologies	Inadequate technical infrastructure of partners	Failure to invest sufficiently in catalog development	Poor value proposition for the supplier
Lack of integration with business partners	Inefficiencies in locating information and infrastructure	Insufficient return on investment	Upper management support
The lack of standards for e-commerce software development	Lack of technical expertise	Uncertainty surrounding the costs and benefits of e-business	Inadequate business processes to support e-procurement
Data exchange standards lacking	Lack of information and education	Regulatory and legal controls	
Security	Lack of technically-skilled staff	Lack of knowledge about e-procurement concepts and solutions	
	Immaturity of technology		

product X and the material is not there, then there is a problem, and if it is there, it is not a problem in their perspective.

Looking forward to the future, Company B's top priority is to develop a better and easy method of communicating electronically with their supplier base. Table 4 illustrates the barriers that were identified from the analysis of the above studies. Barriers could be broadly classified into *hard* and *soft*. Hard barriers are those which have to do with things and regulations. Soft barriers are the problems related to people.

Hard barriers could further be segregated into:

- Technical integration problems
- Technical infrastructure problems
- General problems

As can be inferred from the table, technical problems and integration problems dominate the barriers, followed by lack of knowledge and awareness about the benefits offered by e-procurement. Many studies have clearly demonstrated that cost is the primary focus of drivers, while technology and business partner integration are the main focus of barriers (Hawking & Stein, 2004).

The Application of Web Services in E-Procurement

Today, a typical organization consists of a range of diverse systems, each utilizing different protocols for communication and different formats for data representation. Previously, the need for communication among these heterogeneous systems was minimalist. But with the ubiquitous Internet, connecting to worldwide markets in search of new business partners or communicating with suppliers for better coordination of supply chain activities has become very affordable for even the small and medium enterprises. Business-to-business (B2B) e-commerce has arrived in big style and is now considered the future of businesses.

Collaboration has become the latest trend of doing business, and it is beneficial from both business and customer points of view. A new concept called *co-opetition* has emerged, replacing the concept of competition. Co-opetition is where competitors cooperate for the benefit of customers. Laura D'Andrea Tyson, (lawson, 2000) one of the world's most distinguished economists says that "it was innovate or die, but here are the days when it is co-operate or die." All companies, small, medium, and large can experience increased growth through tightly-integrated partnerships (Samtani & Sadhwani, 2003; Themistocleous & Chen, 2004).

For these collaborations to occur in real-time, all of the participant organizations systems (both intra- and inter-) need to be seamlessly integrated in real-time. This process involves opening up organizations' systems to the outside world which need to be highly compatible and at the same time non-comprising on the security front. Large corporations have the necessary resources to implement costly integration programs. Small and medium enterprises, which generally are limited by resources, are not able to fully exploit the benefits of collaborative commerce. The extraordinary benefits of this new digital age are being hampered owing to the lack of systems integration among the diverse and complex systems used by organizations. Thus, B2B integration has become the most important issue for SMEs. B2B integration can be defined to cover all business activities of an enterprise that have to do with electronic message exchange between it and one or more of its trading partners (Bussler, 2003).

In today's new global economy, it is data, information, and knowledge that have value. Any information technology solution that is designed needs to center on data and information, rather than the platform itself, that is, the solution must be platform-agnostic. The emergence of XML Web services standards attempts to solve this complex problem of integration in an affordable manner at reasonable costs. Web services are a set of XML standards-based technology which promises to provide solutions plaguing the current world of information technology through a simple and standards-based approach.

Web services represent a significant opportunity in tying together the various participants of the global supply chain puzzle in a very cost-effective manner. The key to the successes of Web services lies in its simplistic approach and the usage of industry-wide protocols like XML, HTTP, and TCP/IP. Web services leverage the ubiquitous Internet for application communication. Web services represent the fulfillment of an unprecedented cooperation among industry leaders. At no other instance in the history of Information Technology has there been such a wide industry support in the formation of standards. Old adversaries, Microsoft and IBM, have worked together with Ariba to develop simple object access protocol (SOAP), Web Services Description Language (WSDL), and universal discovery and description interface (UDDI) as cross-platform standards, in a spirit of community-oriented constructive engagement.

Web services are an evolution of the previous attempts by the industry like CORBA and DCOM. Primarily, the lack of universal acceptance of these two approaches could be attributed to the absence of a common network to share information and the lack of a common data format. The emergence of the Internet provided a common ubiquitous network, and the development of XML provided a universal data format. Web services are the killer applications of XML, and of the Internet protocols like HTTP and TCP/IP. This represents a huge leap forward in the way applications are built, communicated, and distributed.

The need for Web services arises owing to the demands for:

- The need for collaboration among different organizations of various sizes with the internet as the backbone
- The strategic importance being attributed to the supply chains as a way to be more competitive among organizations
- The need for real-time seamless communication among various tiers of the supply chain
- The expectation among CEOs of organizations for an instant return on investment.

Figure 5. Convergence of business, technology, and the Internet

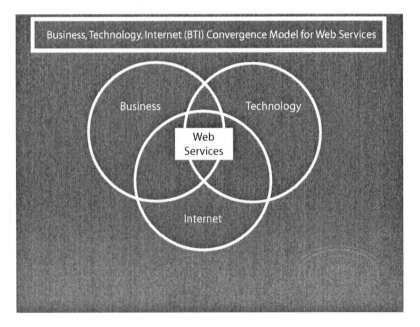

Technical Definition

Web services are defined as "loosely coupled, reusable software components that semantically encapsulate discrete functionality and are distributed and programmatically accessible over standard Internet protocols" (Stencil, 2003).

Business Definition

Web services are an approach that helps the business connect with customers, partners, and employees in a seamless manner with standard open interfaces by leveraging the investments in existing IT infrastructure. The benefits offered by adopting and developing Web services are manifold in nature, both on the technical and business fronts. Let us look at a list of business benefits of Web services.

Benefits of Web Services

By enabling applications to share data across different hardware platforms and operating systems, Web services provide many benefits, including:

- Opening the door to new business opportunities by making it easy to connect with partners
- Delivering dramatically more personal, integrated experiences to users through the new breed of smart devices, including PCs
- Saving time and money by cutting development time
- Increasing revenue streams by enabling businesses to easily make their own Web services available to others (Microsoft, 2003)

Web services use three kinds of new technologies which are purely XML-based, which makes it even more easy to use because of its relative merits and also due to the widespread acceptance of XML. The use of XML standards is very important in the overall scheme of the Web services universe. XML is a data format that represents data in a serialized form that can be transported over the network from one endpoint to another. "XML is nearly as widely accepted as the TCP/IP protocols on which the Internet itself is built (Fu, 1999)." Web services using XML standards is a new paradigm in the way B2B collaborations are modeled. It provides a conceptual and architectural foundation which can be implemented using a variety of platforms and products.

Put simply, a service provider deploys Web services. A service broker lists various services and arranges transactions, helping service providers and service requesters find each other. A service requester uses an application programming interface (API) to discover Web services, asking the service broker about the services it needs. When the service broker returns results, the service requester can then invoke those services it needs to create applications.

The whole process of how Web services work is explained below:

- Just build your system normally.
- Expose them as Web services.
- Any service requester wishing to use the Web services will send in a SOAP request to the application which is exposed as a Web service.

Figure 6. The relationships among the core Web services components (Source: Gottschalk, Graham, Kreger, & Snell, 2002)

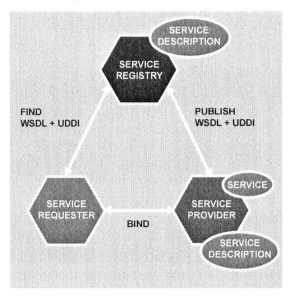

- If you intend to use third-party deployed Web services, look into the UDDI registry to locate the required Web service. Next, Web services Description Language (WSDL) associated with the particular Web service provides technical details about how Web service could be consumed by the required applications.

The following are the three standards on which Web services are based. We will take a closer look into these three XML-based standards:

1. **UDDI** (universal description, discovery, and integration)
2. **WSDL** (Web Services Description Language)
3. **SOAP** (simple object access protocol)

Universal Description, Discovery, and Integration (UDDI)

UDDI stands for universal description, discovery, and integration. Before a business partner can make any Web service request, it must first understand the technical details and perform some activities which include discovering the call interface and semantics, and writing or configuring their software to collaborate with the service. To enable this discovery, a platform is needed to publish these Web services. UDDI fulfils this requirement. UDDI registry is the central database which contains information on all Web services. It provides a platform for Web services requesters to discover or query for new services and to understand their technical details like the WSDL nature of Web services in a common XML format. The UDDI registry is organized into various categories to facilitate the easy discovery and invocation of the Web services. This categorization resembles the yellow pages which are commonly found in telephone directories. A white pages section provides business contact information, a yellow pages section categorizes businesses and services, and a green pages section provides technical information about the services that a business offers. Once a Web services requester validates the details found in the White pages and the Yellow pages section, the Green pages provides the necessary technical details necessary to invoke the services.

Web Services Description Language (WSDL)

Once a business discovers the service it wants to use from the UDDI registry, it needs to understand the call syntax and semantics prior to actually making a call which can be found in the green pages section of the UDDI registry. The WSDL specification is an XML document which describes the interface and semantics of a call to the Web service. It defines how service providers and requesters communicate with each other about Web services. This allows for simple services to be quickly and easily described and documented. Like XML, WSDL is extensible to allow the description of endpoints and their messages, regardless of what message formats or network protocols are used for communicating. WSDL can be used to design specifications to invoke and operate Web services on the Internet and to access and invoke remote applications and databases.

Simple Object Access Protocol (SOAP)

The simple object access protocol is the specification which leverages the power of XML and HTTP. It provides the specification for the exchange of structured information in a decentralized distributed environment. SOAP utilizes the XML for exchanging messages over a variety of underlying protocols, such as HTTP or SMTP. Also, XML is utilized owing to its massive industry support, language-neutrality, and extensibility. HTTP is utilized as any Web-enabled application communicates, using sockets, and it utilizes the Port 80, which makes HTTP traffic firewall-friendly. Simplicity is what makes SOAP powerful. The original specification of SOAP 1.1 was made in 1997. However, the original definition was limited in scope. However, the current version 1.2 has enhanced the specification to serve to a broader audience. SOAP is a "lightweight," very easy-to-understand technology, and it is also easy to implement. It has industry momentum and buy-in from all major e-business platform vendors. Zhao (2001) clarifies the meaning of "lightweight" and notes that "SOAP is an XML marshalling and unmarshalling mechanism and does not need heavy libraries like CORBA and DCOM. The main objective of SOAP is to achieve interoperability by using XML to interact with interoperable Web services."

Earlier protocols such as Internet inter-ORB protocol (IIOP) for CORBA or Java remote method protocol (JRMP) for Java remote method invocation

(RMI) did not utilize the XML. This made it difficult to debug them, as binary streams tend to be more complex to read than simple XML structures. Also, sending information through text-based protocols like SOAP over the HTTP enhances the success rate of the information passing through firewalls as HTTP utilizes port 80, which is open to Internet traffic. However, there might be some performance penalties as text-based information requires more bandwidth than binary streams. But this slight inconvenience can be ignored when considering the bigger benefits related to interoperability that it provides. Once a potential partner who wishes to use the service looks at the WSDL using UDDI, he can make a request to one or more of the services offered in our Web service utilizing the simple object access protocol (SOAP).

Integration Made Easier

Sending and receiving invoices and purchase orders across corporate boundaries, with partners who often employ a complex jugglery of Information Technology solutions, is a daunting challenge. Web services enable these kinds of external communications by exposing internal functions as Web services which could be invoked by other applications. This can be achieved by wrapping the internal functionalities of the system with SOAP wrappers. Web services have been used to wrap a legacy system's functions to support application-to-application integration inside a firewall (Vecchio, 2001). Thus, not compromising the security of the systems and also reaching a wider audience with heterogeneous platforms. The deployment of Web services reduces the integration costs associated with achieving extended enterprise, as well as improves service levels that would otherwise not be achievable (Adams et al., 2003, Samtani & Sadhwani, 2003).

The Application of Web services in e-procurement is a very recent area of development. Very few researchers have concentrated on this area, and very little empirical data exists in this area (Chen & Meixell, 2003).

Many large organizations like Dell and Dollar One have successfully demonstrated how they could effectively use Web services in improving the agility of their supply chain operations without changing the existing infrastructure. This represents a significant opportunity for SMEs because they can participate in the new initiatives of large companies by making minimal investments and not foregoing their existing IT investments. E-procurement is a supplier-facing operation which involves integrating with suppliers' systems which are often asynchronous and located outside the corporate firewalls. Integration of systems becomes a very important aspect in this kind of scenario.

Ncff (2001) clearly notes that e-procurement is still in its infancy because it involves integration with other systems. Integration is one of the most contentious issues facing the world of information technology. But fortunately, Web services with its standards-based approach attempts to provide solutions to integration issues by allowing communications among software applications in a neutral way. The widespread adoption of Web service standards in e-business will address that area of concern.

The key to the success of any supply chain is the ability to share information seamlessly. A study conducted jointly by Stanford University and Accenture (formerly Anderson Consulting), looked at 100 manufacturers and 100 retailers in the food and consumers products industry. The results were revealing; Companies that reported higher than average profits were the ones who were engaged in higher levels of information sharing (Lee & Whang, 2001).

Web services take a service and process-oriented approach in addressing integration issues in supply chain management. An application enabled with Web services can provide streamlined capabilities by consuming Web services from legacy systems (such as for checking inventory status) and external suppliers (such as requesting price quotes from suppliers). These Web services are composed transparently behind the scene in the application to give users access to more supply chain functions from a single application (Chen & Meixell, 2003).

Web Services and B2B Marketplaces

As emphasized earlier, B2B marketplaces are the preferred method for conducting external e-procurement. But of late, we have seen the demise of many marketplaces. One of the main reasons attributable for the closure of many marketplaces is the closed-systems approach followed by many of them. McKertich (2004) emphasizes that "the challenge of integrating quickly, easily, and still maintaining much of the functionality that is offered by e-marketplaces, has been exceptionally difficult." For the marketplace to be successful, there are various aspects on the technical front that needs to be addressed. The following are the IT requirements of a B2B marketplace as highlighted by Ganesh, Das, Chatterjee, Verma, Chawla, and Marwah (2004):

- Ability to integrate with buyer and seller systems
- Ability to integrate smoothly with other partners (e.g., credit card firms, courier companies, etc.)
- Ability to configure/reconfigure services
- Ability to match the information of the participants in a transaction

Previous generation information technologies did not provide much leeway in designing a loosely-coupled system. But, with the anvil of Web services, designing a loosely-coupled system, where heterogeneous systems could communicate using industry standards and open interfaces, has become a reality.

From the above scenarios, we can conclude that Web services can be applied in e-procurement in a variety of ways. This is primarily due to the excellent support for providing dynamic data from a plethora of platforms, which is the basic requirement of e-procurement as it is a supplier-facing operation.

Procurement Transformation Framework Enabled by Web Services

The need for an exhaustive framework detailing the complete procurement process, with the role played by information technology in enabling this process, is much desired. The procurement transformation framework enabled by Web services provides a comprehensive set of structured information on how information technology could aid in the procurement process, in particular how deploying Web services would simplify the task of integration, which is a prerequisite of the new digitally-networked economy.

Step 1: Procurement Process Reengineering (PPR)

Grouping procurement tasks into *strategic* and *transactional* allows SMEs to focus more on the strategic aspects and automate the transactional element. This reduces the cost of order generation and also provides ample time to the buyer who can focus more on the strategic aspects rather than the mundane operational ones. On the strategic side, the company should perform a review

Figure 7. Procurement transformation framework enabled by Web services

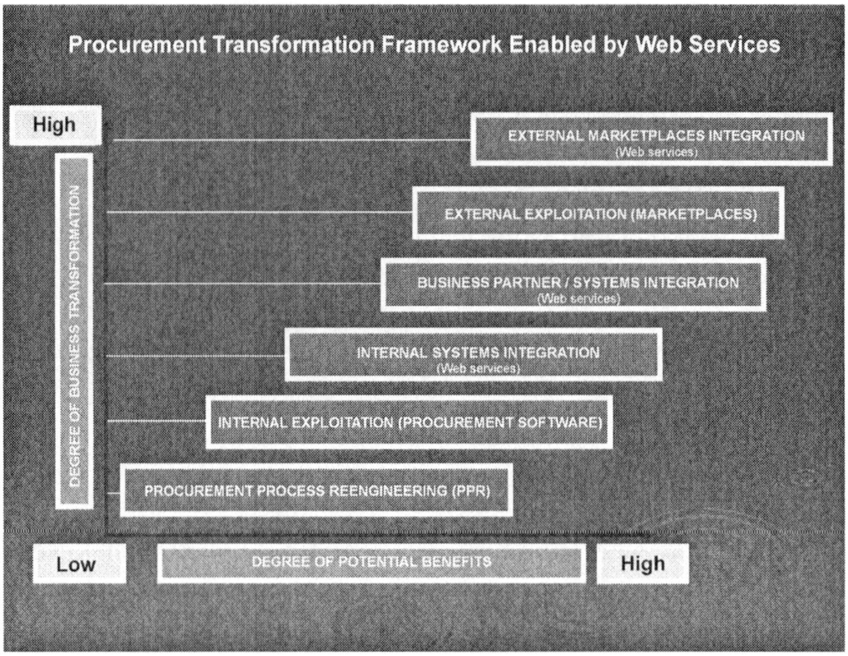

of expenditures, determine market complexity, develop a sourcing strategy, and review the entire procure-to-pay cycle.

Step 2: Internal Exploitation (Procurement Software)

After clearly segregating the procurement tasks, focus should be shifted to the automation of the *internal procurement* tasks. Information technology should be exploited internally to aid in streamlining the internal procurement-related activities. This could be achieved by the utilization of an internal procurement software which could be either in the form of an added functionality to an ERP system, or in-house software.

Step 3: Internal Systems Integration (Web Services)

The automation of the internal part of the procurement process is followed by the integration of the procurement software with the financial and stock management or any other relevant software specific to the particular organization. This is very crucial as often procurement-related information provides valuable inputs for various other information systems. Web services, with its unique standards-based approach, enables SMEs to perform this internal integration tasks in a very cost-effective way and also leverages investments in existing IT systems.

Step 4: Business Partner Systems Integration (Web Services)

Procurement systems sit on the edge of the enterprise and are required to "talk" to a multitude of partners. These partners often employ a complex jugglery of information systems. Without integration with these partners, real-time seamless flow of information is hampered, which defeats the very purpose of having an integrated procurement system. Web services can be used to seamlessly integrate with partners' systems outside the corporate boundary without the problem of firewall. As Web services are built on open standards like XML, HTTP, TCP/IP, organizations do not run into the risk of being locked into proprietary data formats. Also, these kinds of communications do not warrant upfront commitment and significant investments, which makes them ideal for small and medium enterprises.

Step 5: External Exploitation

External exploitation is defined as looking at the possibility of external modes of procurement. This usually involves leveraging the potential of the Internet. E-marketplaces, e-auction, and e-bidding are the preferred way for SMEs to conduct e-procurement. These provide valuable services like aggregation of buyers and sellers, and are an economic way for SMEs to tap into more sourcing opportunities.

Step 6: External Integration with E-Marketplaces

Internal procurement software can contain a number of features and can host a catalogue service. E-marketplaces could be integrated with that of Internal Marketplaces of SMEs. This provides extraordinary benefits and a host of security-related features without any costly investment.

Future Trends

We see that over the coming years the strong business value proposition offered by the Internet will impact the SME community in a tremendous way. We see the increased usage of the Internet by the SME community over and above the existing levels. At the heart of all this activity will be procurement and also the need for seamless loosely-coupled interactions among the various participants of the supply chain, who predominantly are SMEs. The concept of Web services will help SMEs tremendously in their ability to deal with the integration puzzle in a cost-effective way. With Web services crossing the chasm and gaining widespread acceptance over the next few years, we envision a world where a host of marketplaces and e-procurement solution vendors will be offering a suite of products based on Web services. McKertich (2004) emphasizes that "e-marketplace providers will be quick to see the opportunity, and modify their software technology to incorporate Web Services support so that they can continue to 'build the bridges' between buyers and sellers of disparate computing technology, and disparate business priorities."

Chen and Meixell (2003) asserts that companies may soon participate in dynamic e-business via collaborative XML-based Web services that provide remote access to programmable business services and use XML for data interchange.

Conclusion

The above discussions clearly indicate that supply chain integration and information sharing are the key factors which will determine the success of any organization in the future ahead. E-procurement, due to its potential for savings and also because of its high importance in the supply chain, is an important area of focus for SMEs.

Web services with its standards-based approach are clearly the path SMEs should take in the integration of supply chain activities. Soon, innovative business strategies and business models, as well as supply chain integration relying on Web service-based architecture, will become the driving force for XML and Web services adoption (Sullivan, 2002). The fact that Web services can be used internally to provide programmable interfaces to legacy systems, and to integrate Web-enabled applications directly with some legacy systems, make it an ideal choice for its adoption in supply chain context, especially in e-procurement which involves interaction with suppliers' systems and vice versa (Samtani & Sadhwani, 2003; Vecchio, 2001).

Apart from the solutions to barriers on the technical arena, for the widespread adoption of e-procurement among SMEs, a concerted effort needs to be made by the SME managers at the organizational level and by the regional and the national governments at the regional and the national levels, respectively. For example, in developed countries like the United Kingdom (UK), the national government has initiated an ambitious National E-Procurement Project (NEPP). As per the government mandate, all SMEs dealing with the local authorities should possess the ability to deal with them electronically by the end of 2005, and participation in an electronic marketplace would count as one of their criteria for evaluating a supplier. The challenges faced by SMEs in adopting e-procurement are more profound in developing countries. Therefore, the government in those countries needs to play an even more proactive role in enabling SMEs to harness the full potential of e-procurement. A noteworthy example in India is the state government of Andhra Pradesh. The government has been very proactive in the implementation of e-procurement technology. As of 1-1-2005, all departments of the state government have shifted towards e-procurement, which is an extraordinary achievement. This mandates that all suppliers to the government trade electronically. This kind of strong commitment on the part of government in embracing e-procurement goes a long way in providing fresh stimulus to SMEs in adopting e-procurement.

Also, the local and national governments should make a concerted effort in collaboration with the academic community in the dissemination of hype-free, unbiased information to the SME community, who are soaked in the unrealistic, hyped-up, biased information promoted and marketed by product vendors.

References

Aberdeen Group. (2001). *Best practices in e-procurement, the abridged report*. White paper. Retrieved June 2, 2004, from http://www.ariba.com/com_plat/white_paper_form.cfm

ABI. (2003). *Are you e-ready? An initial assessment of e-procurement potential.* Research report. Retrieved July 30, 2004, from http://www.abi.co.uk

Adams, H., et al. (2003). *Custom extended enterprise exposed business services application pattern scenario.* Retrieved February 24, 2004, from http://www-106.ibm.com/developerworks/webservices/library/ws-best5/

Bakos, J. Y. (1991). A strategic analysis of electronic marketplaces. *MIS Quarterly, 15*(3), 295-310.

Bakos, J. Y. (1998). The emerging role of EM on the Internet. *Communications of the ACM, 41*(8), 35–42.

Benbasat, I., Goldstein, D. K., & Mead, M. (1987). *The case research strategy in Berkeley.* 1999.

Bhattacharaya, A. K., Coleman, J. L., & Brace, G. (1996). The structure conundrum in supply chain management. *International Journal of Logistics Management, 7*(2), 39-49.

Bigonline.org. (2005). *Report on the e-procurement benchmarking survey.* Research report. Retrieved July 30, 2005, from http://www.bigonline.org

Boston Consulting. (2001). *Report on the Canadian e-business opportunity roundtable.* Retrieved April 2002, from http://www.bcg.com/practice/022201_FINAL_Canada_Roundtable_English.pdf

Bradley III, D. B., & Peters, D. (1997, June). Electronic marketplaces: Collaborate if you want to compete. In *Proceedings of the 42nd World Conference International Council for Small Business*, San Francisco.

Bussler, C. (2003). *B2B integration concepts and architecture.* Springer-Verlag.

Cagliano, R., Caniato, F., & Spina, G. (2003). E-business strategy: How companies are shaping their supply chain through the Internet. *International Journal of Operations and Production Management, 23*(10), 1142-1162.

Cash, I. J., & Konsynski, B. R. (1985). IS redraws competitive boundaries. *Harvard Business Review, 63*(2), 134-142.

Chan, J. K. Y., & Lee, M. K. O. (2003). SME e-procurement adoption in Hong Kong: The roles of power, trust and value. In *Proceedings of the 36th Hawaii International Conference on System Sciences (HICSS'03).*

Chen, M., & Meixell, M. J. (2003). Web services-enabled procurement in the extended enterprise: An architectural design and implementation. *Journal of Electronic Commerce and Research, 58*(3), 259-279.

Christensen, E., Curbera, F., Meredith, G., & Weerawarana, S. (2001). *Web Services Description Language (WSDL) 1.1*. Retrieved February 19, 2004, from http://www.w3.org/TR/wsdl

Christopher, M. (1998). *Logistics and supply chain management* (2nd ed.).

Cuthbert, C., Hamzic, D., & Archer, N. (2003). *Barriers to SME e-procurement solutions in Canada: A survey*. Hamilton, Ontario: McMaster E-Business Research Centre (MeRC), DeGroote School of Business, McMaster University.

Dai, Q., & Kauffman, R. J. (2000, January). Business models for Internet-based e-procurement systems and B2B EM: An exploratory assessment. In *Proceedings of the 34th Hawaii International Conference on Systems Science*, Maui, HI.

Davila, A., Gupta, M., & Palmer, R. (2003). Moving procurement systems to the Internet: The adoption and use of e-procurement technology models. *European Management Journal, 21*(1), 11–23.

Day, G. S., Fein, A. J., & Ruppersberger, G. (2003). Shakeouts in digital markets: Lessons from B2B exchanges. *California Management Review, 45*(2), 131-150.

DTI. (2003, August 28). National statistics: Statistical press release. *Department of Trade and Industry, UK*, 03/92.

Eisenhardt, K. M. (1989). Building theories from case study research. *Academy of Management Review, 14*(4), 532–550.

Fu, S. (1999). A practical approach to Web-based Internet EDI. *IBM*. Retrieved from http://www.research.ibm.com/iac/papers/icdcsws99.pdf

Gallivan, M. (1997). Value in triangulation: A comparision of two approaches for combining qualitative and quantitative methods. In A. Lee, J. Liebenau, & J. DeGross (Eds.), *Information systems and qualitative research* (pp. 417-443). London: Chapman & Hall.

Ganesh, J., Das, A. S., Chatterjee, A. M., Verma, A., Chawla, M., & Marwah, A. (2003). Web services-based inter-organisational architectural framework for B2B marketplaces. *Infosys Technologies Ltd*. Retrieved February 19, 2005, from http://infolab.uvt.nl/~fjl/mikep/demos/3.pdf

Gebauer, J., Beam, C., & Segev, A. (1998). *Procurement in the Internet age—current practices and emerging trends*. Fisher Center for Management and Information Technology, Haas School of Business, University of California.

Gottschalk, K., Graham, Kreger, S. H., & Snell, J. (2002). Introduction to Web services architecture. *IBM Systems Journal, 41*(2), 168-177.

Grewal, R., Comer, J. M., & Mehta, R. (2001, July). An investigation into electronic markets. *Journal of Marketing, 65*, 17-33.

Hauser, E. (2000). *SMEs in Germany: Facts and figures* (Bonn: Institut fu¨r Mittelstandsforschung).

Hauser, H. -E. (2000). *SMEs in Germany. Facts and figures.* IfM Institut für Mittelstandsforschung Bonn. Retrieved from www.ifm-bonn.de/ergeb-nis/sme.zip

Hawking, P., & Stein, A. (2004). E-procurement: Is the ugly duckling actually a swan down under? *Asia Pacific Journal of Marketing and Logistics, 16*(1).

Henderson, D. R. (1984). Electronic marketing in principle and practice. *American Journal of Agriculture Economics, 66*(5), 848–853.

Heywood, B. J., Barton, M., & Heywood, C. C. (2002). *E-procurement managing successful e-procurement implementation.*

IBM. (1998). *Small and mid-sized business in the global networked economy.* White paper. Retrieved August 18, 1999, from http://www.ibm.com/ibm/publicaffairs/smbus1998

IMPAQ. (2004). *UKPLC not realizing full payback from e-procurement, reveals new study.* Retrieved November, 2004, from http://www.impaq.co.uk/press/news34.htm

Kalakota, R., & Robinson, M. (2000). *E-business: Roadmap for success.* Canada: Addison–Wesley.

Kaplan, S., & Sawhney, M. (2000). E-hubs: The new B2B marketplaces. *Harvard Business Review, 78*(3), 97–104.

Kaufmann, L. (1999). Purchasing and supply management: A conceptual framework. In L. Kaufmann & D. Hahn (Eds.), *Handbuch Industrielles Beschaffungsmanagement: Internationale Konzepte: Innovative Instrumente—Aktuelle Praxisbeispiele* (pp. 3-32). Wiesbaden, Germany: Gabler.

Kaufmann, R. J., & Mohtadi, H. (2004, Summer). Open vs. proprietary systems in B2B e-procurement: A risk-adjusted transaction cost perspective. Forthcoming in the *Journal of Management Information Systems.*

Knusden, D. (2003). *Improving procurement performance with e-business mechanisms.* Doctoral dissertation, Lund University, Sweden.

Lamming, R. (1995). *Strategic procurement management in the 1990's: Concepts and cases*. Stamford, CT: Earlsgate Press.

Lawson, D. (2000). *Home procurement*. Retrieved November, 2004, from http://specials.ft.com/eprocurement/FT33SC3ALFC.html

Lee, H. L., & Whang, S. (2001). E-business and supply chain integration. In *Proceedings of the Stanford Global Supply Chain Management Forum (SGSCMF-W2-2001)* (p. 20).

Leonard, S. R. (n.d.). *Electronic Procurement*. President EDS E.solutions EMEA 2813– 2837.

Levi, D. S., Kaminsky, P., & Levi, E. S. (2003). *Designing and managing the supply chain: Concepts, strategies, and case studies* (2nd ed.). New York: McGraw-Hill.

MacGregor, R. C., & Vrazalic, L. (2005). A basic model of electronic commerce adoption barriers: A study of regional small businesses in Sweden and Australia. *Journal of Small Business and Enterprise Development, 12*(4), 510-527.

Malone, T. W., Yates, J., & Benjamin, R. I. (1987). Electronic markets and electronic hierarchies. *Communications of the ACM, 30*(6), 484-497.

Markham, W. J., Morales, J. T., & Slaight, T. H. (2000). Creating supply advantage by leveraging the strategic nature of procurement. In J. Cavinato & R. Kauffman (Eds.), *The purchasing handbook* (6th ed.). New York: McGraw Hill Publishing.

McKertich., A. (2004). *What do SOAP, ebXML, UDDI, and OASIS all have in common?*

McMillan, J. (2002). *Reinventing the bazaar*. A natural history of markets. New York: W W Norton and Company Inc.

Microsoft (2003).*What is .NET?* Retrieved February 1, 2004, from http://www.microsoft.com/net/basic.mspx

National e-Procurement Project. (2004). *Overarching guide to e-procurement*. Retrieved February 11, 2005, from http://www.idea.gov.uk/knowledge/eprocurement

Neef, D. (2001). *E-procurement: From strategy to implementation*. London: Prentice Hall/Financial Times.

NEPP. (2004). *Local e-gov national e-procurement project, overview of solutions*. Retrieved December 13, 2006 from http://www.localegovnp/default.asp?sID=1100774743609.

New, S., Meakin, T., & Southworth, R. (2002). *Understanding the e-market-space: Making sense of B2B.* Retrieved June, 11, 2005, from http://www.achilles.com

New, S. J., & Payne, P. (1995). Research frameworks in logistics: Three models, seven dinners, and a survey. *International Journal of Physical Distribution and Logistics Management, 25*(10), 60-77.

Obrecht, J. (2000). Playing e-hub name game. *Netb2b.com, 3*(July, BtoB), 9. Retrieved from http://www.economist.com/editorial/freeforall/20000226/

OGC. (2002). *A guide to e-procurement for the public sector.* Office of Government Commerce, UK.

OGC. (2005). *E-procurement in action: A guide to e-procurement for the public sector.* Report. Retrieved February 30, 2005, from http://www.ogc.gov.uk/sdtoolkit/reference/ogc_library/procurement/bluefrog2.pdf

Presutti, W. D. (2002). Supply management and e-procurement: Creating value added in the supply chain. *Industrial Marketing Management, 32*(2003), 219-226

Price Waterhouse Coopers (PWC). (2002). Electronic business outlook: E-markets realism, not pessimism. *Price Waterhouse Coopers.* Retrieved May 15, 2002, from http://pwcglobal.com/ebusinessinsights.

Poon, S., & Swatman, P. (1998), A combined-method study of small business Internet commerce. *International Journal of Electronic Commerce, 2*(3), 31-46

Puschmann, T., & Alt, R. (2005). Successful use of e-procurement in supply chains. *Supply Chain Management: An International Journal, 10*(2), 122–133.

Samtani, G., & Sadhwani, D. (2002). Return on investment and Web services. In P. Fletcher & M. Waterhouse (Eds.), *Web services business strategies and architectures* (pp. 9-24). Birmingham, UK: Expert Press, Ltd.

Schmid, B. (1993). Elektronische Markte. *Wirtschaftsinformatik, 35*(5), 465-480.

Schmid, B. F., & Lindemann, M. A. (1998). Elements of a reference model for EM. In *Proceedings of the 31st Hawaii International Conference on System Sciences (HICCSS-31)*, HI (Vol. 4, pp. 193–201). IEEE Computer Society Press.

Scott, C., & Westbrook, R. (1991). New strategic tools for supply chain management. *International Journal of Physical Distribution and Logistics Management, 21*(1), 23–33.

Segev, A., Gebauer, J., & Faeber, F. (1999). Internet-based electronic markets. *EM—International Journal of Electronic Markets, 9*(3), 167-176.

Shimada, T. (2004). *The challenge of B2B exchange operators on Southeast Asia*. Unpublished manuscript.

Stencil Group. (2001). *Defining Web services.* Retrieved from http://www. stencilgroup.com/ideas_scope_ 200106wsdefined.pdf

Stevens, G. C. (1989). Integrating the supply chain. *International Journal of Physical Distribution & Materials Management, 19*(8), 3-8.

Stockdale, R., & Standing, M. (2004). Benefits and barriers of electronic marketplace participation: An SME perspective. *The Journal of Enterprise Information Management, 17*(4), 301-311.

Sullivan, T. (2002). *App dev on the Web services path.* Retrieved from http:// www.infoworld.com/articles/fe/xml/02/06/10/020610feapp.dev.xml

Themistocleous, M., & Chen, H. (2004). Investigating the integration of SMEs' information systems: An exploratory case study. *International Journal of Information Technology and Management, 3*(2/3/4), 208–234.

UN-ECE (1997, November 13-14). *SMEs—their role in foreign trade.* Background paper prepared by the UN/ECE Secretariat for the BSEC Workshop, Kyiv, Ukraine.

Vecchio, D. (2001). Legacy software: Junkyard wars for Web services? In *Proceedings of the Gartner Symposium/ITxpo*, Orlando, FL.

Yin, R. K. (2003). *Case study research: Design and methods.* London: Sage.

Zhao, Y. (2001). *XML-based frameworks for Internet commerce and an implementation of B2B e-procurement* (SE-581 83). Linköping, Sweden: Linköpings Universitet.

Zheng, J., Caldwell, N. D., Harland, C. M., Powell, P., Woerndl, M., & Xu, S. (2004). Small firms and e-business: Cautiousness, contingency, and cost benefits. *Journal of Purchasing and Supply Management,* (Special Issue IPSERA 2003), *10*(1), 27-39.

Chapter XI

Complementary Features of Reverse Auction Web Sites:
A Survey

Aayush Shrivastava, Indian Institute of Technology, India

Gautam Gupta, Indian Institute of Technology, India

Pratap K. J. Mohapatra, Indian Institute of Technology, India

Abstract

The objective of this chapter is to study the features of reverse auction sites. Twenty-five features of 38 reverse auction sites have been studied. The features are divided into core and complementary features. These sites are broadly divided into B2B/B2G and B2C/C2C groups. We show the differences that exist in the site design of these two groups insofar as the inclusion of these features are concerned. We derive weights, signifying the importance which the site designs have assigned to various complementary features. These weights are used in two ways: to provide benchmarks to evaluate the design of the Web sites, and to find out the site evaluation index of any Web site for comparison with the benchmark. Using their complementary features, we derive weights for the features and develop site evaluation indexes for them.

Introduction

All around the world, managers, analysts, researchers, and the business press have been contemplating that the Internet will change everything. And indeed, since the advent of the Internet, we have seen it challenge nearly every aspect of marketing practice. Emerging technologies like broadband and Wi-Fi have pushed the Internet to new limits, enabling data transfer at enormous speeds. In the future, new and exciting business models are likely to emerge that will give the Internet a new meaning. It has been predicted that the Internet will bring about $1 trillion worth of efficiencies, to the annual $7 trillion that is spent on the procurement of goods and services worldwide (Boult, 2000).

The biggest segment of e-commerce revolves around purchase and sales of supplies and services, specifically referred to as e-procurement. E-procurement (or electronic procurement) uses the Internet as well as other information and networking systems, such as electronic data interchange (EDI) to connect with enterprise resource planning (ERP) for the procurement and purchases. The participating companies expect to be able to control parts inventories more effectively, reduce purchasing agent overhead, and improve manufacturing cycles. Online reverse auction is one of the most frequently employed tools for e-procurement. Many large organizations have identified reverse auction as an effective tool to achieve procurement savings. As the name suggests, reverse auction is the opposite of a traditional forward auction. A traditional auction normally involves a seller offering an item for sale while potential buyers compete with one another for the purchase. The highest bid is awarded the item. In a reverse auction, multiple sellers vie for the business of a single buyer; therefore, the price is driven down. Bidding continues until a preestablished bidding period ends or until no seller is willing to bid any lower. It is also known as a procurement auction or upside-down auction.

In this chapter, we will focus on the features required for successful deployment and operation of online reverse auction sites. Such features can be broadly classified into two categories: core features and complementary features. Core features are essential for the very existence of a site. Besides having these features, the sites also provide many complementary features to enhance users' experience with the site. Today, there are many reverse auction Web sites. It is interesting to study what features make a site successful. Since a site has to have the core features, it is likely that the presence or absence of complementary features contributes to the popularity of the auction sites. Our study explores this issue by surveying the complementary features of 38 reverse auction sites.

The rest of the chapter is organized as follows. In the next section we present a brief review of the related work. We then describe our survey, which is followed by results.

Literature Survey

Merson (2000) identified reverse auctions as the wave of the future, and initially termed the process as "unsealed bidding." Reverse auctions had started gaining popularity by that time, as a result of the emergence of Internet-based online auction tools. Early adopters of this online tool included General Electric and United Technologies. Merson (2000) also observed that reverse auctions were most suitable for government procurements, but stressed the need for tools to assure the minimum required level of specified quality.

Although reverse auction was initially considered more suitable for government, Jap (2002) noted that, unconstrained with any social and economic programs that are a part of the federal procurement process, the private sector has pioneered reverse auction with more significant success. Examples included car manufacturers (General Motors, Daimler Chrysler, and Ford Motor Company, who have merged their parts requirements) and aerospace firms (Lockheed Martin Corporation, Boeing Company, Raytheon Company, and BAE Systems, who have formed a buying consortium).

Despite so much success, reverse auction seems to be on shaky ground. Some critics like Merson (2000, p. 4) feared that reverse auctions are "a gimmicky practice that will lead to the purchase of shoddy products." Emiliani and Stec (2001) argued that online reverse auctions rarely deliver savings that are as great as advertised by auction service providers. They said that savings from reverse auctions are difficult to measure and do not account for extra expenses resulting from problems such as poor quality, late deliveries, and supplier non-performance. Jap (2001) found reverse auctions to be highly toxic for buyer-supplier relationships. Similarly, Emiliani and Stec (2001) found that suppliers who are forced to bid in reverse auctions look for opportunities to retaliate by charging higher prices.

Security is a major concern in online reverse auctions to counteract faulty bidders and information leakage. Hawking, Stein, and Wyld (2003) feel that reverse auctions must ensure that the security concerns are taken care of beforehand. Similarly, Emiliani and Stec (2005) feel that legal complications must be cleared before actual transactions take place.

The literature in regard to reverse auctions is still young, and the survey done by us is unique in its approach and scope. Despite its late and comparatively dubious emergence, reverse auction is gradually strengthening its foothold and popularity among both government and private firms. Recently, Indian government organizations like Northern Railways and private companies like Tata Steel have also started using reverse auctions.

Methodology

This section explains how the survey was conducted. The entire process of Web sites selection and the procedure for data collection is described here. This survey covered 38 reverse auction Web sites operating on the Internet. The aim of the survey was to understand the current state of online auctions, with an emphasis on studying the features and services provided by the reverse auction Web sites.

Selection of Sample

A sample of 38 Web sites was selected using Google (www.google.com), Yahoo (www.yahoo.com), Khoj (www.khoj.com), and Rediff (www.rediff. com) search engines and auction site listings at Rediff and www.internetauctionlist.com. Rediff and Khoj were used for selecting Indian Web sites. Internetauctionlist.com lists auction Web sites from across the world. The sample was selected, keeping Indian Web sites in focus. The idea was to study the differences in the features of Indian and foreign auction Web sites. Among the 38 Web sites selected, 10 Web sites were Indian. The Web sites were randomly selected as far as the auction formats and business models are concerned. This was to get an overall picture of the auction Web sites. Since almost all the prior work referred to in this study surveyed an almost similar number of Web sites, the sample size selected for this work can be considered reasonable.

While selecting the sample, it was found that although there were many auction Web sites that had been included in auction listings and search results, a number of these Web sites did not operate any longer. In some cases, it was found that as many as 60% of the links were not working properly. When some of the links given by Lucking-Reiley (1999) were checked, they were found to be not working properly. Hence it can be said that most of the Web sites that are not popular last only for a few years. Beams and Segev (1998) had a similar opinion, when they said that nearly 33% of the auction Web sites that they surveyed were less than a year old, 28% were less than two years old, and the rest (39%) were more than three years old. A few popular Web sites had multiple domain names registered with them; for example, www.priceline.com could be accessed by another domain name, www.travelbids.com. So even though there were many domain names and search results that showed up while searching for online auctions, the segment was actually dominated by a small number of popular Web sites. Appendix A gives the Web site addresses.

Selection of Features

The selected Web sites were studied for various core and complementary features. The survey of the literature helped in identifying four core features and nine complementary features. Being the most popular site and the choice for many such studies, e-Bay (www.ebay.com) was used as a representative Web site to select one more core feature and nine more complementary features. Two features, demo software and legal details, were studied considering their specific importance in reverse auction Web sites. Thus a total of 25 features were studied, which are:

- **Core/Functional features:** These are the features that define an auction Web site. These are the basic or core features that directly affect the functionality of the Web sites:
    1. Business models (B2B, B2G, B2C, C2C, and C2B) (Dans, 2002)
    2. Auction formats (Dans, 2002)
        - Open/sealed
        - Base (Price, choice, multifactor)
        - Ending criteria (time, price limit, customer-defined)
    3. Categories of products (products were divided into six broad categories, explained in results section with details in appendix B) (Beam & Segev, 1998)

4. Payment methods (Wurman, 2003)

5. Phases of auction

- **Complementary/Non-functional features:** These complementary features are an addition to the functional features. They add value to the Web site functionality and enable them to perform better:

6. Faulty bidder/seller identification (Wurman, 2003)

7. Seller's ranking (Wurman, 2003)

8. Shopping basket

9. Search facility (Jenamani, Mohapatra, & Ghose, 2002; Wurman, 2003)

10. Advertisements (Jenamani, Mohapatra, & Ghose, 2002)

11. Career-oriented services (Jenamani, Mohapatra, & Ghose, 2002)

12. Links to other sites

13. Help and support

14. Newsletter

15. Auction update notification (Wurman, 2003)

16. Customer feedback forum

17. Language customization

18. Site map (Jenamani, Mohapatra, & Ghose, 2002)

19. Other services

20. Bookmarking

21. Scripting language

22. Text-graphics ratio (Jenamani, Mohapatra, & Ghose, 2002)

23. Security (Huhns & Vidal, 1999)

24. Legal details

25. Demo software

Most of the features were checked for their presence and absence only, marked by 1 and 0 respectively. However, features like business models, auction format, phases of auction, payment methods, and scripting language were marked for each category in these features. Text-graphics ratio was approximated for each Web site based on the design of its home page.

Data Collection

All the Web sites were visited and scanned for relevant data. In particular, feature information was collected from home page, help and support pages, site map, and registration page for both seller and buyer along with few active auction pages. In most of the cases, home pages provided information for such features as faulty bidder/seller identification, search facility, advertisements, career-oriented services, links to other sites, help and support, customer feedback forum, language customization, sitemap, other services, customer counter, legal details, bookmarking, scripting language, and text-to-graphics ratio. Help and support pages provided information for business models followed, auction formats used, and payment method available. The site map was used for finding the broad categories of products that were purchased on the Web site. To get information about newsletter and auction update notification, registration pages for both buyers and sellers were visited. Besides this, relevant auction-related pages were also visited to know about the shopping basket and phases of the auction.

Results

The section is divided into subsections describing the results for each feature separately. The sample consisted of 38 Web sites with 10 Indian sites, 7 sites from Singapore, China, and Japan; 15 sites from U.S., UK, Canada, the Netherlands, and the rest of Europe; and 6 sites from the rest of the world. Twenty-two percent of the sites did not allow browsing before registration. The survey had 18% government sites, including two from India. The procurement for a wide range of products from agriculture to defense equipment was done through these government sites. Ten (26%) such sites involving companies, like Tata Steel, L&T, and Arsenal Football Club, had their own reverse auction sites. The various inferences drawn from the survey and the numerical results obtained are as follows.

Core/Functional Features

Most of the Web sites in the survey were open-bid B2B models with price as base and time as ending criteria. All Indian Reverse Auction sites were

B2B or B2G. B2G sites and were treated as a separate category because of the specific popularity of reverse auctions in government sectors.

Business Models

The Web sites were mainly studied for the business models **B2B**, **B2G**, **B2C**, **C2C**, and **C2B**. B2G can be grouped with B2B as government can be considered as a business entity. B2C model consisted of intermediary Web sites that allowed other businesses to use their sites for transaction. C2C were those sites that followed the system of barter and swap, that is, the consumers were also the vendors for numerous and diverse product categories. There was one C2B site in the survey where the consumer created and supplied bakery products for a company using reverse auction, and later they themselves also bought the packaged product from the same company. B2C and C2C dominated the forward auction. But in reverse auction, majority of the sites (**58%**) were B2B/B2G. The number of sites of a particular model is as follows: B2B - **22** (7 were B2G); B2C - **13**; C2C - 2; and C2B - 1.

Auction Format

The Web sites were studied for their format based on criteria like type of auction, basis of winner determination, and the auction ending condition. The number of sites using open-bid format was 58%, and sealed-bid format was 42%. Fifty-seven percent of the sites used only price as the basis of bid evaluation, while 22% of the reverse auction Web sites had multi-attribute evaluation schemes based on past performance of the bidder, delivery time, and the quality of the product. Most of the Web sites (69%) used predefined time limit, while 29% of them used price limit as their ending criterion, and the remaining used either both of them or other user-defined criteria.

Product Categories

Most of the reverse auction sites were single-category sites with exclusive procurement auction for a particular item. There was a wide variety of products. For the purpose of surveying, the products were divided into six broad categories, that is, Travel, FMCG, Financial, Final Goods, Intermediate Goods, and Specific purchases. The detailed list of the categories and the products in it is given in appendix B. Category-wise analysis of the Web sites is as follows.

Travel

This category includes sites which sold travel-related services like hotels, cruises, flight tickets, holidays, maps, and so forth. This was the most popular and profitable category, with 32% of Web sites offering these services. These B2C sites had a larger number of active auctions going on at one time compared to other categories.

FMCG

This category includes the fast-moving consumer goods. It mainly comprised of food, fashion, and beauty products. Fifteen percent of the Web sites had these products for auctions. All of them were either B2C or C2C.

Financial

This category includes reverse auction sites auctioning mortgages, market shares, and bank loans of different types. There were two such sites.

Final Goods

These are the consumer goods which were being procured in their final form. This category includes a wide range of products like books, antiques, merchandise, software, hardware, vehicles, and so forth. Twenty-nine percent of Web sites (all B2C/C2C) sold these products.

Intermediate Goods

These are goods used to make the final goods. These include spare parts, components, materials and manufacturing requirements, peripherals, and so forth. These were mainly B2B sites which used reverse auction to select its vendors. Seven sites (five sites belonged to specific companies) dealt with these products.

Specific Purchases

This category refers to those auction sites which procure single and specific products through their Web sites. The products being procured in such a manner were defense equipment, used scientific equipment, metals, chemical products, real estates, flowers, scraps, and so forth. Six B2B sites and one B2C site (selling flowers) exclusively sold these products.

Payment Mode

Most of the B2C /C2C Web sites use online *PayPal* services or credit cards. Other options were checks, bank transfers, and money orders. Only a few payments (44% in total, 13% exclusive) were done off-line by cash, checks, demand draft, and so forth. The number of sites (out of the total of 38) with particular payment mode is as follows: Bank transfers - 3; Money Orders - 2; Checks - 4; Credit Card - 21; Cash - 10; PayPal - 14; and Not Specified - 7.

Complementary/Non-Functional Features

We give below along with discussions wherever necessary, the number and percentages of the Web sites that have incorporated a particular non-functional feature.

Faulty User Identification

Auction Web sites collect users' feedback based on their interaction with the sellers via their Web sites. On the basis of these feedbacks, Web sites rate the sellers, so that other bidders can get information about the sellers. This is one of the mechanisms that auction Web sites use to prevent frauds. Out of 38 Web sites, 28 (74%) sites used faulty user identification before registry and access. A majority of them did not allow browsing and access unless the registration process was complete and verified. For user identification, 15 sites took user feedbacks, 13 of them scanned the history of the user, and two even conducted personal interviews. Twelve sites had compulsory registration by providing e-mail, and in one case SMS registry was done.

Advertisements and Links

Revenues for any e-commerce Web sites not only come from the product they are selling, but also from advertisements. Twenty-five of the 38 sites had advertisement and sponsored links. The links were mainly to the following sites: Google—6; Self or subsidiary—8; Bidder—9; Web site host—7; and others—9.

Demo Software

As reverse auctions are comparatively new, seven sites had demo software that explained the functioning and potential benefit to the bidders. While three sites sold demo software, four were freely downloadable for appraisal and study.

Scripting Language and Text-to-Graphics Ratio

The distribution of sites according to scripting language was as follows: ASP - 36%; JSP - 24%; PHP - 23%; and others (PL, CGI, and CFM) - 17%. Regarding text-to-graphics ratio, 26% of sites had 90% text in it. Only a few sites (11%) had more graphics compared to text.

Legal Details

Many B2B/B2G sites had clearly defined legal details on the sites itself to avoid future complications. Twelve sites (32%) had this feature.

Seller's Ranking

Web sites collect user feedback based on their interaction with the sellers via their Web sites and accordingly rank the bidding sellers as a mechanism to prevent frauds. Twelve (32%) sites had this feature.

Search Facility

Seventeen (45%) Web sites had the search facility. The facility was offered by Google in most of the sites. Search facility could be used to search within the site as well as the entire Web.

Bookmarking

Web sites also provide a link that allows users to bookmark their site easily for future use. In the survey, four (11%) Web sites had the bookmarking feature.

Career-Oriented Services

The auctioneer or the company which is conducting the auction to make a purchase can use their Web sites as a medium to advertise the job openings in their organizations. It was found that only eight (22%) Web sites advertised their job postings on their reverse auction sites.

Help and Support

Twenty-eight of the sites (74%) had some sort of help pages, but the quality of information varied widely between big and small Web sites. Some sites have categorized the information into FAQs which were easier to understand in the first visit itself and explained the features of the Web site in a lucid manner. This could be one of the reasons why a few sites are more popular than others.

Newsletter

A few sites have an online newsletter that they circulate among their users. To check the presence of this feature, the registration pages of the sites were checked. Usually Web sites ask the user's preference and permission before final subscription. Out of 38 sites, five (13%) had this feature.

Customer Feedback Forum

Many Web sites, especially B2C sites, have a large number of customers across the globe. To get feedback from them and to keep users hooked on to their sites; they provide discussion forums as an additional feature. Eight (22%) of 38 Web sites had this feature. Even B2B sites are implementing this feature to attract bidders from global companies.

Language Customization

Mostly the European and the Chinese Web sites offer this feature. Six (16%) out of 38 sites surveyed, provided the language customization feature. These Web sites could be seen in English and other European languages.

Site Map

For proper navigation through the site, 14 (37%) had the site map feature.

Other complementary services were Katrina relief fund, virtual tools, yellow pages, gifts, news, FAQ, and so forth; these were not considered in the further analysis. The above Web sites were broadly divided into two groups: The first group had **22** B2B/B2G sites, and the second group contained **16** B2C/C2C sites. The reason for this grouping was to analyze the differences in these two groups, and to evaluate the surveyed reverse auction sites. To accomplish this, we have followed the following procedure. We first calculated the weight of a particular feature. Then, depending on its importance with respect to other features, we calculated the relative functional weightage. The formulae used are as follows:

- Number of sites with the feature 'i' = $\mathbf{n}_i$
- Total number of sites with the feature 'i' = $\mathbf{N}_i$
- Feature weightage = $\mathbf{(n/N)}_i$
- Relative functional weightage $\mathbf{(w_i)} = \mathbf{(n/N)}_i / \mathbf{\Sigma(n/N)}_i$

Using the procedure mentioned above, the relative feature weightages were computed separately for both the groups. (Table 1)

Table 1 shows the obtained values for each feature. More the value; more is the relative importance of a particular feature. After obtaining the value, we performed a chi-squared test on the two data sets for the null hypothesis that values in both groups are equal. The larger value of the statistic suggests greater variation in the data values, with due consideration to their relative importance. The shaded portion in the above table shows the features that have a noticeable variation in chi-square statistic (>.01).

From the chi-square test of non-functional features, we infer that faulty user identification and legal details were more important in B2B/B2G sites. This reflects that B2B/B2G sites are comparatively more concerned to have a fairer and fault-free auction. In contrast, seller ranking was more prevalent in B2C/C2C sites which asked its customers to rate the bidding sellers on the basis of their past performance. Career-oriented services were more important in B2B/B2G sites, as most of these sites were owned by business enterprises which also offered career-related information and links on their sites.

Apart from the differences obtained from the chi-square test, few other differences were noted in the data of the two groups. While the first group

Table 1. Relative weightage of non-functional features

Relative weightage			Chi-square statistic
Features	B2B	B2C/C2C	
Faulty User Identification	0.1509	0.1205	0.00684
Seller Ranking	0.0377	0.0964	0.05129
Search	0.0943	0.0843	0.00112
Advertisements	0.0943	0.0964	0.00004
Career-Oriented Services	0.0566	0.0120	0.05783
Links	0.1321	0.1566	0.00418
Demo Software	0.0377	0.0361	0.00007
Help and Support	0.1415	0.1446	0.00007
Newsletter	0.0283	0.0241	0.00068
Feedback	0.0377	0.0482	0.00255
Language Customization	0.0283	0.0361	0.00191
Site Map	0.0660	0.0843	0.00445
Bookmarking	0.0189	0.0241	0.00127
Legal Details	0.0755	0.0361	0.02771
TOTAL	1.0000	1.0000	

(B2B/B2G) had 80.6% text, the second group (B2C/C2C) had only 56.1% text. This basically shows the comparative gravity of the first group, considering they do not need to attract consumers to their sites using graphics. One more difference was that B2C/C2C sites necessarily had online payment options for the ease of their global customers. Also, while B2C/C2C sites had more inclination to open bidding, B2B/B2G tended to have time-limit sealed bid auctions based on price only.

Site Evaluation Index (SEI)

For site evaluation, we used the relative feature weightage ($\underline{\mathbf{w}}_i$) calculated above. As mentioned before, the relative feature weightage shows the relative importance of a particular non-functional feature on a site. After assigning binary flags to these weights, every site was evaluated. The formula used was as follows:

Site Evaluation Index

Binary flag $(\mathbf{f}_i) =$ **0** if the feature 'i' is absent

                     1 if the feature 'i' is present

Site Evaluation Index **(SEI)** = $\sum(\mathbf{w}_i * \mathbf{f}_i)$

The maximum, minimum, and average values of SEI are given in Table 2.

As evident from above, B2C/C2C sites have more complementary features than the B2B sites. This may be because B2C/C2C sites are meant for the general consumers, and they need these complementary user-friendly features to attract consumers to the Web site. As none of the Indian sites have yet entered the B2C model of reverse auctions, the SEI values of Indian sites were compared with the values of the rest of the B2B/B2G sites. The results are given in Table 3.

It clearly shows that Indian sites are comparatively lacking in all the categories. As this is based on non-functional features only, it just gives the relative index of the Indian sites in terms of non-functional features. A more in-depth analysis will suggest the actual inference from the evaluation index.

Table 2. Maximum, minimum, and average value of SEI in two groups

	1st group (B2B/B2G)	2nd group (B2C/C2C)
Maximum	77.36	83.13
Minimum	22.64	22.89
Average	60.82	61.63

Table 3. SEI values for Indian sites

	Indian Sites (all B2B)	Non-Indian B2B Sites
Maximum	71.7	77.36
Minimum	22.64	54.72
Average	56.01	65.09

Evidence for Relating SEI with the Popularity of a Site

In many cases, sites with a high value of SEI are popular sites on the Internet. For example, coolbid.com (SEI - 83) and priceline.com (SEI - 79) are indeed more popular among the reverse auction sites. In defense of this claim, the above values were compared with the values obtained from a user feedback survey. The user feedback survey included a few qualitative features like user friendliness, aesthetics, ease of use, and navigability, and was conducted on 10 frequent net users from diverse backgrounds and age groups. The ratings obtained were compared with the SEI values after conversion to a particular scale and were found to be highly coherent in most cases (Figure 1).

The coherence also proved that the Indian sites were indeed lacking in the area of reverse auctions. As reverse auctions are still not very popular in India, most of the companies were undergoing a trial phase in this regard. Also, the Indian government still continues to use the same old vendor selection method in many sectors.

Figure 1. SEI values compared with user feedback ratings

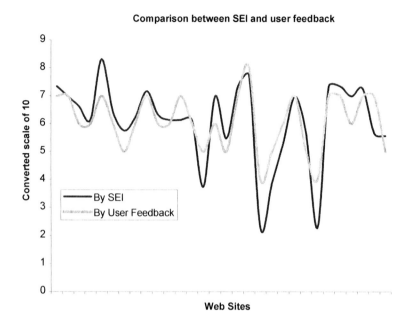

Conclusion

In this work, we broadly classify the functionalities of online reverse auction sites as core and complementary features. We conducted a survey to study the existence of these features on a set of 38 reverse auction sites. We described a scheme to assign importance weights to the complementary features. We proposed a model to evaluate Web sites based on these feature weights. We provide some anecdotal evidences to show that the sites with very high site evaluation (SEI) are indeed the popular ones and concluded that the proposed model can be used as a benchmark to evaluate the functionalities of other online reverse auction sites. Based on the evaluation index, we pointed out some glaring differences between the concept and mechanism of B2B/B2G and B2C/C2C reverse auction sites. This chapter also gave an insight into the Indian reverse auction scenario in comparison to the rest of the world.

References

Beam, C., & Segev, A. (1998). *Auctions on the Internet: A field study* (CITM Working Paper 98-WP1032). Berkeley, CA: University of California.

Boult, M. (2002). Online reverse auctions: Hope or hype? *USA Today*, (2/7/2000).

Dans, E. (2002). Existing business models for auctions, and their adaptation to electronic markets. *Journal of Electronic Commerce Research, 3*(2), 23-31.

Emiliani, M., & Stec, D. J. (2001). Online reverse auction purchasing contracts. *Supply Chain Management: An International Journal, 6*(3), 101-105.

Emiliani, M., & Stec, D. J. (2005). Wood pallet suppliers' reaction to online reverse auctions. *Supply Chain Management: An International Journal, 10*(4), 278-288.

Hawking, P., Stein, A., & Wyld, D. (2003). The 20% solution? A case study on the efficacy of reverse auctions. *Management Research News, 26*(5), 1-20.

Huhns, M. N., & Vidal, J. M. (1999). Online auctions. *IEEE Internet Computing Magazine, 3*(3), 103-105.

Jap, S. D. (2001). *The impact of reverse auctions on buyer-supplier relationships.* Working paper. Atlanta, GA: Emory University.

Jap, S. D. (2002). *Online reverse auctions: Issues, themes, and prospects for the future.* Working paper. Atlanta, GA: Emory University. Atlanta.

Jenamani, M., Mohapatra, P. K. J., & Ghose, S. (2002). Benchmarking for design evaluation of corporate Web sites—a study. *Quarterly Journal of Electronic Commerce, 3*(4), 391-416.

Lucking-Reiley, D. (1999). *Auctions on the Internet: What's being auctioned, and how?* Department of Economics, Vanderbilt University.

Merson, I. R. (2000). *Reverse auctions: An overview, the wave of the future, or just one more addition to the toolkit?* Department of Commerce, National Oceanic and Atmospheric Administration.

Parente, D. H., Venkataraman, R., Fizel, J., & Millet, I. (2001, July). B2B online reverse auctions: What's new? *Decision Line, 32*, 13-15.

Wurman, P. R. (2003). Online auction site management. In *The Internet encyclopedia*. Retrieved from http://www.csc.ncsu.edu/wurman/Wur-article.pdf

Appendix A

B2B/B2G Sites	B2C/C2C Sites
www.dsta.gov.sg	www.priceline.com/www.travelbids.com
www.lntenc.com (L&T)	www.lowbidswin.com
www.auctionindia.com (TVS Electronics Limited)	flower.localstreets.com
www.matexnet.com (Material Stock Exchange)	www.expedia.com
www.chembargains.com	www.smartertravel.com
www.metalbid.com	www.ebay.com
www.traders.co.in	www.carauc.com
www.steelbid.com	www.etruly.com/
www.scrapbid.com	www.bestfares.com
www.abanindia.com	www.kellysearch.com
www.labx.com	www.coolbid.com
www.bidorbuy.co.za	www.28.com
www.hedgehog.com	www.aadvantageeshopping.com
www.Tata Steel.co.in (TISCO)	www.halfbakery.com
www.ftc.gov	www.arsenal.com
www.save33.com	reverse.interauct.com.sg
www.yellowpages.com.sg	
www.FedBid.com	
www.state.mn.us	
cpr.ca.gov	
http://nreps.com	
http://www.eprocurement.gov.in/	

Appendix B

Category-1 Travel	Category-2 FMCG	Category-3 Financial	Category-4 Final goods	Category-5 Intermediate goods	Category-6 Specific purchases
Hotels	Beauty Products	Mortgages	Cars, Scooters	Components	Defense Equipment
Flights	Food	Bank Loans	Cassettes, CDs	Spares	Scraps
Railway Tickets	Fashion Products	Market Shares	Merchandise, Gifts	Materials and Manufacturing Requirements	Used Scientific Equipment
Cruises	Health Products		Hardware, Software	Services and Jobs	Metal
Holidays			Mobiles	PC Peripherals	Chemical Products
Road Maps			Sports and Toys		Real Estate
Maps			Apparels		Flowers
			Antiques		
			Books		
			Electronics		

Glossary

Country code top level domain is the registration of domain names with two-letter country code such as .au, .ca, .jp, .it, and .uk; ccTLD are administered by country-code managers.

Digital divide is the difference between those who possess the material and cultural conditions to exploit new technologies, and those who do not, or those who lack the crucial ability to adapt to the rapid continuous changes instigated by the Internet.

Digital subscriber line is broadband technology replacing mostly the much slower dial-up connection. Via DSL, subscribers can use a telephone both for voice communication and Internet connection at the same time.

Domain name specialization ratio indicates the extent to which a region is specialized in domain names compared to the United States.

E-business refers to the use of electronic and associated networks to enable, improve, enhance, transform, or invent a business process or business system, which results in superior value for current or potential customers. It is a more generic term than e-commerce because it refers to not only buying and selling, but also servicing customers and collaborating with business partners.

E-commerce is the exchange of information using a combination of structured messages (EDI), unstructured messages (e-mail and documents), data access, and direct support for business processes using the Internet technology: fax server, e-mail, World Wide Web, EDI (EANCOM, EDIFACT, XML).

Electronic data interchange is a technical platform rooted in the set of standards, which enables informational exchange among participants.

Electronic marketplaces are sophisticated Web sites where buyers and sellers meet to buy and sell their goods or services. Since there are many buyers and/or sellers, prices are competitive.

Em-procurement is the usage of both electronic and mobile technologies and networks to carry out procurement activities.

Enterprise resource planning is the information pipeline within an organization, which enables efficient flow of internal information for collaboration and decision support. It is an enterprise-wide set of forecasting, planning, and scheduling tools, which employs proven processes for decision-making, and coordinates various functions such as sales, marketing, operations, logistics, purchasing, finance, product development, and human resources.

Environmental context is the arena where an organization operates; this arena includes its industry, suppliers, customers, and the government.

E-procurement deals with the linking and integration of inter-organizational business processes and systems, and commences with the automation of the requisitioning, approval, purchase order management, and accounting processes using Internet protocols.

Estimated cost value procurement is typically prepared for public works procurement and for some types of services procurement. The schedule of rates (a price list maintained by government departments) forms the basis of ECV preparation.

E-supply relationships refer to supply relationships that are enabled by the use of Internet technology.

Gini index is a measure of distribution inequality, defined as the ratio of area between the Lorenz curve of the distribution and the curve of the uniform distribution, to the area under the uniform distribution. It is often used to measure income inequality. It is a number between 0 and 1, where 0 corresponds to perfect equality (i.e., everyone has the same income) and 1 corresponds to perfect inequality (i.e., one person has all the income, while everyone else has zero income).

Guanxi is a Chinese term which refers to a special kind of relationship, characterized by implicit rules, both of obligation and reciprocity. It is briefly translated as human relationship or personal connections on which an individual can draw to secure resources or advantages when doing business as well as in their social life.

Innovation is an idea, practice, or object that is perceived as new by an individual or organization.

Innovation diffusion is the process by which an innovation is communicated through certain channels over time among the members of a social system.

Instant messenger (IM) is peer-to-peer service which enables users to send and receive messages in real-time. IM is a more informal communication tool than e-mail.

Institutional theory places greater emphasis on the taken-for-granted nature of the decisions made by organizations.

Inter-organizational information system is an automated information system shared by two or more organizations. An IOIS builds on common EDI standards (when necessary) to design and deploy different functionalities that interconnect multiple organizations.

Legitimacy is a generalized perception or assumption that the actions of an entity are desirable, proper, or appropriate within some socially-constructed systems of norms, values, beliefs, and definitions.

Letter of assumption of responsibility is the document through which the applicant assumes full civil and penal responsibility for the use of the domain name requested.

Lorenz curve is a graphical representation of the cumulative probability distribution function; it is a graph that shows the proportion of the distribution assumed by the bottom y% of the values. It is often used to represent income distribution, where it shows for the bottom x% of households, what percentage of the total income they have. It was developed by Max O. Lorenz in 1905 to represent income distribution.

M-business is the usage of functionalities brought in by mobile technologies to carry out business activities. The ability to exchange data via a mobile network makes it possible to conduct location-independent business practices which were previously unavailable.

Mimetic pressures imply that organizations change over time to be more similar to other organizations in their environment.

Multilateral Development Bank E-Government Procurement Group is a working group created in the beginning of the year 2003 by a few leading Multi-Lateral Development Banks (MDB): Asian Development Bank, the Inter-American Development Bank, and the World Bank. Subsequent to the constitution of the working group, the Nordic Development Fund and the African Development Bank have also joined the group. For further details, refer to www.mdb-egp.org.

National Telecommunications and Information Administration is an agency of the United States Department of Commerce that serves as the President's principal adviser on telecommunications policies and regulation of the telecommunications industry.

Normative pressures imply that strategic processes taken by organizations are subject to values and norms shared among the members of their social network.

Penetration rate is an index used to measure the digital divide and the Internet diffusion among demographical/geographical regions.

Private-public-partnership is defined by the Canadian Council for Public-Private Partnerships as a cooperative venture between the public and private sectors, built on the expertise of each partner that best meets clearly-defined public needs through the appropriate allocation of resources, risks, and rewards.

Process integration means the networking of business processes, human resources, their tasks, and the information and communication technology used.

Process reengineering is a methodology for introducing a fundamental and radical change in specific business process for achieving organizational and technological efficiencies.

Procurement is a broader term than purchasing or sourcing. Procurement covers the entire cycle from purchase requirement notes (PRN) to feedback about suppliers and products. Thus it is often referred to as a closed process.

Rate contract refers to the activity handled by a central agency for empanelment of one (single rate contract) or more (parallel rate contract) suppliers for delivery of a good/service for a price to all agencies within a given jurisdiction, which could be a nation, a state, a department, or an office, for a defined period of time. The empanelment of suppliers is done based on a tendering process.

Réseaux IP Européens Network Coordination Centre (RIPE NCC) is one of four regional Internet registries that supply and administer IP addresses.

Service-flow refers to a sequence of logically-related activities that are executed upon a service request during which information or tasks are passed from one service-provisioning unit to another, according to a set of predefined procedures.

Service orientation is an approach to model software systems around the notion of service, which represents an encapsulated unit of functionalities hiding the internal processing details, thereby enhancing the interoperability and reusability of heterogeneous applications.

Service point represents a physical or logical unit that extends a set of well-defined services, which can be invoked by users through service requests.

Small and medium enterprises are those enterprises which employ fewer than 250 persons and which have an annual turnover not exceeding EUR 50 million, or an annual balance sheet total not exceeding EUR 43 million.

Software agent is a programmed artifact that can act on behalf of its user by exhibiting autonomous, reactive, proactive, and flexible behavior.

Supply chain management can be described as the chain linking each element of the manufacturing and supply process, from raw materials to the end user, encompassing several organizational boundaries.

Technology assimilation entails the infiltration of the technology across the various sub-units of an organization and progressing through the various stages such as awareness, evaluation, utilization, and institutionalization.

Technology migration is the evolutionary change to a better state or level of technological sophistication.

Transaction cost economics suggests market and hierarchy as two mechanisms of coordination, and any middle-range solution is considered to be inferior. Over the years, transaction cost economics has been revised to reflect the empirical reality that middle-range solutions could be actually more effective.

Typology is a system of grouping to aid demonstration or inquiry by establishing a limited relationship among phenomena.

Web services are defined as loosely-coupled, reusable software components that semantically encapsulate discrete functionality and are distributed and programmatically-accessible over standard Internet protocols.

About the Authors

Ashis K. Pani is the chairman of information systems area, XLRI Jamshedpur, and the coordinator of the Center for e-Business. His research and teaching focus on how businesses can effectively use information technology (IT) in general and the Internet in particular. His current areas of interest are e-business, e-SCM, e-procurement, e-CRM, e-security, IT outsourcing, and application of AI techniques. Presently, he is a member of the Indian Association of Research in Computing Sciences (IARCS), and the Computer Society of India (CSI).

Amit Agrahari is associated with Infosys Technologies Ltd, Bangalore, India. He is currently working with the Software Engineering and Technology Labs, where he is involved in research on experience co-creation and business transformation. He is a fellow of XLRI – Jamshedpur and holds a Bachelor's degree in mathematics and statistics. His area of interest includes social network, e-procurement, and application of game theory. His research appeared in several international journal and conferences.

*   *   *   *   *

Gautam Gupta is a B.Tech (Hons) in industrial engineering from IIT Kharagpur and is pursuing his M.Tech in industrial engineering and management from the same institute. His research interests are in the areas of e-business and supply chain management.

Faruk Karaman holds BS in electrical and electronics engineering from the Bosphorus University, Istanbul-Turkey (1993) and MBA from the Marmara University, Istanbul-Turkey (1997). In 2001, he was awarded a PhD in management at the Marmara University, Istanbul-Turkey. Currently he is giving graduate and undergraduate level lectures of e-commerce and financial management at Okan University, Turkey, and consults SMEs in the Istanbul area. His research interests include e-commerce, Internet security, intellectual property laws, content protection, technological trends, and futurism.

Kiran Maringanti is a research fellow at the University of Bolton specializing in the applicability of Web services for SMEs in the supply chain management domain. His current research interests include Web services, SMEs, e-procurement, and service-oriented architecture (SOA). His PhD research area was investigating the adoption of e-procurement systems by small and medium enterprises. Kiran holds a master's degree in computer science and a bachelor's degree in finance.

Maurizio Martinelli graduated in Computer Science at the University of Pisa in 1992. He is technologist at the Institute for Informatics and Telematics, Italian National Research Council - Pisa. He is the head of the "Technological Services" department of the Institute, the technical manager of the .it Registry and the Italian technical contact for the .eu Registry.

Pratap K. J. Mohapatra is a professor with the Department of Industrial Engineering and Management. He has published many papers in journals like *International Journal of Electronic Commerce, International Journal of Operations and Production Management, Quarterly Journal of Electronic Commerce, IEEE Intelligent Systems, International Journal of Systems Science* and *OMEGA*. His current research interests are in the area of system dynamics, software project management, and e-business.

Joe Nandhakumar is a professor of information systems in Warwick Business School at University of Warwick, UK. He has wide-ranging experience in industry and gained his PhD from the Department of Engineering, University of Cambridge, UK. Dr. Nandhakumar's research focuses on the human and organizational aspects of information systems development, organizational consequences of information technology use and theoretical and methodological issues in information systems research. He has widely published in these areas.

Stanley Oliver is the academic leader of the Department of Business Logistics and Information Systems at the University of Bolton. His current areas of research include SMEs, e-business, e-procurement, Web services, supply chain management, ERP systems, and knowledge management. He is also the president of the Society of Automotive Engineers (SAE) in the UK. Professor Oliver holds a PhD, MSc and is also a certified chartered engineer.

Manas Ranjan Patra is a senior faculty member in the Department of Computer Science, Berhampur University, India. He holds a PhD degree in computer science from University of Hyderabad. For some time, he has worked in the International Institute of Software Technology, Macau, South China, as a visiting United Nations fellow. He has been actively engaged in teaching and research in computer science. Some of his research interests include service-oriented computing, multi-agent systems, and electronic business. He has published about 40 research articles in different referred journals and conference proceedings. He is a visiting faculty to different universities and institutes.

Mateja Podlogar is the assistant professor of the Business Information Systems, Business Process Reengineering, E-Commerce, and MIS course at the Faculty of Organizational Sciences, University of Maribor, Slovenia. She completed her PhD at the University of Maribor in November, 2002, with the dissertation titled: "A model of electronic commerce critical success factors in procurement process." She is a head of the E-Procurement Laboratory. Since 1994, she has been involved in E-Center and its several research and e-commerce activities as, for example, the Annual International Bled E-Conference. She was also a conference chair assistant of ECIS 2001. She participates in the Slovenia's E-Commerce Project involving 20 business and government organizations. She also serves as an ISACA Academic Advocate from September, 2004. Her current research includes: electronic commerce and new business models in supply chain, RFID technologies, business process reengineering, ERP systems and ACL usage in the auditing process.

Irma Serrecchia graduated in computer science at the University of Pisa in 1993. She is a technologist at the Institute for Informatics and Telematics, Italian National Research Council - Pisa. She is part of the technical staff of the .it Registry. She is currently working for the "Statistical Project" of the .it Registry as information technologist.

Michela Serrecchia graduated in Economic Science at the University of Pisa in 2003. She is a researcher associate at the Institute for Informatics and Telematics, Italian National Research Council - Pisa. She is currently working for the "Statistical Project" of the .it Registry as statistician.

Aayush Shrivastava is a B.Tech (Hons) student in industrial engineering at IIT Kharagpur. His current research interests are in the area of e-business with reference to e-procurement functions.

Ramanathan Somasundaram (RS) is employed as project manager of e-procurement at the National Institute for Smart Government, India. RS holds a PhD in information systems from the Department of Computer Science, Aalborg University, Denmark. He studied the diffusion of electronic public procurement in Denmark for his PhD work. He has previously held offices at the Erasmus University Research Institute for Decision Information System (EURIDIS), The Netherlands; Florida International University, USA and Copenhagen Business School, Denmark. Currently, he is looking into the implementation of e-procurement in Indian government organizations.

Kishor Vaidya is a PhD student at the University of New England, NSW, Australia. He completed his master's degree in information systems from the Central Queensland University, Australia, in 2001. His research interests include adoption, implementation and performance measurement issues in the areas of e-procurement, e-government, and public procurement. Kishor's articles have been published in a number of international conference proceedings and journals including *The Journal of Public Procurement*.

Susanna Xin Xu is a post-doctoral researcher at the Centre for Innovation and Structural Change, J. E. Cairnes Graduate School of Business and Public Policy, National University of Ireland, Galway. Dr. Xu gained her doctorate in School of Management, University of Bath, UK (Centre for Information Management and Centre for Research into Strategic Purchasing and Supply). Her doctoral work investigated the dynamics of formation and transformation of e-relationships of a new breed of Chinese enterprises with the rest of the world. It focused on social, cultural and organisational aspects of the development and use of information systems in such organisations. Previously she worked in the marketing department of IBM China for several years to develop relationships with business partners.

Gonca Telli Yamamoto is an associate professor in the School of Business Administration at Okan University. She was formerly founder and director of Social Sciences Institute of Okan University, Turkey. She currently teaches, consults, and conducts research on mobile and integrated marketing, customer relations, and new learning technologies in business. She has been studying integrated marketing, technological developments, and customer value about 10 years in the academic field. She is also interested in the broader business, social, and policy implications associated with the emerging information society. She also has some books related in sales and integrated marketing. She has several articles in the national and international journals.

Index

E

e-customer relation management (e-CRM)
  234
e-government procurement (e-GP) 76
e-supply chain management (e-SCM) 234
ebXML 247
economic variables 165
ECV-based procurement 82
educational variables 165
electronic auction (e-auction) 234, 235
electronic business (e-business) 271
electronic catalog (e-catalog) 52
electronic commerce (e-commerce)
  strategy 55
electronic data interchange (EDI)
    1, 235, 270, 307
  -based
    IOIS 197
  -based IOIS 9
  systems 202
electronic dyads 7
electronic governance (e-governance) 107
electronic hierarchy (e-hierarchy) 8
electronic market (e-market) 8
electronic market place (e-marketplace)
  234
electronic monopolies 7
electronic MRO (e-MRO) 235
electronic payment (e-payment) 234
electronic procurement (e-procurement)
    1, 21, 42, 78, 102, 107, 233, 23
    5, 237, 265, 307
  activities 236
  added value of use 47
  adoption 21, 101, 197, 202, 210
    barriers 101
    impact of 21
  assimilation 21, 32
    intensity of 25
  barriers 278
  benefits 79, 273
  business model 45
  challenges 238
  collaboration 51

definition 43
excellence 53
frequency of use 54
impact of systems 204
implementation 76
  in India 85, 89
initiation 200
market 76
organizational assimilation of 21
participants 52
portfolio of systems 197, 207
positive experiences 51
practice 101
process 44
  type 52
space framework 3
state of 84
subprocess frequency use 54
success factors 42, 62
system 197
systems 7
use 55
electronic relationship (e-relationship) 127
electronic supply relationship (e-supply
    relationship) 127
electronic tendering (e-tendering)
    234, 235
electronic transaction (e-transaction)
  factors 65
  volume of factors 54
endogenous metrics 161
enterprise resource planning (ERP)
    235, 236, 307
  e-procurement integration 45
  use 55
environment changing response 51
European Economic Community (EEC)
  107
European Union (EU) 107
  accession 106, 107
Extensible Markup Language (XML) 244
external exploitation 297
external integration with e-marketplaces
  297

procurement 267
  in line departments 83
  international 109
  process 44
procurement process reengineering (PPR)
    295
procurement software 296
procurement transformation framework
    295
public marketplace 277
public procurement 26
Public Procurement Authority (PPA)
  of Turkey 116
public sector units (PSU) 199
purchasing
  process 43

Q

qualified workforce 106, 111

R

railroads transportation infrastructure (RTI)
    114
rate contract negotiation 81
rate contract ordering 81
request for information (RFI) 236
request for proposal (RFP) 86
request for quotes (RFQ) 236
revenue expenditure 83
reverse auction Web site 306
RosettaNet 246
  partner interface process (PIP) 246

S

scripting language 316
search facility 317
service
  collaboration 252
  composition 251
  consumer 242
  flow 252
  point 251
  provider 242
  registry 243

service-enabling agent 257
service-flow
  diagram 253
  hierarchy 252
service-orientation 240
service-oriented
  agent-based e-procurement model 249
  agent-based model 233
  paradigm 240
simple object access protocol (SOAP)
    244, 291, 292
site evaluation index (SEI) 320
site map 318
skilled personnel 89
Slovenia 57
small and medium-sized enterprise (SME)
    108, 233, 266
small to medium-sized enterprise (SME)
    202
software agent technology 248
sparse planning and outsourcing (SPOS)
    203
state-wide system 76
structurational theory 24
structurational theory of technology use
    33
supplier 43
supplier relationship management 236
  application (SRM) 236
supply
  network 127
  relationships establishments 138
supply chain
  management (SCM) 102
  synthesis (SCS) 103
supply chain management (SCM) 271
surface transportation infrastructure (STI)
    114

T

technological
  factors 34
  variables 167
TelcoX 136
telecommunication
  infrastructure 116

Single Journal Articles and Case Studies
Are Now Right at Your Fingertips!